Roman Woman

ABOUT THE AUTHOR

Lindsay Allason-Jones was Director of the Centre for Interdisciplinary Artefact Studies and Reader in Roman Material Culture at Newcastle University until she retired in 2011, having previously been Director of Archaeological Museums for the University, responsible for the Museum of Antiquities and the Shefton Museum of Greek Art and Archaeology.

Her research into Roman artefacts and Roman women has led to her working across the Roman Empire, particularly in North Africa and the Middle East. She is a Trustee of several of the Hadrian's Wall museums and serves on the Board of Management of the Great North Museum. She is currently Chair of the Marc Fitch Fund and President of the Border Archaeological Society as well as Visiting Fellow at Newcastle University.

Roman Woman

Everyday Life in Hadrian's Britain

Lindsay Allason-Jones

Michael O'Mara Books Limited

MIX
Paper from
responsible sources
FSC® C013604

This paperback edition first published in 2019

First published in Great Britain in 2000 by
Michael O'Mara Books Limited
9 Lion Yard
Tremadoc Road
London SW4 7NQ

A CIP catalogue record for this book is
available from the British Library.

Papers used by Michael O'Mara Books Limited are natural, recyclable products made
from wood grown in sustainable forests. The manufacturing processes conform to the
environmental regulations of the country of origin.

Every reasonable effort has been made to acknowledge all copyright holders. Any errors or
omissions that may have occurred are inadvertent, and anyone with any copyright queries
is invited to write to the publishers, so that a full acknowledgement may be included in
subsequent editions of this work.

ISBN: 978-1-78929-074-5 in paperback print format
ISBN: 978-1-78243-287-6 in ebook format

www.mombooks.com

Cover design by Claire Cater
Cover illustration: Fresco from the Villa dei Misteri, Pompeii / The Yorck Project: 10,000
Meisterwerke der Malerei, Directmedia Publishing GmbH
Designed and typeset by Barbara Ward

Printed and bound by CPI Group (UK) Ltd, Croydon, CR0 4YY

Contents

Place names

Abus	River Ouse
Alauna	Maryport
Calcaria	Tadcaster
Camulodunum	Colchester
Cataractonium	Catterick
Coria	Corbridge
Danuvius	River Danube
Derventio	Malton
Eboracum	York
Isurium Brigantum	Aldborough
Londinium	London
Luguvalium	Carlisle
Manduessedum	Mancetter
Mare Internum	Mediterranean
Moguntiacum	Mainz
Novio Magus	Nijmegen
Noviomagus Reginorum	Chichester
Petuaria	Brough-on-Humber
Tina	River Tyne
Tyrus	Tyre
Verbeia	River Wharfe
Vercovicium	Housesteads
Verulamium	St Albans
Vindolanda	Chesterholm
Vindomora	Ebchester

Ianuarius

SENOVARA SHIFTED HER sleeping daughter onto her other hip, carefully keeping the child's head covered by her own thick, woollen cloak. The air was filled with a fine mist which seemed to seep right through to the skin. Even with her hood up, her hair was damp and escaping from its bun into unruly tendrils. She shuffled her cold feet, trying to ease the ache in her calves and the itching chilblains on her toes. By her side her young son fidgeted and Quintus placed a steadying hand on his shoulder. All around them their neighbours and friends stood in equal discomfort as the ceremony slowly came to a close.

The last centurion had already recited the military oath in full, and Lucius Minicius Natalis, the Legate, was now working his way slowly along the ranks as each soldier solemnly declaimed, '*Idem in me*,' in affirmation of his loyalty to the Emperor. Over the course of the morning the mist had settled on the hundreds of helmets and spears gathered on the parade ground, muting the normal military splendour. Senovara watched the water dripping off the elbows and noses of the soldiers standing closest to her as they stood to attention; everybody on the parade ground, whether soldier or civilian, was cold and wet through, wanting nothing more than for the ceremony to be over. Even the gilded eagle held by the *aquilifer* only gleamed in a half-hearted way, and the coloured ribbons on the standards hung limply instead of fluttering bravely in the breeze.

Senovara remembered the first time she had witnessed this ceremony, just a few weeks after she married Quintus Flavius Candidus. On that occasion the sun had shone and she had been thrilled by the drama and pageantry of it all. She had never seen so many soldiers gathered in one place before and had thought the brightly polished metal of their helmets and cuirasses, and the bright scarlet of their tunics, a glorious sight. Her new husband had looked so proud and so at home on the military parade ground! Looking back, she realised that that day had been a turning point in her life; the moment when she had finally understood that she had married not a childhood friend, as most of the other girls of her tribe had done, but a man who had been a Roman legionary and that, as a result, she had become part of a new way of life. She could still remember the wave of happiness – and terror – which had surged through her on that day. Since then the Kalends Ianuarius had had special significance for her; but this year the usually proud and inspiring ceremony seemed dull and unimpressive and Senovara hoped that it was not an ill omen for the year.

At last the rites were over, and people started to move away as the soldiers marched back into the fortress. After the solemn silence of the occasion everyone seemed to feel a need to talk and a hubbub of chatter broke out on all sides.

'Quintus! A Fortunate and Happy New Year! How are you these days?' An elderly man clapped her husband on the shoulder and as he turned to respond Senovara felt a tug on her skirts. 'Mater, can we go home now? I'm cold.'

She smiled down at her son: his tone was firm rather than

whingeing, simply stating a fact with every expectation that she would deal with it. He had been very good, considering how long he had had to stay still and quiet; but he had a point – there was no sense in risking the children catching a chill. She looked towards her husband. Raindrops glistened on his bald head and on his long nose but he was impervious to the cold and damp, like all old soldiers. He had been drawn into a group of fellow traders and was clearly planning to stay for a while. She moved across, trying to catch his eye, and Ertola woke up with a wail. Quintus looked up and she mouthed, 'I'll take them home,' pointing to the children. He nodded and turned back to his conversation, which was getting heated to judge from the flaying hands and red face of one rather plump trader.

Senovara bounced Ertola gently on her hip to quiet her and took Lucius' hand. 'Let's go home and have something to eat. Pater will come when he has finished solving the Empire's ills.'

Lucius' brown eyes brightened and he shook the raindrops out of his curly hair. She had heard his tummy rumbling off and on for the last half-hour but, luckily, he had appeared too overawed by the silence of the adults round him and the presence of the soldiers in their parade armour to complain out loud. No doubt he was keen to get back home so that he could carry on playing with the wooden horse he had been given as his New Year's present that morning. Thanking the Fates that they didn't have far to go, as their shop was close to the southern corner of the fortress, just beyond the *porta principalis sinistra*, and not across the river where the newer parts of the settlement lay, Senovara led her children from the parade ground. As they skirted the fortress walls and made their way past the whitewashed, half-timbered houses and shops, Senovara greeted a number of friends and acquaintances who were also hurrying home, but it was too cold and wet to linger more than civility required. Most people were concerned to check if their fires had gone out in their absence, or eager to have something to eat or drink after their long vigil on the parade ground – a number of the men, indeed, were heading purposefully towards the taverns near the fortress gates or to the broken amphorae at the street corners which served as public urinals.

Although there were more people about than usual, the streets were strangely quiet. Building work had stopped in the fortress while the official religious business of the day claimed the soldiers from their usual tasks. For months there had been a terrific din as the masons cut stones and gangs of men hauled them up the wooden scaffolding into position. Even in the growing civil settlement, the importance of the day meant that few of the shops or workshops had opened for business, although no doubt most of them would resume work as soon as their owners got back; the soldiers might be able to take the whole day off but most of the civilians needed to keep working. Even as Senovara and her children made their way through the drizzle towards their home, wooden shutters were being drawn back from shop windows and doors were being opened.

Lucius kept up his usual chatter, commenting on everything he saw, questioning everything he did not understand. 'Why do the soldiers have to tell the Emperor every year that they are loyal to him, Mater? Surely if they are his soldiers they have to be loyal to him?'

'You had better ask your father when he returns,' replied Senovara, her mind already occupied with the tasks facing her on her return. 'We have to go through all this again the day after tomorrow, you know, when we have to make our own vows for the welfare of the Emperor and the Empire. Today was only for the soldiers. We go along to watch because your father was once a soldier and he likes us to be there. The day after tomorrow is the ceremony for the people who live in the town.'

Senovara sighed. As he grew older Lucius was beginning to ask her a great number of questions, many of which she felt unqualified to answer. Questions which related to the alien life she had married into. Questions which made her feel that it was she, a member of the Parisi tribe who had occupied the lands to the east of Eboracum since time immemorial, who was the foreigner, not the incoming Romans. These were uncomfortable feelings and she usually tried to shrug them off, but Lucius' innocent persistence often left her with a nagging feeling of strangeness.

As far as her family was concerned, isolated on their farm three hours' walk away along the road to the coast, the changes which had crept over the country since the invasion of the Roman army ninety years ago had been insidious and hardly noticed. None of them had been a warrior; none of them had been involved in the rebellions which had shaken many of the neighbouring tribes. They had lived on the same parcel of land for generations and had simply gone on farming in their old way. She had felt secure there, part of a way of life that seemed to stretch back to the time when the old gods had first put the animals on the land. But the presence of the army had slowly begun to alter even her parents' lives, particularly after the road to the coast had been built past their farm.

After he had eyed the situation for a few years, her father had started to bring his surplus produce in to Eboracum along the new road to sell to the army and the civilians who had begun to settle round the fortress. She and her brother had always considered it a great treat to visit Eboracum, but when she had come in with her father as a child she had presumed that if everything was strange it was just because things were different in a town, not because the world was changing. Even when she was older, and more used to visiting Eboracum, she had not been a questioning child like Lucius; she had simply accepted that in the town things were not the same as in the country, but noisier and busier and endlessly fascinating to a country girl.

Her family had been pleased when Quintus, a respected member of the veteran community with a thriving business as a shoemaker, had asked to marry her. Even her grandmother had grudgingly admitted that, though he was one of the invaders and twice her age, he was a steady, sober man who would be well able to provide for a wife and family. Senovara recalled with a smile that she herself had been more taken with his tall figure and kind eyes than with his financial position or community status. She had been twenty-one – just the right age to marry, in her family's opinion – and she had quickly become used to life in the settlement. She had already been able to speak some Latin and was now so fluent that she could change from her local dialect to Latin and back without thinking, though she couldn't always understand Quintus when he lapsed into the language of his childhood. Nowadays it was only occasionally that something happened which made her aware that her tribal lands were governed by foreigners, and that she herself was married to a German who, as a legionary in the Sixth Victrix, had been involved in 'subjugating our people', as the rabble-rousers claimed. Her grandmother, the redoubtable Enica, had been born in a round house and was proud of it, still wearing her hair in long plaits, scorning the modern pinned hairstyles of the Roman women and grumbling about the newfangled ideas, but the rest of the family had adapted over the years to the new fashions and customs, worshipping the gods they were encouraged by the authorities to worship, but still continuing to accord special respect to the old gods; speaking the language of the incomers when they had to, but using their native tongue automatically between themselves; experimenting with the new imported foods after a visit to the town, but sticking to their familiar soups and stews most of the time. Their rate of change was slow; Senovara's had had to be rapid and she sometimes found it disturbing.

Before Lucius could continue with his questions about the morning's ceremony they arrived at the door of their shop. Senovara reached her hand behind the wooden window shutter and found the hidden bone latchlifter to unlock the door.

There! That was exactly the sort of thing which she had come to take for granted without realising it. At the farm there had been no need to lock the door; there were so many people around, what with family, servants and slaves, there was always someone at home, but here, with only Quintus, herself and the children, the house was often left empty; and Quintus insisted on the door being locked when they went out because, as he said, there were some very odd people about these days from every corner of the Empire and the barbarian territories beyond. At the farm they had always known of someone approaching before he came anywhere near the end of the track. Her brother reckoned that their grandmother knew a stranger was coming even before the visitor had left home. Having been used to knowing every detail of the lives of her neighbours at the farm, Senovara found it very uncomfortable not knowing even the names of the people who lived in the same street.

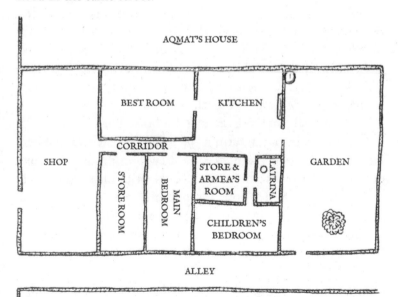

Senovara pushed Lucius over the threshold from the street into the shop, by now thoroughly irritated with her train of thought. Normally the sight of the neat, well-maintained, single-storey building with Quintus' workshop at the front and their snug living quarters behind would have comforted her, but today she felt restless and the normal sense of wellbeing she derived from her home eluded her. She made her way round Quintus' workbench and led the way down the passage, past the closed wooden door to the best room on the left and Quintus' storeroom and their bedroom on the right, into the kitchen.

'Let's get these wet cloaks off.' She put Ertola down on the floor while she took off her own cloak and helped Lucius to hang his up on one of the iron hooks by the back door. She gave the charcoal on the stove an experimental poke with an iron rod and sighed with relief as a dull red glow appeared under the ashes. She added some more charcoal from the baskets under the stove. When the fuel started to catch she went into the bedroom and came back with a linen towel. Sitting down on the stool by the stove, she scooped Ertola onto her knee and gently dried the child's fair curly hair. Lucius, having stood still all morning, was determined to make up for lost time and started to prance about the kitchen.

'Look at me! I'm the Legate on his horse,' he shouted.

Senovara shot out an arm as he galloped past and grabbed him by the back of the neck. She drew him towards her and proceeded to rub his hair and face briskly with the rough towel.

He squirmed in her grip. 'Even legates can't gallop around soaking wet,' he was informed as Senovara finished with him.

She stood up; then, moving a folded woollen rug onto the stone-flagged floor to protect Ertola from the cold, she put the child down on it and handed her her new doll. She was rewarded with a wide grin. She would have preferred an attempt at words but knew she had to be patient. 'Some children,' her grandmother had reassured her, 'do not talk early. Just because

Lucius was *born* arguing loudly doesn't mean to say that Ertola need be the same.' She had laughed at that, as had Quintus when she reported this conversation to him.

'It's probably from your revered grandmother that Lucius has inherited his noisy nature,' he'd declared.

She prodded the fire again and held her hand over it, assessing the heat. She had made some soup before they went out, so it was just a matter of warming it up. She wondered how long Quintus was likely to be. Once he started to talk to friends he sometimes lost all sense of time, and on a day like this, when he would probably be reminiscing with his old comrades, he might be ages.

The door opened just as she was trying to decide whether to feed the children or wait.

'You didn't stay long, Quintus.'

'Carinus and Felicius Simplex started to argue about taxes so I left them to it.'

He took his cloak off and hung it up, before pouring himself a tankard of beer. He stood by the stove warming his hands.

'The ceremony seemed to take for ever this morning, even though most of the legion is still in the north,' he commented.

'Did you hear when the rest are due to return to Eboracum?' Quintus was always eager to hear news of his old legion, most of the cohorts of which were still up in the north building a wall of stone to separate the province of Britannia from the tribes beyond. But his main concern these days was to get news of his brother, Gaius Flavius Naso, who was a centurion at the fort of Vercovicium on the new frontier. Gaius was often able to send letters to his brother via the messengers who went back and forth from the frontier to the legionary headquarters, but they hadn't heard from him for some weeks and Quintus was getting anxious.

'Not really. There are rumours flying about as usual but no one has any definite news.' He looked worried and Senovara was glad when their son distracted him.

'Pater! Pater!'

'What are you bellowing about now?' Quintus drew his son to him and held him against his side.

'He wants to ask you why the army has to renew its oath of allegiance every year. I thought you would explain it better than me.'

'The oath of allegiance, eh? Well, you see, son, when soldiers first join the army as recruits, they have to take a solemn oath to follow their general wherever he may lead them, and vow not to desert their standards or break the law. The ceremony this morning is to remind them of their promise and of their loyalty to the Emperor, the general of generals.'

'But if they have promised once, why do they have to do it again?' Lucius was determined to get to the bottom of this.

'Because not all the soldiers have seen the Emperor or even been to Rome. They come from provinces all over the Empire, and sometimes they need reminding that although they may have been born a German, like me, or a Briton, like your mother, or a Gaul, like my friend Sacer, they are all Romans and must be loyal to Rome.'

'So do the soldiers all over the Empire renew their oaths today?'

'Yes – in every province, all over the world, from Pannonia to Britannia and from Mauretania to Cappadocia, soldiers will have been standing on their parade grounds today reciting their oaths. I can tell you, it used to make me feel very proud thinking about that when I was a soldier.'

'Does every soldier feel like that?'

'It would be good to think so, wouldn't it, but there are always troublemakers and the army doesn't always agree to renew its oath of allegiance. My father – your grandfather – told me that once, when he was still serving, some legionaries in Germania refused to take the oath to the Emperor on the Diem Kalendarum. That was the Emperor Galba. They reckoned they should have been given more rewards for their part in Virginius Rufus' campaigns against Vindex.'

'What happened to them?'

'Nothing much, as far as I know. Galba was killed a few days later and I suppose everyone was too bothered about sorting out the succession to worry about a few disobedient soldiers in Germania, luckily for them.'

'How did he die?' Lucius was insatiably curious.

Quintus hesitated for a moment. The story of an elderly emperor, however disliked, being cut down by his own cavalrymen was probably not the most edifying story for a five-year-old. 'Well, he was seventy-three . . .'

Luckily, Lucius lost interest in the demise of old emperors as Senovara placed bowls of soup on the table. He climbed onto his stool, took the wooden spoon his mother handed to him and started eating noisily. Senovara lifted Ertola onto her high stool and stirred a small bowl of soup vigorously to cool it for her daughter.

'What will happen when we go to make our vows, Pater?'

'You mean on the third day?' Lucius nodded. 'Well, we all make our way to the parade ground at the fortress and an ox is sacrificed to Jupiter, Best and Greatest. We traders then declare our loyalty.' Quintus broke some bread off the round loaf on the table and dunked it in his soup.

'Do you have to recite something in front of everyone?'

'No, thank the gods. We all chorus the words together these days, otherwise we'd be stuck there all day. Afterwards the Legate, Lucius Minicius Natalis, has to write a letter to the Governor of Britannia, Sextus Julius Severus, in Londinium, telling him that we have sworn our loyalty, and he in turn lets the Emperor know.'

Lucius was impressed by this and stopped asking questions as he concentrated on his meal.

The rest of the day passed quietly, even though it was a holiday. The family had made no plans to visit friends and it was too far to visit even Senovara's family in winter. Quintus' only surviving relatives, his brother's family, had only been down from Vercovicium to visit Quintus and Senovara once since their marriage. Senovara sometimes rather regretted being no longer part of a large family. She had been brought up in an extended family, as was usual with the Parisi. With her grandparents, her uncle and his family, and a number of farmworkers' families, both slave and freed, living in the same compound as her parents, her brother and herself, any celebration had been a noisy affair. But that afternoon, as the temperature started to drop and the fog rolled in from the river, she was thankful that she had no need to go out on duty visits.

She spent the afternoon preparing a stuffed pig's stomach, as this was the first day of the year and something special was required for the evening meal. It was a fiddly job picking the stringy bits out of the calves' brains and pounding the meat with the eggs, oats, pepper, rue, lovage and liquamen before stuffing it into the cleaned stomach. It was also a lengthy business, because she had to boil it up, then hang it over the stove to smoke for a few hours before boiling it again. Even though she had done much of the preparation the day before, there was still a lot to do. Luckily, Lucius and Ertola were happy playing with their new toys and didn't get under her feet, so she could concentrate on her cooking.

Eventually dinner was ready and she called Quintus in from the shop, where he was checking his stock of leather and hobnails. Lucius climbed up on to his stool eagerly, ready for his meal; Senovara lifted Ertola onto her high chair and tied a piece of cloth round her neck. She placed two pottery bowls of mashed turnips and braised leeks on the table and then put the plate with the stuffed stomach in front of Quintus.

'Are you ready, everyone?' Quintus asked, as he sharpened a knife with a whetstone. Senovara nodded, smiling.

'Go on!' urged Lucius, squirming on his chair and waving his spoon in anticipation.

'Right.' Quintus plunged the knife into the brown, gleaming, steaming, neatly tied pig's stomach, and he and Lucius cheered as the contents burst out of their tight jacket and oozed onto the plate. Ertola banged her spoon on the table in excitement while Senovara shook her head despairingly – they went through this ritual every time she served pig's stomach and there was great gloom if she had made the mixture too dry so it didn't burst out.

Quintus scooped a little of the food into a small bowl and handed it to Senovara. She added some turnip and leeks, stirring the mixture briskly before putting it in front of Ertola. She put a bone spoon in the child's hand and watched for a few seconds as she tucked in. Lucius was already helping himself to vegetables, which was a relief – leeks were not his favourite but there was little else at this time of year. She blamed her grandmother for his dislike of leeks. He had eaten them without complaint until Enica told him they were newfangled imports of the Romans and that no real Briton would eat them. Lucius, already confused enough as to whether he was a Briton, a German or a Roman, had come out strongly against leeks for several months.

She poured some water into four beakers, adding red wine to two of them, but then, after a thoughtful look at Lucius, she turned to her husband. 'Shall I give Lucius some wine? He's old enough now.'

'It is the first day of the year so he could have a little, I suppose. Well watered, it will be good for him.'

Lucius' already rosy cheeks glowed even more brightly as he realised the significance of being considered old enough to drink wine. His parents both laughed when he grimaced at the sour taste and Senovara ruffled her son's brown curls affectionately.

'This is a good pig's stomach. Do you want some more, Lucius?' Quintus asked his son, who nodded with his mouth full. 'Does Ertola need any more, Senovara?' he added.

'No, she's still working her way through her first plateful. But don't eat too much, either of you. Remember, we're having two courses today because of it being the Kalends.'

When the plates were empty Senovara cleared them away and put out fresh bowls, placing her best dish in the centre of the table. The pale cream of the pudding contrasted well with the shiny red surface of the pottery, and she was pleased with the effect. She ladled the egg custard with its bottom layer of apple and its thin top coating of honey and pepper into the bowls and handed them round. Lucius' eyes gleamed and he attacked the food with gusto.

Quintus pushed his bowl away. 'That was excellent. A good omen for the rest of the year's meals, I hope.'

Senovara reddened. Quintus didn't often pay her compliments, particularly about her cooking, which he tended to take for granted. Sadly, it was rarely possible to shine as a cook because ingredients were often limited to the same cuts of meat or tired vegetables at the end of their season. The recipe for the stuffed pig's stomach had come from her mother and was a family favourite, but the new way with egg custard she had learned from her Greek friend, Basilia, at the bathhouse last month. She must remember to tell her friend how successful it had been.

While she swilled the dishes in the half-barrel set on legs by the side of the stove and tidied the kitchen, Quintus sat on the bench playing with Ertola and Lucius. 'What are you going to call your horse, Lucius?'

'I don't know. Do you know any good names for horses, Pater?' Quintus picked up the wooden horse and eyed it consideringly, spinning the wheels with his finger. 'It's definitely a horse good enough for an emperor,' he said at last. 'Look at its proud eyes and long tail. I think we should name it after one of the Emperor's horses. Why don't we call it Borysthenes after Hadrian's favourite hunting horse?'

'Borysthenes.' Lucius tried the unfamiliar word a few times and then nodded. 'It's a good name for a good horse. Is Ertola's doll going to have a name?'

'Well, we could call her Sabina after the Empress.'

'But she hasn't got any clothes yet – it's not very respectful,' Senovara broke in.

Quintus grinned at her, biting off a ribald comment about the activities of empresses with or without clothes. 'True. Let's call her after a goddess then. What about Venus – she never seems to wear any clothes! Can you say "Venus", Ertola?' but the child just gurgled at him, unwilling or unable to speak.

'It's time for bed, you two,' announced Senovara. She picked Ertola up off Quintus' knee and took her into the children's bedroom. 'Can you supervise Lucius washing his face, please? There's water in the bowl on the bench.'

Both children fell asleep quickly, tired by the long day at the ceremony and by the larger than usual meal. Quintus checked that the doors were both bolted, and Senovara damped down the fire on top of the stove for the night, making sure that there was dry tinder ready for the next morning.

'It's very cold out there,' Quintus announced as he came back into the kitchen. 'The fog is even heavier – I couldn't see across the street – and it's freezing hard. If you've finished in here, I'm ready for bed.'

Senovara woke several times in the night feeling cold. Eventually she got up and, throwing her clothes on as quickly as was possible in the dark, went through to the kitchen and opened the shutters. Fog swirled in through the small opening but little light entered so she closed them again – there was no point in letting in cold air if there was no daylight. She riddled the fire and groped under the stove for the tinder. As she added it, she blew gently on the charcoal to encourage it to take. This was not the morning to have trouble lighting the fire! Small tongues of flame started licking round the edges of the grey ashy lumps of charcoal and soon a cheerful little fire was burning. She held a thin taper of wood to a flame and lit the candle, which was standing ready in its iron holder at the edge of the stove. The fitful light threw shadows round the kitchen walls but at least she could now see what she was doing. She added more fuel to the fire; she would need to have plenty of hot charcoal ready so that she could provide Quintus with a brazier for the shop.

Quintus came in from the bedroom. 'You're up early.' He helped himself to a beaker of water and cut a lump off the remains of the bread on the kitchen table.

'It was too cold to stay in bed. It's warmer moving about.'

'I doubt if I'll get many customers today; they'll all be staying indoors round their fires getting over yesterday. I'll get on with those boots I'm mending for Sacer.'

'Bring the brazier through and I'll fill it – I think this is warm enough now.'

Quintus came back carrying the iron bowl from the tripod brazier and Senovara picked some of the burning charcoal out of the fire using a pair of long tongs. 'Have you got any charcoal in the workshop?'

'Enough to keep this going for today but we'll need to get some more tomorrow. Viducus isn't due to deliver any for a few more days and I notice we're quite low.'

Lucius wandered into the kitchen looking dishevelled and rubbing his eyes.

'Help yourself to some bread while I deal with your sister,' Senovara instructed. 'Then you can wash your hands and face and get dressed properly.'

When she came back into the kitchen Lucius was sitting on the floor with a large lump of yesterday's bread in one hand, running his horse's wheels back and forth across the flagstones. She cut herself some bread and picked up the water jug. It was empty. Looking at the two wooden buckets by the side of the stove, she groaned. There was hardly any water left. She should have refilled the buckets yesterday before dinner.

Senovara looked out of the kitchen door and shivered. There was only the slightest hint of dawn. The freezing fog, which had made the night so cold, hadn't lifted and the ground was thick with frost. It was on days like this that she regretted leaving the farm, where the well was just outside the back door and there were plenty of people around to share the duty of making sure there was enough water for the day's chores. But there was no putting it off; she needed more water. She lifted her thick woollen cloak off its hook and, wrapping it round her shoulders, fastened it with a large round brooch decorated with cheerful red and white enamel.

Quintus looked up from his bench as she walked into the shop carrying the two buckets. 'You aren't going out in this cold, are you?' he asked.

'If you want a wash tonight or a hot meal, I'll have to get water.'

He nodded. The constant need for water was a fact of life, or rather a fact which tended to dominate their life.

'I'll tell you what,' he said. 'Why don't you put a pair of my old socks on over your boots? That might give you a better grip.'

She thought about it for a few moments. She would look ridiculous but there would be few people about and her long skirts would hide her feet. She nodded. 'Good idea.'

He put down his hammer and went into the bedroom. She could hear him rummaging about in his old army box.

'Here you are,' he said, holding up a disreputable pair of old tubular drawstring socks. 'These stood me in good stead when I was on the frontier, though they're past their best now.'

She sat down on the stool provided for customers, pulled the socks on over her boots and stood up. She took a few tentative steps.

'Very elegant,' laughed Quintus.

'I'm hoping no one will see me,' she retorted and picked up the two wooden buckets by their rope handles. She put them down again; she had been so concerned about her feet that she had forgotten her hands. She went back into the bedroom and returned with her gloves. These were just bags made from strips of an old cloak, with a separate tube for each thumb, which she had made herself, but they were perfect for carrying heavy buckets of water back from the trough.

Fully equipped, she looked out of the front door again with a distinct lack of enthusiasm; then, throwing her cloak hood over her hair, she said, 'Ertola has gone back to sleep and Lucius is playing on the floor by the kitchen door with his horse. I'll be as quick as I can – it's not a day for gossiping, even if there is anyone else at the trough.'

Quintus nodded and, after casting a look at the door to the living quarters to be sure that he could see his son, returned to hammering hobnails into a boot sole.

Senovara closed the door behind her and shivered. She advanced down the street, keeping close to the sides of the buildings where the overhanging eaves had protected the ground from the worst of the frost.

Her feet slithered a few times on the occasional flagstone outside shop doorways but the socks seemed to be helping to keep her upright. Her nose began to hurt with the cold and her cheeks were stinging. As she walked along she heard the horn in the fortress signalling the start of the military day. Soon there would be bustle and activity, but there was no one else around yet.

In the open space beyond the end of the row of buildings the water trough gleamed. Her heart sank; the water was frozen. She must be the first person to get there that morning. Please the gods that it was just frozen on the top, otherwise she would have to go on to the well.

She shifted both buckets to one hand and tested the ice with the tip of a gloved finger. Nothing moved. She put down the buckets and, holding on to the edge of the trough to stop herself slipping on the frozen puddles, she looked around for the stone that was kept there to break the ice.

'Curses be on any man or woman, slave or free, if they've dropped the stone into the water before the trough froze,' she muttered. But no, there it was, tucked under the end of the trough. She bent down to pick it up and swore again when she found it had frozen to the ground.

'By Jupiter and the Genius of This Place,' she exclaimed, 'now what do I do?'

She bent down again and, getting the gloved fingers of both hands under the edge of the stone, she heaved. She felt the ice give a little. She pushed and pulled at the stone until it eventually gave way, and stood up panting. Turning to the trough, she brought the stone down hard onto the surface of the ice and sobbed with relief as the ice cracked. She brought the stone down again and this time it went through into the water below. Taking off her gloves, she dipped the two buckets into the water, dredging up a mixture of water and ice.

Now came the worst bit. She would have to get the stone out of the water in case the trough froze over again. Pushing back her cloak, she rolled up her right sleeve and plunged her hand into the water. She gasped as the cold hit her fingers. She picked out the larger lumps of ice and threw them behind the trough; that would help stop the water freezing over before anyone else had a chance to fill their pails. She continued to grope around in the dark water, unable to see the stone among the icy lumps in the uncertain light. At last her fingers found the edge of the stone and she drew it up from the freezing depths and propped it by the side of the trough. She quickly dried her hands on the hem of her cloak and pulled her gloves back onto her hands, one of which was now blue and numb with cold.

She got as sure a grip as she could on the bucket handles and set off for home, her teeth beginning to chatter. As usual, a drip formed on the end of her nose as soon as she had both hands full. Slowly she edged back along the street, extra cautious now in case she fell and lost the precious water. There was still no one else about. No bustling shoppers; no one standing by open doors. All the shops had their shutters up and their doors shut. She could see chinks of light through the gaps under doors and could hear voices and the sound of hammering. Life was going on inside the buildings; it was just out in the street that it was so eerily quiet.

Just at that moment a jingling caught her attention and she looked up. Through the freezing fog came a soldier leading a horse. The man was completely enveloped in an enormous army cloak and had his head down. The horse had a sack covering its saddle and its ears were well back; neither man nor horse was enjoying their outing. The bundles tied onto the saddle indicated that the man was an army messenger, and she hoped for his sake that he was only going to a nearby town like Calcaria or Isurium rather than further afield. He didn't seem to be in a hurry so she presumed he was on a routine trip and not taking news of any emergency. She noticed with wry amusement that both horse and man had sacking tied round their feet.

The soldier became aware of her presence and raised his head. 'Hail, lady,' he muttered.

'Hail,' she replied.

Neither of them slackened pace. They carried on, the only people out on the coldest day of the winter so far.

Senovara reached the door of their shop thankfully. She put down a bucket, wiped her nose on her glove and lifted the latch. She hauled one bucket in and slid it just inside the door, not wishing to let any of the cold fog into the shop. She pulled in the other bucket and slammed the door shut behind her. Quintus put down his tools and came over to pick up the buckets. As he led the way into the kitchen she rubbed her hands together and stamped her feet to get warm.

'You look frozen,' he said mildly. 'Come and get warmed up.'

'The trough was iced over. No one else had been out. The only person I saw was an army messenger leading his horse.'

She bent over the glowing charcoal on the stove, still rubbing her hands together. Her fingers began to ache as the feeling came back and she fumbled as she took off her cloak.

'Put this on the chest in the bedroom,' she directed Lucius.

He sighed, not wanting to leave his wooden horse, but obeyed. For a few seconds he struggled to get a hold on the heavy, damp material and then he trotted into the bedroom.

'Here,' said Quintus, 'have some wine to warm you.' He held out one of their pottery beakers.

'Thank you.' She gulped the red wine and found that it was comfortingly warm and had less water in it than usual. Quintus must have had it sitting by the fire waiting for her return. She looked up at him gratefully, but he was already on his way back to his bench.

The fog and frost hardly lifted all day. Lucius lost interest in his horse and wanted something to do, but it was too cold for him to go out into the garden at the back of the house to play and none of his friends had ventured out into the street. He started to play with his sister but she seemed more interested in trying to push crumbs down into the cracks between the flagstones of the kitchen floor. The midday soup was a welcome distraction but by the middle of the afternoon Senovara was becoming irritated with him.

'Go and talk to your father,' she sighed, knowing that Quintus was unlikely to have many customers that day and might well welcome the company of his young son.

Once again Senovara recalled her life on the farm, where there had been the companionship of her brother and cousins.

She had never been bored as a child. Even on the occasions when the boys made it clear that they didn't want a girl joining in their games there had been the house slaves to talk to, her mother and the farmworkers to help, and her father, uncle and grandmother to tell her stories of the old life.

She let Lucius into the shop and stood for a moment watching her husband hammer nails into a boot sole. It had been too dark in the shop all day for him to cut out or sew or decorate the leather – there was too much danger of wasting the expensive hides. But it was also far too cold to open the shop shutters to let in what little daylight there was, and the light from the candles was too fitful in the draughts to do close work.

'Hello, Lucius. Have you come in here to cause trouble?'

'No. I've come to help you. Mater said I should.'

Quintus caught Senovara's eye and grinned at the mixture of outrage and virtue in the boy's voice.

'Very well, then. Why don't you help me by sorting out these hobnails?'

Lucius drew nearer and looked at the boot on the big iron last set into the top of a great block of wood.

'Why do you put the nails in patterns?' he asked.

'Well, boots need to have most of their hobnails here, just under the balls of the feet, do you see? And here, under the heel. Those are the bits that touch the ground and need to have the most grip. I have to use different numbers of hobnails in the different parts of the sole, so I like to make patterns so people can recognise my shoes from those of other shoemakers.'

'Do you always use the same pattern?' Lucius was interested now; he had often watched his father hammering in the nails but had never thought about the patterns.

Senovara continued to listen; Quintus rarely talked to her about how he made shoes and she was just as curious as her son about the skill in turning animal hides into stout, comfortable boots and sandals.

'No. I use different patterns for different shoes. If I'm making a woman's boot, I might make the hobnails into a flower pattern. Here's one you can have a look at. I've put the petals under the ball of the foot, do you see? Here's the stem along the edge of the instep and here are the leaves under the heel. Look, Lucius, why don't you sit up here on the bench and sort through this bag of hobnails? Check that they all have proper shanks and aren't bent. Put the bad ones in this box here so I can take them back to Sudrenus. You can make patterns with the good ones if you promise not to bend their shanks. I'll pick them out from your patterns as I need them.'

Lucius agreed that this would be a fine way to spend the afternoon and was lifted up onto the bench. Quintus turned back to his work and Senovara returned to her kitchen, thankful that they were both occupied and she could get on with making some honey cakes. She rather hoped that Lucius would become interested in shoemaking and want to follow his father in the trade instead of joining the army, but it was a faint hope – veterans' sons were expected to enlist when they were seventeen and Lucius, like all boys of his age, was already enthusiastic about the prospect.

Father and son laboured on together, both content at their tasks. A gentle peace fell on the workshop, interrupted only by the rhythmic tapping of Quintus' hammer on the iron hobnails. When he finished the boot he was working on, he placed it on the bench and squinted at it sideways to check that none of the nails was protruding further than any of the others – he had a reputation to uphold for producing comfortable, good-quality boots. He tapped a few down a bit more. When he was satisfied, he put the completed boot on a shelf, ready for finishing, reached into the basket by his side for its pair, and began again.

Before he started he glanced at Lucius sitting on the end of the bench and chuckled as he recognised one of the patterns Lucius had produced. Having started with simple flowers and triangles, the child had moved on to more interesting designs, and instead of placing the hobnails with their points up he had laid them on their sides and made a picture of a hedgehog, with the bent shanks pointing outwards like prickles. He was fascinated by hedgehogs, and Quintus recalled with a wry smile the previous summer when Lucius had found a hedgehog in the garden and carried it into the kitchen, keen to adopt it as a pet. He had been furious when he was told he couldn't keep it in the house and had stormed back into the garden to sulk, still clutching it. He had then spent a tearful night scratching the flea bites which had been the result of his meeting with the prickly creature – Senovara had been up most of the night applying a soothing ointment of bear's grease and dock leaves which she had bought from the *seplasarius* who had set up a shop in Eboracum.

The door opened suddenly and a blast of cold air accompanied by swirling fog interrupted his thoughts. A shrouded figure stood inside the door with only one black, glittering eye visible among the folds of the dark-blue cloak. Lucius took one look and fled into the kitchen to the safety of his mother.

The shrouded figure laughed and threw back her hood.

'Hail, Aqmat,' Quintus courteously greeted their new neighbour.

'Hail, Quintus. Is Senovara willing to receive a visitor?'

'In the kitchen.' He nodded in the direction of the door, which his son had left open in his flight. 'Just go through, if you will.'

Aqmat smiled and strode through into the passage leading to the kitchen.

'Oh, Aqmat! I wondered who it was. Come on in – please do not mind us being in the kitchen. It's too cold to sit in the other room.'

'It is good of you to accept a visitor.' The Palmyrene woman spoke slowly so that Senovara could understand her eastern accent. 'Hairan is away at Cataractonium and this weather is making me feel very miserable.' She picked Ertola up from the floor and gave her a hug. 'Hello, young lady.'

'Come nearer the stove and warm yourself,' invited Senovara. 'I suppose you are not used to such cold weather.'

'It is not the cold – we get very cold nights in the desert in winter. It is this fog. Everything is so grey and dark and damp and . . .' She groped for the right word. 'Muffled,' she finished with an exasperated snort as she sat down with Ertola on her knee. 'I don't know how you stand it here in Britannia. I thought Gallia was bad enough but this sort of weather frightens me. I long so much for the bright, white light of the Palmyrene desert with the haze shimmering in the distance. I hate not being able to see anything around me and everything blurred and dull.'

Senovara was sympathetic. She couldn't imagine the desert, although Aqmat had tried to describe it to her when they first met, but she could understand how it felt to be far from home, even if her home was only a few hours away and not across provinces and oceans. She also realised that Aqmat was missing her son, who had stayed behind to look after his father's business in Palmyra, and her daughter, who was married to a merchant in Damascus.

'Can I pour you some wine?' Senovara knew there was no point in offering Aqmat Celtic beer.

'Thank you, but well watered, if you would.'

Senovara was glad to see her new neighbour, who always fascinated her with her exotic appearance and tales of life in other provinces. Before coming to live in Eboracum, Senovara had never seen anyone like Aqmat. From her veiled hair, dressed in a wall of braids over her forehead, to the tips of her fingers, this woman sparkled with jewellery. Bronze pins with glass heads fixed her fine veil and hair in place. In her ears there were gold earrings with more glass beads hanging from them.

Round her neck there were several necklaces, some of plain chain, some with green beads which caught the light. She had several jangling bracelets of bronze on each wrist and at least three rings on each hand.

Senovara handed Aqmat a beaker of wine. 'I hope this is mixed to your taste.' She put down a plate of the freshly baked, small, oval honey cakes. 'Help yourself.'

Lucius edged closer, not wanting to take his eyes off their guest but definitely interested in the honey cakes. Aqmat took one and, breaking it in half, popped a piece in her mouth and held out the other piece to Lucius. After a second he grabbed it and through the spray of crumbs was understood by his anxious mother to have said, 'Thank you.'

He ran the wooden wheels of his horse over the tabletop then suddenly asked, 'Why do you wear so much jewellery? Mater doesn't.'

'Lucius!' Senovara was scandalised by her son's audacity, although she was equally curious to know the answer.

Aqmat laughed. 'I don't think I wear a lot of jewellery. You see, I come from a city called Palmyra, a long way from here in the eastern province of Syria, and Palmyrene women always wear lots of jewellery. If I was at home, this amount would be thought very modest. Here in Britannia, though, women, like your mater, don't like wearing most of their dowry all the time.'

Senovara tried to imagine herself going about her daily chores in such finery, but failed. She also wondered what Quintus would have to say about the idea and decided mischievously to suggest it to him later to see his reaction.

'Are you going to the loyalty ceremony tomorrow, Aqmat?' asked Senovara quickly, before her son could ask something else outrageous.

'Oh, yes. That's why I called in. Even though Hairan is away I would like to be there, but it would be nice to go with someone – can I go with you?'

'Of course you can. Shall we call for you as we pass your house?'

'That would be kind. But I had better not hold you up any more today. You will be wanting to start preparing your evening meal. I will see you tomorrow. Goodbye, Lucius. Goodbye, Ertola.'

Senovara showed her guest out through the shop. Quintus was busy talking to a customer and just smiled as Aqmat nodded her farewell.

Later that night, when they were getting ready for bed, Senovara said, 'Quintus, I promised Aqmat that we would take her with us to the ceremony tomorrow. I hope you don't mind.'

'Not at all – it may start rumours that I'm taking up the eastern habit of having more than one wife; but I'm all for that, particularly if one of the wives is as exotic as Aqmat.'

Senovara took off her linen shift and threw it at him, then sat down on the edge of the wooden bed to untie the laces at the top of her stockings. 'If you want an exotic wife I'll start wearing all my jewellery at once and pile my hair on the top of my head, but your customers will probably begin to suspect that you're overcharging them if I'm covered in glitter and curls.'

'No. You'll do fine as you are,' Quintus answered, handing her back her shift. He flung back the blankets and climbed into bed. 'What are you doing now? I want to go to sleep.'

'I'm just rubbing some axle grease and barley-ash handcream into my hands. They got very chapped when I was getting the water this morning and my fingers are itching.'

'I've been thinking about that. I may not want an exotic Palmyrene wife but I don't want the one I've got working herself to the bone, particularly as that handcream smells terrible. What would you say to us getting a slave?'

Senovara checked as she was about to get into the bed. 'A slave? But we couldn't afford a slave! And where would we put one? This is just a small house.'

'Your brother and I were talking about this the last time he was in Eboracum. One of the girls on his farm is now twelve and he doesn't need any more house slaves. He asked if we wanted her. Her name is Armea – he thought you would remember her: she's the daughter of Docilis and Alogiosa – so you wouldn't have a stranger in the house.'

'I know Docilis and Alogiosa well. Alogiosa has worked in the kitchens at home for years, and Docilis is reckoned to be a good farmhand. If their daughter takes after them she'll be a good worker, but I probably wouldn't recognise her now. Can we afford her?'

'Matugenus doesn't want a lot for her. Because he's known her since she was born he isn't looking for the market price if he can get her settled somewhere where she'll not be badly treated.'

'But we'd have to feed her and keep her.'

'How much can a twelve-year-old girl eat? Are you interested in the idea? Shall I let Matugenus know we want her?'

'Yes, I suppose so, if you think we can afford it. We could clear some space in the storeroom for a bed for her.' Senovara's mind was racing through the problems and possibilities. 'It would be wonderful to have someone to look after the children when I want to go out shopping. Shopping with Lucius in tow can be hard work!'

'And she could fetch the water from the trough and do the gardening, and a multitude of other tasks. You could become a lady of leisure, like Aqmat. I'll talk to Matugenus about a contract next time he's in town.'

Quintus turned over in bed. The conversation was over as far as he was concerned and it was time to sleep. Senovara snuggled into his back and he gave a grunt. She smiled into the darkness with her cheek against his tunic. A slave! She was going to have a slave! And what was even better, it was to be someone she knew, who knew her family and her home. There would be someone else to go to the water trough on bad days. Someone to look after the children while she went to the market. Someone else to chap her hands preparing vegetables on winter days. Someone else to scratch their hands rubbing sand across the surface of iron pans to remove the inevitable rust spots. The more she thought about it, the more the loss of privacy, the bringing of a stranger into their home, ceased to be an issue. She had been used to having slaves around the house and farm when she was a child, but they were local people who had been bound to her family for generations. In Eboracum it was more usual to buy a slave and, although Quintus made a good income from his shoes, she had never expected they would be able to afford the price of a servant. Even if they had, she would have felt a little unhappy about bringing a foreign slave into their house. She had discussed this once with her friend Basilia, who had scoffed at her concern and said, 'If you don't like a slave, you simply sell it and get another one and go on until you get one you like.' Senovara had been astonished by this, for she had been brought up in a tradition in which slaves were regarded as part of the extended family and few were ever bought or sold. To have a slave from her brother's farm solved the problem nicely. She moved a little to make herself more comfortable, careful not to disturb Quintus, and fell asleep making plans.

Februarius

IANUARIUS HAD CONTINUED miserably with fog and rain, snow and frosts, and everyone in the town had had colds, including Senovara and her family. Luckily, they had avoided the winter sickness, which Senovara had dreaded annually since her uncle and both her parents had died of it five years earlier. During the winter she always paid particular respect to the healing gods, just to make sure. This year only Quintus had felt well enough to attend the celebrations of the Emperor's birthday on the ninth day before the Kalends of Februarius, and even he had merely attended the religious ceremonies in the morning and had not gone on to the military displays. Lucius, in particular, had been very ill and she was worried that he still hadn't got rid of a chesty cough which racked his little body painfully. Senovara had been up with him almost every night for a fortnight and she was beginning to feel worn out. She was looking forward to this afternoon, when her brother, Matugenus, was due to bring the new slave girl. At last she would have someone to help her with the chores, which had been building up while they had all been ill. Today, however, she would have to do the shopping herself if she was going to have any food and drink in the house to offer her brother. Quintus would have to look after Lucius – the child was still too ill to go out – but she would take Ertola with her.

As she was working out what she needed to buy at the market, there was a knock at the kitchen door.

'Hail, Senovara. Pervica and I are off to do some shopping and wondered if we could get anything for you.'

Senovara whirled round, startled. It was as if she had summoned up the Shades! Her friends Surilla and Pervica were standing just inside the door, shaking the rain off their woollen cloaks. As always she was delighted to see the two of them, both competent middle-aged women who had befriended her when she came to live in their street. Surilla came from the same Danubian tribe as Quintus and was of a similar age to him so he always enjoyed her visits, which gave him an excuse to speak the language of his childhood and exchange reminiscences about Germania. Surilla had come to Britannia with a soldier of the Sixth Victrix and when he had died ten years ago had stayed on, supporting herself, like many women in a similar situation did, by taking in soldiers' laundry. She was a wiry little person with dark hair, now streaked with grey, held in a snowy white linen cap. Senovara had been drawn to this tactful, cheerful woman immediately they had met and often found herself relying on Surilla for advice and support.

Pervica was very different, in both appearance and temperament. A huge woman with wild, curly red hair and piercing blue eyes, she loomed over Surilla and Senovara. But it was not just her size which made her dominate any gathering. She held firm views and was never afraid to express them. A Brigantian by birth, she stuck to her tribe's principle that men and women had equal rights, and had no opinion of the Roman view that females needed guardians all their lives. Senovara well remembered the row there had been when Marcus Anicius

41

Ingenuus, the fortress doctor and husband of their friend Basilia, had tried to explain this rule to Pervica by quoting the Roman lawyer Cicero, who had written that women needed guardians because of their weakness of intellect. Pervica's quick wit and sharp tongue had briskly proved that theory inaccurate, and Anicius Ingenuus had retired to his hospital, muttering that he would have liked to have heard Cicero himself arguing the point with Pervica, and that his money would not have been on the famous advocate. Pervica was married to a *gubernator* – a river pilot – and was the mother of two strapping sons who worked with their father. Surilla had once said there were times when the noise that came through the wall between her house and Pervica's when the family was arguing sounded as if all the gods of thunder, war and lightning were failing to see eye to eye. No one ever asked for advice from Pervica – you didn't need to: she gave you advice whether you wanted it or not.

'Come on in. I was just thinking I need to do some shopping – I'm expecting my brother this afternoon and there's hardly any food left in the house. Let me pour you some beer while I work out what I need.'

'A beer is just what I could do with. Wine's no good when the weather's as wet as this.' Pervica had never taken to wine, preferring the Celtic beer she had grown up with.

'Do you want it warmed?' asked Senovara.

Pervica shook her head but Surilla nodded: 'Yes, please.'

Senovara poured three beakers of beer and handed one to Pervica. She pushed the iron poker into the hot charcoal on the stove and waited for it to warm before plunging it first into Surilla's beaker and then into her own.

Pervica lowered her bulk onto a stool and Senovara held her breath as she waited to see if the stool would take the weight. Pervica was famous as a destroyer of furniture, either through sitting on it too heavily or by throwing it at her husband. But the three legs of the sturdy little oak stool stood up to the challenge.

'And how are you, young Ertola?' Pervica's massive arm scooped up the small child. 'Are you going to talk to me today?' Ertola gazed at her and shyly shook her head, sticking her thumb in her mouth to make the point. Pervica laughed. 'One day she'll suddenly come out with a full senatorial oration and give us all a shock, won't you, my pet?'

'Stop teasing the child, Pervica.' Surilla turned to Senovara. 'How are you all now?'

'Well, Quintus and I are fine, and Ertola seems to have got over her sniffles, but Lucius is still in a bad way.'

At that moment Lucius wandered into the kitchen. On seeing his mother's friends he tried to greet them but could manage only a choking cough. Senovara picked him up and held him on her knee, offering him some of her warm beer as she rubbed his back.

'My, that's a good cough you've got, Lucius. You sound like a croupy bear.'

Lucius tried to giggle at Surilla's description but only succeeded in coughing again.

'You need to give him something for that cough,' said Pervica.

'I've been giving him spoonfuls of honey flavoured with rosemary.' Senovara tried not to sound resentful. Although she was very fond of Pervica, the older woman often made her feel defensive and incompetent.

'That might work for a tickly cough' – Pervica's voice implied that this was highly unlikely but she was willing to be gracious – 'but he sounds as if he needs something stronger. What you should do is burn hare's dung until it's just ashes, then mix it with wine and give the child a beakerful every evening. It always worked with my two.'

Senovara blinked. Where was she going to find hare's dung in Eboracum in Februarius? There was no point trying to dissuade Pervica, however. 'Thank you. I might try that,' she said.

Surilla grinned at her sympathetically. 'I've always found Albanus' cough mixture containing hyssop, rue and figs to be excellent for coughs. I have some at home; I'll drop it in later if you wish. It'll save you having to prepare a new mixture.'

'Oh, that is kind.' Senovara was relieved. Pervica was quite capable of checking that her advice had been taken and it would be difficult to put her off.

Pervica snorted. 'You shouldn't give children anything with rue in it, I was always told, but no doubt you know best.'

'Have you thought what you want us to get you at the market?' Surilla was practised in moving the conversation on when Pervica was being bossy.

'I've made some soup so I think all I need is some meat for tonight's meal and a loaf of bread – I haven't had time to bake. A three-*as* loaf will be enough: I might mill some flour and do some baking tomorrow. I've got some turnips and onions in the storeroom, so that should do.'

'What sort of meat do you want?'

'Oh, whatever there is. I'll just do a stew – that's more to Matugenus' taste – so it doesn't need to be anything tender. Pork or mutton would be wonderful, if you can find any. Enough for us three adults, the children and the new slave.'

'Matugenus is bringing the slave, then?'

'Yes, thank Jupiter. He hasn't been able to get her here before this, with the weather being so bad. The carter brought a message yesterday to say that Matugenus reckoned they could get here today if he waited until the light was full before he set off. He'll stay the night so he's not trying to make it back before the fog comes down or it gets dark.'

'Sensible man. Even though this is the Nones of Februarius and officially supposed to be the first day of spring, it's still nasty out on the roads. Right, Pervica, we'd better get on, otherwise Matugenus will be here before we've got Senovara anything to feed him with.'

'If you'll wait a minute I'll get some money from Quintus to pay for the meat.' She went into the shop and came back with a couple of bronze *sestertii*. 'Here, this should be enough.'

'See you later.'

The women threw their cloak hoods over their heads and picked up their baskets as she opened the door for them. It was still raining but it didn't seem to be as bad as it had been, and by the time they returned a watery sun was trying bravely to show itself.

'There was absolutely nothing in the meat market except some scrawny chickens and some pig's liver. The rest I wouldn't feed to a goat.' Pervica's tone was derisive. 'I don't know how they have the nerve to sell some of it.'

'All the decent meat seems to go north to the troops on the frontier these days,' commented Surilla. 'There were plenty of cows and sheep being herded towards the fortress – the news in the market is that another cohort is due back from the frontier in the next few days – but there was little for us poor civilians. We found some hares at Sangus's stall but we didn't know if Matugenus would eat hare.'

'Oh, he'll eat anything but Quintus doesn't like it much – it's too rich for his taste. So what did you manage to get?' Senovara stored away the snippet of news about the legion's movements to tell Quintus later, but no doubt he had heard already and her more immediate concern was with their evening meal.

'We reckoned the pig's liver was the best. We got it from Bonosius. The kind man put it in a bowl so I could carry it, but I promised to take the bowl back straight away.' Surilla handed over a grey pottery dish covered by a dirty piece of cloth.

Senovara lifted the bloody contents out and sniffed it before putting it into one of her pots. 'It smells all right. I can make a good stew with this and some onions. I've got plenty of lentils and eggs to make a *patina* to serve it with.'

'Here's your loaf and your change – one *as*. We'll leave you to get on with it. See you tomorrow.'

'Many thanks. That was really kind.'

When her friends had left, Senovara lifted a bronze cauldron off its hook, threw in a couple of handfuls of lentils and covered them with water to soak. At least the liver stew wouldn't take long to cook, so she would have time to tidy the house a bit before Matugenus arrived.

Lucius coughed again and Senovara looked at him with concern. She took down a small wooden box from the shelf and lifted its lid off.

'Here, Lucius,' she said, picking up a sharp knife and cutting into the box's contents, 'Try chewing some honeycomb. That might help.'

Lucius brightened. He loved honeycomb. No matter how long you chewed it, there always seemed to be some left stuck round a tooth to be sucked. He took the small, sticky square from his mother's hand and retired to a corner the better to concentrate.

His sister wandered over eager to share the treat.

'No, my love, you can't have any honeycomb but you can lick my fingers clean.'

Senovara sat down with Ertola on her knee and let the child suck her honey-covered fingers for a few minutes.

'I can't do this all day; I'll have to get on with the housework, Ertola. Otherwise Uncle Matugenus will be rude about the mess we live in.'

An hour later, Quintus stuck his head round the door into the kitchen, where Senovara was trying to wash Lucius' face. 'Matugenus is here.'

'I'll be right with you once your son has stopped squirming like an eel and let me wash the honey off his face. Do stand still, Lucius. Uncle Matugenus won't want to see you if you're all sticky.'

Ertola trotted across the kitchen after her father, eager to see her uncle. Senovara made a grab for her as she went past but, not wanting to let go of Lucius, she couldn't reach the toddler.

'Quintus, Ertola is right behind you. Don't let her out into the street. It's too busy today with all the waggons and animals on their way to the fortress.' She held the top of Lucius' head in a vice-like grip and energetically scrubbed his face with a cloth. 'There. That's better. Not as beautiful as the young Apollo but acceptable.'

Lucius' face emerged from the cloth glowering at his mother as a stocky, dark-haired man in the baggy tartan trousers and woollen cloak of a local farmer entered the room holding Ertola in his arms, followed by a young girl.

Matugenus hugged his sister. 'Hail, Senovara. Do I find you well?'

'Indeed you do, but Lucius still has a horrible cough, so don't make him laugh,' she said warningly as her brother started to tickle his nephew. 'Is this Armea?' She looked at the young girl with interest.

'Yes. You probably won't remember her. She's grown quite a bit since you last saw her. She's still only small, of course, but she's stronger than she looks and no trouble. I've brought you a brace of duck as well; hand them over, girl.' He gave the young slave a kindly shove towards Senovara.

The girl was slightly built with light brown hair hanging in a plait down her back. She was wearing a drab brown tunic, which reached only to her calves, and a tweed cloak which was too big for her. She looked at Senovara and smiled nervously as she passed her the duck, tied together by their feet.

'Oh, thank you, Matugenus – those look good. Hail, Armea. Welcome. If you come with me I'll show you where you're to sleep. This is Lucius, by the way, my son, and Ertola there is my daughter.'

'Thank you, Mistress.' The girl's reply was barely a whisper but Senovara started at the response. Until that moment she hadn't really taken it in that she was to have a slave. There had always been slaves at the farm, of course, but her grandmother had always been the mistress of the house. She suddenly felt very matronly.

'Are you coming to live with us?' Lucius demanded.

'Armea is coming to help me look after you and Ertola,' Senovara intervened quickly to save the girl from having to respond and then, seeing a mulish look appear on Lucius' face at the idea that he needed looking after, showed Armea into the small room off the kitchen that was usually used as a pantry and for storage.

'Here,' she said, pointing to a small truckle bed fitted into a space she had cleared by the wall, 'this is where you will sleep. The mattress has fresh straw in it and you can keep your things in that old crate over there. The children's bedroom is behind. We have a *latrina* in the room opposite.' She couldn't keep the note of pride out of her voice and was pleased to see Armea looked suitably impressed. 'Now come and have some soup to warm you after your journey.'

When they got back into the kitchen they found Quintus and Matugenus established at the kitchen table with a large jug of beer at their elbows and a small sheet of wood in front of them.

'Why don't you show Armea round, Lucius, so she'll know where everything is, while I warm up some soup?'

Lucius looked at the girl in front of him consideringly and then, as she clearly had passed some secret test, took her by the hand and pulled her out of the kitchen.

'What's that you've got there? It looks very official.' Senovara peered over her brother's shoulder.

'It is. It's the contract for Armea.'

Quintus held the rectangular sliver of wood out to her and she sat down on the bench to read the words inked onto one of its faces.

Matugenus, son of Totius, who resides in the territory of the Parisi, by this document acknowledges to Quintus Flavius Candidus, son of Lucius Flavius, that he accepts as valid this handwritten sales contract made concerning the female slave Armea, twelve years of age and with no distinguishing marks. Quintus Flavius Candidus here takes possession of her from Matugenus, son of Totius, just as she is. She is non-returnable, except for epilepsy or external claim. The price exchanged is fifty *denarii*, which Matugenus here acknowledges has been received in full. For this amount Quintus Flavius Candidus will pay the sales tax on the aforementioned slave. A warranty on this slave has been given by Matugenus according to all claims made in this contract. Signed Matugenus, son of Totius of the Parisi. Q. Flavius Candidus of Eboracum. Nones Februarius, XVI *trib. pot.* Hadrian.'

Senovara blanched when she read the price – she could buy ten tunics for that amount! – but she knew it was nowhere near the current market value for a healthy female house slave.

'This is very formal – I bet you didn't write it, Matugenus.'

'Of course not. I wouldn't know how to word it so that it was legal. We stopped at the scribe's house by the fortress gates and he wrote it up for me. Quintus has just signed it.'

'And what does "external claim" mean?'

'Jupiter only knows!' her brother replied cheerfully. 'I think it covers the possibility that someone might be able to prove that she wasn't mine to sell.'

'But how could they? She was born on the farm.'

'I know, but these things have to be done properly.'

Senovara got up and started pouring soup into bowls. All this legal talk was beyond her.

'How are Grandmother and Ahteha getting on?' Matugenus had not been married long, and Senovara knew only too well how difficult her grandmother could be.

'Remarkably well, I'm glad to say. Ahteha is very patient and realises that the old woman is set in her ways, so hasn't tried to alter anything much. It's probably just as well that Ahteha has known us all since she was a child and understands Grandmother.'

Senovara was relieved. Her own mother had never been able to wrest the running of the house from her independently minded mother-in-law and there had been some prime battles between them over the years. Her two cousins had both moved away soon after the death of her parents, Bodenius to join the Roman army, Amatus to work on his own wife's family farm near Petuaria on the coast. Senovara sometimes thought her grandmother missed them all and made life difficult for her remaining relatives more out of habit than through any real desire to control their lives.

'Have you heard anything of Bodenius or Amatus recently?' she asked.

'No, but no news is good news. I'll call in on Amatus when I next go to Petuaria, but that probably won't be for a few more months. The last I heard of Bodenius, his unit had been sent to Pannonia – you know, of course, he's been promoted to *optio*?'

Senovara nodded and he turned to his brother-in-law. 'Have you had any news of the First Cohort of Britons, Quintus?'

'No more than you. But I have old colleagues who have contacts in Pannonia; I'll see if I can get any news of Bodenius for you.'

The next day her brother was up early, keen to be off as soon as it was light enough. The pig's liver stew with slices of lentil *patina* had been devoured with enthusiasm and the two men had sat up long into the night talking by the meagre light of the charcoal on the stove and an oil lamp. Armea had proved amiable and efficient as she helped to put the children to bed but was obviously tired from her journey. Senovara suspected the girl had not slept the night before because of anticipation and fright, so had sent her off early to get some sleep. She'd checked that her husband and brother had enough ale and that there was plenty of fuel for the lamp and then had gone thankfully to her own bed – the men's talk of the rising in

Judaea and whether the Emperor Hadrian had really gone there to sort the rebellion out himself, as the official reports stated, or had stayed in Athenae and left Judaea to the legate, Teneius Rufus, to deal with, as some of the gossipmongers claimed, had not interested her in the least. Now that it was morning she was keen to start showing Armea her duties, but that would have to wait until Matugenus had gone on his way.

She filled his flask with beer and handed it to him. 'Do you want any food for the journey?'

'No. A piece of bread will do me fine. Ahteha will have a meal waiting for me when I get home.'

'Give her my greetings and Grandmother as well.'

'I will. See you when I'm next in town.' Matugenus gave his sister a hug then waved a hand at the slave. 'Be a good girl, Armea. I'm sure Senovara will be a kind mistress. I'll tell your parents you arrived safely.'

Armea's face went suddenly blank as Matugenus, her last link with home, was about to leave. She smiled tremulously at her former master but he was already on his way through the shop, exchanging farewells with his brother-in-law and the children. Senovara felt pity for the girl, no more than a child, who had been left with strangers. It would be as well to keep her occupied and busy or she'd be in tears.

'Put your cloak on, Armea, and we'll go and do some shopping. On the way I'll show you where the water trough is. It'll be your job to get the water each day.'

Senovara called to Lucius, who was still in the shop with his father: 'Lucius, I'm going shopping. Do you want to come?'

'Yes, please.' Lucius ran in, with Ertola. His cough was much better today. The hyssop mixture that Surilla, true to her word, had brought round seemed to have worked and it would do him good to get out. She handed him his cloak and pinned Ertola into a smaller version.

Armea reappeared and Senovara passed a basket to her.

'Right, we'll be on our way. I need some money, Quintus. A couple of *sestertii* should do,' she said as they went into the shop.

He reached into the box under the bench and threw her some large coins, which she wrapped in a twist of fabric and tucked into the bottom of the basket.

'Are you all going?' he enquired as he took in the little crowd before him.

'Yes, it will give me a chance to show Armea where everything is. We won't be long, though.'

She led the way down the street to the water trough, with Ertola in her arms and Lucius running along in front, Armea bringing up the rear carrying the rush basket. At the trough she put Ertola down while she showed Armea where the stone was kept to break the ice.

'It's not like getting water from a well. You need to dip the bucket right into the water,' she warned. 'If you just skim it across the top you get all the flies and leaves on the surface, but you also shouldn't drop it right in because if you scrape it across the stone you dredge up the mud and stones that collect on the bottom.'

Armea looked with interest at the water trough and its wooden pipe. 'Where does the water come from, Mistress?'

'The pipe runs from the aqueduct that brings the water into the town from the River Verbeia over near Calcaria – or so I've been told,' Senovara added quickly. She, too, had always found this feat of engineering amazing, and sometimes wondered if it was really true.

'Does it ever run dry?'

'In the summer it can do and then we have to get our water from the well at the next crossroads. If the trough freezes solid, we also have to go to the well. We'll pass it on the way to the market, so I can show you where it is. Come on, you two.' She gathered up Ertola and set off again. Lucius dragged himself away from two friends he had been playing with in the mud behind the trough.

'Haven't you been to Eboracum before?' Senovara asked, seeing Armea's astonishment at the bustle of the marketplace with its wooden shops with raised shutters and the trestle tables and carts of the travelling traders who had just set up for the day.

'Just once. It's so big and noisy!' She shrank against her mistress as a group of off-duty soldiers on their way to a tavern pushed past her, laughing loudly at a ribald comment one of them had made. Senovara had to agree that it was noisy. The din of people exchanging greetings, arguing about prices, calling out their wares, or just gossiping was always overwhelming as it bounced off the walls of the surrounding buildings. In the background there was the noise of the stonemasons working at the fortress and of the blacksmiths hammering in the workshops by the fortress gate; shouts and crashes from the quayside, where the river boats were being unloaded, added to the general cacophony.

'You'll soon get used to it,' Senovara tried to reassure her. 'Lucius, hold Armea's hand so that she doesn't get lost.' That would also stop him wandering off as he was prone to do, she thought.

They stopped by a brightly painted shop with its shutters pulled back to display a wooden counter piled high with round loaves, each scored with eight lines, like the spokes of a wheel, so that you could break it into equal pieces. Senovara bought a loaf, having abandoned any hope of milling flour and baking bread that day, then moved her small entourage on to another shop further down the row. This one had joints of meat hanging from iron hooks on its back wall, and piles of offal and smaller pieces of meat on its wooden counter. Some of the meat was covered by cloths but most of it was revealed for inspection by customers. A couple of sheep's heads stared back at the passing throng through blank eyes. A small, plump man in a blood-smeared tunic was taking his ease, sitting cross-legged on the counter in the middle of his wares.

'Hail, Senovara.'

'Hail, Bonosius. This is Armea, our new house slave. She'll be doing some of the shopping for me in the future, so don't try fobbing her off with old meat!'

'You wrong me, Senovara. As if I would!'

Senovara grinned amiably at him and turned to Armea. 'Bonosius and I are old friends. I'm sure if you ever have any trouble while you're in the market he'd be happy to help you.'

'Indeed, I would,' Bonosius said stoutly. 'This is not always a good place for a young girl on her own. Can I get you anything today, Senovara? I have some nice beef.' He got down and whipped a bloody cloth off a corner of the table to reveal a small lump of red meat. He picked it up by the bone and showed it off to her.

She prodded it suspiciously. 'Why hasn't it gone into the military supplies?'

'Well, I will admit the cow was a bit elderly for the army's specifications. But it's fresh and it'll stew well. I know you prefer stews.'

Senovara prodded it again and sniffed it. It seemed reasonable. She opened negotiations with Bonosius and, after some good-natured haggling, handed the meat to Armea. 'There's a cloth in the basket. Wrap this up before we go on.

'That was lucky, Armea,' she continued after she had said her farewells to the butcher. 'Bonosius doesn't often get beef these days. Most of the good meat is bought up by the army but they won't have the old milk cows because they're too tough to roast. This will make a good stew and some soup as well. Now all we need is some vegetables. Vindex sometimes has some parsnips; they'll be a bit frosted at this time of year, so you'll have to peel them right back, but in a stew they'll do us very well.'

They went on through the market with Senovara pointing out which stalls and shops she favoured with her custom and which she preferred to avoid. Every now and again she stopped to introduce Armea to traders or friends, feeling rather smug at her new acquisition. Progress was slow, and by the time they got home they were all tired and ready for something to eat. Senovara quickly smeared a little honey over the beef to keep it fresh until she could cook it, and hung it up in a linen bag out of harm's way while she got out the remains of the previous night's supper for their midday meal.

During the afternoon Senovara showed Armea the small garden at the back of the house. 'It doesn't look much at the moment, but it's big enough for us to grow some vegetables and herbs. This year we should get our first crop of apples from that tree – Matugenus brought us that two years ago.' She couldn't keep a note of pride out of her voice and Armea looked a little surprised. Senovara explained. 'Most of our neighbours are veterans or traders who have followed the army, so very few of them are in the habit of growing much – they're too used to having to move on before anything grows. Not many people round here have a garden but, even after six years, I still find going out to shop every day a bit odd and prefer to grow as much as possible myself.'

'Every day, Mistress!' Armea sounded shocked.

'Why, yes. Without our own animals, fields and orchards, food has to be bought in and, as we don't have the storage space here that there is at the farm, we have to get our food as we need it. We get fifteen *modii* of wheat or barley delivered each month, of course, so you won't have to carry that back from the market, and the oil and wine men come round to the door but there's usually something I need each day, no matter how much I plan, so you'll probably have to go to the market most days. I'll tell you what to buy and Quintus will give you the money.'

Seeing the look of worry on Armea's face she stopped. 'You can count and use money, can't you?'

'Not very well, Mistress. I've only counted chickens and dusters and suchlike when I've been working with my mother in your grandmother's kitchen. I've never had any money to count.'

Senovara was annoyed with herself for not having thought of this during their morning's expedition. She'd forgotten how little she had had to do with cash before she came to Eboracum; even now, she preferred Quintus to keep the housekeeping money and give her what she wanted as and when it was required. The problem was one which could be easily remedied, however; Armea didn't seem to be a stupid girl and would no doubt learn quickly. 'Don't worry. I'll come with you until you get the hang of it. I'm teaching Lucius his numbers at the moment so you can join in with his lessons. Can you read?'

'A little, and I can write my name,' Armea was quick to assure her mistress.

That was less of a problem. A domestic slave didn't really

need to be literate but Senovara could teach her and Lucius together. It might provide some stimulus for her son to learn. Senovara smiled to herself as she remembered her mother, who had been brought up in the civilised town of Isurium Brigantum, struggling to teach Matugenus, Bodenius, Amatus and herself their letters in the face of their grandmother's opposition. Enica had never learned to read or write and had her own way of counting; she couldn't see why her grandchildren needed to be educated. As it was, it was just as well Bodenius had learned and learned well, otherwise he would not have been promoted so fast in the Roman army. For the rest of them, being able to read and write had become increasingly important in their daily lives, whether for trading, shopping, dealing with the authorities over their taxes or just keeping in touch with friends and family. In Enica's day one married locally and rarely moved further than a few hours' walk away; these days people could be scattered all over the known world and if one couldn't write one lost touch. Senovara shook her head, as the strangeness of it all struck her anew, and pointed out to Armea some of the potherbs growing in the garden.

The rest of the day passed quickly as Armea was shown a bewildering array of duties both inside and outside the house. Finally, when the young slave was preparing the vegetables for their supper, Senovara took pity on her.

'Quintus is going to the temple of Mithras this evening. As soon as he has gone and we've tidied up you can go to bed. You look tired.'

'Thank you, Mistress. Shall I go and get the children ready for their supper?'

'Yes. I won't be long now.'

As the slave went out of the room to look for the children Quintus came in from the shop.

'I heard that. I hope the girl isn't going to be sickly. A slave who needs to go to bed early isn't going to be much use.'

'No, she'll be fine. It's just her first day and everything is new and confusing.'

'Well, remember she's here to help you. Don't be too kind-hearted.' He poured a bowl of water and washed his face and hands. 'I'll be off now. I shouldn't be too late back tonight.'

Senovara nodded. She knew the pattern of his Mithraic ceremonies through the year now, even if she would never know what Quintus and his fellow worshippers actually did at their secret rituals – other than eat. Quintus never missed his visits to the Mithraeum if he could help it; it kept him in touch with some of his old army friends and Senovara sometimes wondered if it was the ritual or the chance of a good gossip which drew her husband to the temple by the fortress wall.

Armea carried Ertola into the kitchen, closely followed by Lucius, and Senovara applied herself to dealing with the more immediate needs of her family. They were all tired after their long morning in the market and the children ate their suppers quickly, although rather querulously. Senovara was glad when they had been put to bed and Armea had said her own goodnights. She made her way back into the kitchen and, by the light of the candle by the stove, settled down to make a dress for Ertola's wooden doll out of a scrap of woollen cloth, a task she had not yet had time to do, despite her best intentions.

There was a loud knocking at the door. Senovara started; she must have dozed off. Ertola started to cry in the children's room. She looked at the candle; it was almost burned out. It must be quite late.

Who could it be at this time of night? she thought. Surely it couldn't be Quintus; the door wasn't bolted and he had the latchlifter with him.

The knocking came again, more loudly. Ertola responded by crying more loudly as well. Senovara went into the bedroom and shushed her child as she tried to decide what to do. It was not likely to be one of her friends at this hour – besides, they would call out her name if they needed her attention urgently. The hammering was becoming persistent; she was going to have to answer the door. She wished Quintus was back, but on the nights when he went to the Mithraeum he was rarely back early, despite always claiming he wouldn't be late.

She carried Ertola into the kitchen and put her down on the bench. 'Shush. Sit there quietly and don't move.'

Picking up the iron frying pan from its hook by the stove, she gripped it firmly in her right hand and advanced through the shop to the door, her heart thumping painfully.

'Who's there?' she asked.

'Aulus Postumus.' The voice was low but authoritative.

'Who?' Senovara could not remember anyone called Aulus Postumus.

'Aulus Postumus, *optio* of the First Cohort of Tungrians, with a letter for Quintus Flavius Candidus from his brother Gaius Flavius Naso, centurion at Vercovicium.'

'By the Shades,' thought Senovara, 'what a time to deliver a letter!'

Should she let him in? She never knew what to do in these situations. Back at the farm she would not have hesitated; her father would have expected her to offer hospitality to anyone arriving at the door, but then there would have been more people – at home she had rarely been alone. In Eboracum the rules were different; there was no one else in the house but her children and Armea, and Quintus took the Roman view that a wife did not entertain male visitors in her husband's absence, particularly late at night. But surely someone bringing a letter from a member of his family should be given some sort of welcome? She could hardly send him away. She struggled to unlatch the door.

Outside a tall figure loomed in the fitful light from the one candle she had left burning just inside the door to give Quintus some light when he came home. A large cloak enveloped the man completely; all that was visible was the gleam from his eyes and the shine from the browband of his helmet.

'Hail, lady.'

'Hail,' replied Senovara hesitantly.

The visitor threw back his cloak, took off his bronze helmet and came further into the light. Senovara's eyes widened as she took in the size of the tall, imposing figure in his bright red tunic and winter trousers. A broad grin lit up his rather squashed, lived-in face as he caught sight of the frying pan. Senovara looked at her right hand sheepishly and found herself grinning back.

'It's very cold out here,' the face said ingratiatingly.

Senovara hesitated and then drew back, opening the door more widely. 'Enter,' she said, 'and welcome. My husband's out at the moment but he should be back soon.'

She led the way through to the kitchen where she saw, with some relief, that Armea had been woken up by the noise and had come in to quieten the whimpering baby. 'Be seated by the fire. May I offer you some wine or would you prefer beer?'

She indicated a stool by the stove. The stool looked hard and the fire on top of the stove was almost out. She should have shown him into the best room, but she hadn't been expecting guests and the brazier was not lit. She also wasn't too sure how tidy it was in there; because of the illness in the house it was a while since she had dusted.

'Wine please.' The soldier settled himself at the table and put his helmet on the floor beside the stool. He smiled encouragingly at Armea, who blushed and looked confused.

Senovara poured half a beaker of rich red wine from a cream-coloured pottery jug and handed it to the soldier, indicating the water ewer on the table.

'Many thanks, lady. This will warm me through.' She took the hint and added some more charcoal to the fire, with a few small sticks to encourage a more homely blaze. The sticks caught immediately, so the charcoal must have been hotter than she had thought. She lit the pottery lamp hanging from the wall with a stick from the fire – Quintus always preferred her to use oil lamps when they had visitors, rather than the cheaper candles they usually relied on; luckily she had trimmed the wick and refilled its reservoir before supper. She took her daughter from Armea, both of whom were gazing at the soldier with wide eyes.

'I am sorry it is so late, lady. It took longer than I'd expected on the road and I had to present my orders at the fortress before I could get away.'

He handed her a small pile of wooden strips held together with string and with a small blob of wax at the knot.

She looked at it. '*To Quintus Flavius Candidus, at Eboracum*' was written on the top slat. She nodded and put the letter on the table. Her husband would want to open that himself, glad to have some news of his brother at last. He would let her know the contents in his own time – or as much of the contents as she needed to know. The letters between the brothers tended to consist mostly of private jokes, which made Quintus laugh but which just left her puzzled.

'Were the roads bad?' she enquired, trying to think of something to say and wishing fervently that Quintus would return.

'There was ice on the roads around Cataractonium. That stretch of road is bad enough on any day but in this weather it's treacherous. I could only go slowly.'

She nodded again. 'And my brother-in-law is well?'

'He was when I saw him two days ago,' was the reply. 'His lungs were certainly in full working order. He was bellowing at some new recruits when I left. They could probably hear him at Vindolanda. He was giving them a good dressing-down. Accused them all of being hairdressers who had got into the army by lying about their occupations.'

Senovara laughed. That sounded like Gaius. He was a kindly man, but he had a short temper and a fine line in invective when roused.

A small figure appeared at the door, rubbing his eyes. Senovara sighed. She might have known that the soldier's hammering at the door would have woken her son but she couldn't be cross; somehow his presence made her feel safer.

'Hello, young man,' said Aulus Postumus.

'Hello,' said Lucius, his eyes widening as he took in the polished iron strips of the soldier's cuirass with its brass buckles and studs, the sword in the red leather scabbard at his right side, and his helmet on the floor beside him. 'Are you a soldier?'

Aulus Postumus laughed. 'I certainly am. Are you going to be a soldier when you grow up?'

Lucius nodded enthusiastically and scampered over to the *optio*, giving his mother a wide berth in case she stopped him. He stood in front of the stranger with his feet planted sturdily apart and looked the soldier in the eyes.

'Which unit are you in?'

'First Cohort of Tungrians, sir.'

'That's the same unit as my Uncle Gaius.' Lucius sounded accusing and the soldier's grin spread.

'It is indeed. I know your uncle well. In fact, I've brought a letter from him for your father.

'Did he tell you about me?' demanded Lucius.

'Lucius! Really!' Senovara was appalled.

'He told me he had a nephew who would probably plague me with questions if I met him,' Aulus replied, trying not to laugh.

'Oh.' Lucius considered this. 'Does that mean you don't mind me asking questions?'

Senovara winced. Quintus was really going to have to have a talk with his self-confident son.

'I don't mind at all. Ask whatever you like.'

The questions came thick and fast. How long had he been in the army? Since he was seventeen, answered the soldier tolerantly. Why didn't he have a shield with him? Because he was on horseback. Was his sword sharp? The soldier drew it a little way out of its scabbard so that Lucius could see the iron blade.

'Too sharp for you to touch, little man.'

'Have you ever killed anyone with it?'

'I don't think so. I did use it in battle many years ago and inflicted some damage with it, but whether any of the enemy died of their wounds or not I can't say. I'm more of an administrator these days.'

Lucius looked disappointed. How bloodthirsty small boys were, thought Senovara despairingly.

'Don't you fight battles any more?'

'No. We've been busy building a wall further north, in order to keep the northern tribes out of the province, so we don't have time to fight battles,' explained Aulus Postumus. Lucius looked as if he thought little of this strategy. 'You see,' the soldier continued, 'a soldier's job is to protect Roma's citizens and Roma's territories. Sometimes that's better done by keeping the enemy out than by fighting them all the time. In some provinces, like Germania, the frontier runs along a great river so that we only have to defend the river – stop the enemy getting across. In Britannia there isn't a river right along the frontier, so we've had to build a wall joining the River Tina to the coast beyond Luguvalium.'

'But why doesn't the Emperor conquer the northern tribes and stop them being enemies?'

Senovara nodded. She had never fully understood this herself.

'It's been tried, believe me. When Agricola was Governor we overran the whole area, but it's difficult country. Lots of narrow, wooded valleys in which small groups of tribesmen can ambush a column of marching soldiers. The hidden men can attack the rear of a column as they enter a valley, and those at the front of the line can't get back to help. By the time the rest of the column has turned, the enemy have melted back into the woods leaving no one to fight. The Emperor Hadrian decided that it wasn't worth losing men like that and ordered the legions in Britannia to build a wall. I don't think he has any plans to advance north in the foreseeable future, though no doubt, one emperor or other will do so one day.'

There was a sudden cold draught as the front door was opened, letting the damp night air through the shop and into the kitchen.

'This will be my husband.' Senovara hoped that her voice didn't sound too thankful or, indeed, too nervous. What would Quintus say when he found the soldier settled in his kitchen?

The kitchen door opened and Quintus stood there with the candle from the front door in his hand. He surveyed the assembled company in astonishment. Senovara rushed to explain Aulus Postumus' presence as the soldier stood up and saluted his host.

'This is Aulus Postumus, from Vercovicium. He's brought a letter from Gaius.' She indicated the pile of wooden slats on the table.

'Hail, Quintus Flavius Candidus. I bring greetings from your brother at the fort of Vercovicium. I apologise for the lateness of my visit but I had trouble getting through because of the weather. Your wife has been gracious enough to take pity on my cold plight and allowed me to wait for you.'

'You're welcome, Aulus Postumus. My brother has spoken of you. You hold the rank of *optio*, don't you? Did you leave my brother in good heart?'

Quintus sat down on the bench and frowned at his son, who took the hint and disappeared quickly back to bed.

Senovara handed Ertola to Armea and indicated silently that she should take the baby and retire as well. She took a beaker from the shelf and placed it on the table beside her husband's elbow. The soldier was confirming who he was and repeating his description of his last sighting of Gaius. Quintus laughed and poured himself a drink before starting to question the soldier about the situation on the frontier. Senovara relaxed as her husband appeared to take to the soldier and busied herself tidying the kitchen while they talked.

'Have the troops finished building yet?'

'I sometimes wonder if they'll ever finish, the way the officers keep changing their minds! There's a rumour that yet another fort is to be built on the frontier to the east of Vercovicium, just when everyone thought all was complete. Each century is hoping that the job will be given to another unit! We all expected the legions to have been withdrawn by now, leaving the auxiliaries in place.'

Quintus nodded sympathetically – he had heard much the same complaint from Gaius in previous letters.

'Are you in Eboracum for long?' he enquired.

'No. I'm carrying correspondence to the Procurator at Londinium so I'll have to be off again tomorrow morning at first light.' He drained his wine and set the beaker on the table. 'I must be off to claim my bed in the *mansio*. Many thanks, lady, for allowing me to visit and for the opportunity to meet your son. He's a lad to be proud of, sir.' Quintus' face showed mixed emotions at this. 'I'll be passing back through Eboracum in a week or two's time when I have carried out my commission. If you wish, I will call again – earlier in the day! – and collect any letter you want carried to Gaius.'

'Thank you. It would be good to know a letter was sure to get to my brother.'

He picked up the oil lamp and ushered the soldier out through the shop. Senovara waited by the stove, listening as her husband showed the soldier out and slid the door bolts into place.

Quintus came back into the kitchen and stood by the door. 'Well!'

Not sure how to interpret this cryptic comment, Senovara started to explain herself breathlessly. 'I didn't know what to do. It was so cold and wet outside but it was so late and there was only me and Armea and the children, but he had a letter from Gaius so I thought you'd want me to ask him in but I didn't know . . .' Her voice trailed off, aware that she sounded as panicky as she had felt.

'How did you know he had a letter from Gaius before you opened the door?' Quintus enquired mildly.

'He said so, through the door, and he knew your name and Gaius'. So I thought you might think it was rude if I told him to come back tomorrow, so I opened the door to take it from him, but I was so frightened . . .' Again her voice trailed off as she caught back a sob. Then she drew herself up. 'But I took the frying pan with me and if he hadn't really had the letter I'd have hit him with it!'

Quintus laughed at this brave declaration and drew her to him. 'I'm sorry if you were frightened and, as it turned out, you did do the right thing. But don't do it again. Next time it might not be a real messenger; there are some very strange people coming through Eboracum these days, with all the traders and worse going north to the frontier to live off the troops there.'

'I won't.' Senovara buried her head in his shoulder, feeling reassured. 'But it's often frightening here when you're out. Couldn't we get a dog? There were always dogs at the farm and they always seemed to know who were friends and who enemies. I'd feel much safer if we had a dog.'

'Hm. I don't know about that. A dog as well as a slave? We're becoming quite a household and dogs can be more of a nuisance than anything with their barking. Just look at that great brute of the baker's. Whenever I go past there after dark he sets up such a howling, like a soul that has got lost on its way to the Underworld – and he knows me perfectly well. I don't know how anyone in that household gets any sleep. And a new puppy wouldn't give you much protection, not to mention how we'd feed it. Would we have enough scraps left over? You never seem to waste much.'

Senovara ignored this last comment, not sure if it was meant as a compliment or not. 'We could ask Matugenus if he has a quiet, older dog we could have.' She raised her head and looked at her husband, pleadingly. 'Please.'

'Very well. I'll ask him next time he visits if he has such a beast. It might help to keep the vermin down; the bigger this town gets, the more mice we seem to have and rats as well now. You go to bed. I'll read Gaius' letter while I finish my wine.'

Senovara carried the remains of the candle with her into the bedroom, smiling to herself. Quintus reached for a knife to cut the cords holding the slats of the letter together.

She was just dozing off when Quintus came into their room and climbed into bed.

'What news is there from Vercovicium?' she asked.

'I thought you'd be asleep by now.'

'Not yet. Did Gaius send news of Flavia and the children?'

'Just to say they're all well. I don't believe we'll be seeing them until at least the autumn; Gaius seems to think he'll be kept at Vercovicium to carry on working with the auxiliaries and not transferred back to the legion.'

'Weren't you hoping he'd be coming back to Eboracum soon?'

'Yes, but that's army life for you. They move you when you've just got settled, and then don't move you when you want to go! At least Gaius and I are in the same province, so there's always the chance of meeting. If he got posted to Dacia or somewhere in Africa, we might never see each other again. If they want him to stay with the First Cohort of Tungrians while the auxiliaries take over at the frontier, there's a chance that he'll be in Britannia for some time yet, thank Jupiter.'

Senovara murmured sympathetically. The thought of being separated from close relatives by thousands of miles, across oceans and deserts, always appalled her, though she had met many such cases in army families since her marriage.

Quintus acknowledged her concern by kissing her shoulder, and carried on with his news. 'Anyway, Gaius was mainly writing to tell me that a fellow centurion and old friend of his is going to be in charge of the next unit of the Sixth to be transferred back to Eboracum, and he wants to know if he can tell him and his family to call on us when they get here. He's a man of Aquincum – that's in Pannonia, you know. He's called Veturius, son of Teutonus.'

'That's where Bodenius has just been posted to! What family does Veturius have?' Senovara was fully awake now. She was always interested in meeting new people and she couldn't remember having met any Pannonians before. She would be able to find out what the province of Pannonia was like and imagine her cousin there.

'A wife and a sister. No' – he forestalled her next question – 'Gaius didn't say what their names were, how long they've been married, how old they are or if they're fat or thin, just asked if we'd welcome them. No doubt you'll find out all about them when they arrive.'

Senovara grinned into the dark; she couldn't help being curious about people. 'Did he say when they're coming?'

'Next month sometime – I doubt if there's a definite date yet. Now, let's get some sleep, woman. It's been a long day.'

Next morning Quintus showed Senovara Gaius' letter. She was flattered – he rarely showed her his letters, preferring to relay their contents to her in his own way. She sat down, the better to concentrate on reading the spidery brown writing on the slats.

To Quintus. Greetings, brother. Flavia and the children
are well and send their best wishes to you and our sister
Senovara. Two centuries are to be sent back to
Eboracum next month and I recommend to you the
centurion and my old messmate, Veturius, son of
Teutonus, a man of Aquincum. On my behalf welcome
him and his wife and sister. I continue here with the
Tungrians and will do so for some months to come.
Farewell, brother. May you continue to prosper. Gaius
Flavius Naso.

'He doesn't say when next month.'

'I doubt if he knows, and it may be even longer, so I wouldn't start baking for them just yet.'

'No, but I'd better start baking for you, otherwise there'll be nothing for any of today's meals.'

Senovara started bustling about the house – there was a great deal of lost time to be made up and it would be a while before Armea could take many tasks off her mistress's shoulders. But as she refilled the oil lamps, she wondered about the people from Aquincum and whether she would like them. There were always new faces in Eboracum, but many people were just passing through. Senovara was looking forward to meeting two new women from another province.

Martius

SENOVARA OPENED HER eyes and was immediately aware that her mood had changed. After several weeks of feeling weary and lethargic, she suddenly felt energetic and ready to tackle any task. She jumped out of bed and flung open the shutters, craning her neck to see what the sky looked like in the gap above the alley separating their house from Ursa and Lurio's next door. The air coming through the opening felt mild and dry and what she could see of the lightening sky looked blue, with only an occasional fluff of high, white cloud. The sound of birds singing in the garden was loud and joyous; clearly they were feeling as energetic as she was.

Quintus grunted as he woke up. 'What are you doing?'

'Trying to see if it's going to rain.'

'You're hardly going to tell from what you can see from that window. If you're so eager to know what the weather's going to be like, look out of the back door, like a sensible woman. Why do you need to know, anyway?'

'I'm in the mood to spring clean.'

'Oh, no!' Quintus rolled over in bed and buried his face in the pillow.

'It has to be done. It shouldn't take so long this time with Armea to help. That sounds like her in the kitchen.'

She stuck her head outside the bedroom door and called down the passage to the kitchen. 'Armea, put a cauldron of water on the fire, will you? We're going to do some house cleaning today.'

Armea could be heard clattering around in the kitchen, setting the big, bronze cauldron on the top of the stove and pouring buckets of water into it.

'Tell her not to use all of it – I need a wash,' directed Quintus as he climbed out of bed.

Senovara went to the kitchen, coiling her long, brown hair into its bun. She took the bone hairpins out of her mouth and rammed them into position one by one, while she peered at the amount of water in the cauldron and in the buckets. Then she saw that Armea had sensibly filled a pottery bowl and set it on the table for the family's washing needs.

She quickly splashed her face and hands in the cold water, then carried the bowl into the bedroom for Quintus. She went into the children's room and opened the shutters. 'Up you get, you two. There's no time to waste. Armea and I are going to be busy today, cleaning.'

Lucius sat up in his low truckle bed, rubbing his eyes and Senovara lifted Ertola out of her cot. 'Come on, little one. Time to get you washed and dressed.'

She carried the child through into the bedroom and pulled Ertola's crumpled cream tunic up over her head. Dipping a piece of linen rag into the bowl of water, she quickly washed the child from head to toe. She dressed her in a clean tunic, the green one this morning. While she was fastening the laces on her daughter's boots, Lucius wandered in with his own tunic in a tangle about his neck.

'Help!' The word was muffled by the woollen fabric and Quintus laughed as she sorted their son out.

'I'll give the children some bread and water, then ask Aqmat if she'll look after them for a few hours. That will give us a chance to get plenty done.'

Quintus nodded. He finished shaving and wiped the blade of his iron razor on a towel. 'I'll take mine into the shop. If you're going to be cleaning all day I want to keep out of the way.'

Aqmat declared herself delighted to look after Ertola and a rather truculent Lucius. He had objected to the idea that he needed to be minded but had been overruled and was duly handed over with strict instructions to behave. Armea went off to the trough to refill the buckets. When she returned, Senovara was ready to start.

'We'll do the best room first, starting with our shrine,' she decided. 'It's only respectful to tidy the house of the gods before we clean anywhere else.'

She led the way into the room behind the shop, which tended to be used just when they had visitors. Most people in Eboracum, following the Roman custom, called this their dining room, but Senovara preferred to describe it, more accurately in her opinion because they rarely had people for dinner, as the 'best room'. She opened the doors of the wall cupboard in which the statuettes of their family gods lived. She carefully handed down the small bronze statuettes of the *lares* and the pipeclay figurine of the Dea Nutrix to Armea, who placed them on the low table. Senovara then lifted out the small stone relief depicting three seated Mother Goddesses, grunting when she took the weight, and lowered it onto the floor. She washed out the cupboard thoroughly while Armea dusted the statuettes. The Mother Goddesses were then put back squarely in the centre of the shrine and the figurines arranged round them. Senovara shut the cupboard doors to keep out the dust, with a sense of satisfaction.

'Right. That's that done. I'll put some fresh flowers in there later. Now we'll really get started.'

Between them the two girls carried the furniture out into the passage, then, tying a scrap of old tunic onto the end of a broom shank, Armea cleaned the spiders' webs from the lime-washed ceiling and dark red walls. Senovara, meanwhile, took the leather cushions out into the garden and banged them against the wall of the house before tying them to the boughs of the apple tree to air. A few green buds caught her eye; she must remind Quintus to prune the tree before it was too late. She looked round the garden and sighed. There was a great number of tasks crying out to be done out here as well, and if they didn't tackle them soon they would have to waste money on buying vegetables later in the year. But they had started on the house, so they had better finish that before dealing with the garden. She went back indoors and began to clean the furniture stacked in the passage. Soon she had the low, rectangular wooden table, the couch and the two small basketwork chairs washed down, and Armea was on her hands and knees scrubbing the stone-flagged floor.

They were just putting the room back together again when a voice hailed them from the kitchen. 'Senovara, are you there?'

'That's Ursa. I wonder what she wants?' Tucking a stray hair back into her bun, she went into the kitchen, where she found her next-door neighbour looking distracted, her brunette curls writhing round her head and her normally neat clothing dishevelled. Senovara noticed with amusement a streak of charcoal dust decorating Ursa's flushed forehead, giving her the appearance of a war-painted Caledonian.

'Hail, Ursa.'

'Hail, Senovara. Apologies for interrupting – you look as though you're busy – but I've had a mishap. I put some water onto the stove to wash some clothes – it's the first good drying day we have had for weeks. Lurio called me into the shop to serve a customer and when I got back the water had boiled over and put out the fire. Could I ask for a brand from your fire to get mine going again?'

'Yes, of course. But you have relaid the fire, haven't you? I know to my cost that it's no good trying to light wet charcoal.'

'Oh yes. I've raked out all the wet stuff and soaked up the water with sacking. New dry twigs are all ready to light, but I can't get a spark. I've been trying for ages. If I don't get it going soon I won't be able to get anything cooked for our evening meal. I've already had to give up on the idea of washing any clothes. Today is turning into a complete disaster!'

Senovara nodded sympathetically. It had happened to her often, and it was always when you needed to light the fire most that you couldn't get a spark from the flint. She chose a promising-looking stick from the fuel baskets under her stove and thrust it into the heart of the glowing charcoal. While they waited for it to light, she explained that she and Armea had just finished turning out the best room.

'I must tackle my own house soon,' said Ursa. 'It's dreadful how dirty everything gets over winter, with mud tracked into the house and the smuts from the oil lamps and braziers.'

Senovara pulled the stick out of the fire and looked at it. 'This looks ready.'

'Many thanks. I'll do the same for you one day. Farewell.'

Ursa took the smouldering stick from Senovara and rushed out of the kitchen door, shielding the burning end of the brand with one hand while she dashed next door through the gate between their gardens.

Armea came into the kitchen with a bucket in both hands. 'Do you want to start on the children's room now, Mistress?'

'No, we'll have a break. The fortress horn has just signalled the seventh hour. Go and tell Quintus that I've got some cold meat and bread here.'

She poured some water into a jug and added a little vinegar, then set out a small piece of meat on the table with half a two-*as* loaf.

Quintus ate his meal quickly and without comment.

'How are you getting on?' he asked when he'd finished.

'Fine. We've done the best room. This afternoon we'll do the children's room. That will be enough for today.'

'Then I'll get back to my bench and leave you to it!'

Senovara and Armea worked quietly and steadily all afternoon and eventually the children's room was cleaned to their satisfaction.

'You go next door and collect the children, Armea, while I start on our meal.'

Armea nodded and rolled down the sleeves of her tunic, but at the kitchen door she was stopped by the sound of uproar coming from the shop. She and Senovara looked at each other in alarm.

'What's going on?' Senovara headed down the passage but before she had got to the end the door was flung open and Quintus was dragged through by a small barking dog on a length of rope.

'This hound of Hades,' he said grimly, 'is for you.'

'For me?' Senovara looked stunned as she backed into the kitchen.

'Yes. You may recall,' he continued, tying one end of the rope to the kitchen table and sinking gratefully onto the bench, 'that you wanted me to ask Matugenus if he had a quiet, mature, well-trained watchdog. This is what he has sent. The carter just dropped it off. It's already had a fight with a passing cur, cocked its leg on the doorpost and tried to bite a customer. Also, the word "quiet" does not appear to be in its vocabulary.'

Armea disappeared through the back door, trying not to laugh.

'Does it have a name?' Senovara patted the barking puppy nervously on its head and tried to quiet it.

'I can think of several, but no official name was provided.'

At that moment Lucius rushed into the room.

'Armea says Uncle Matugenus has sent us a dog, oh, isn't he fine!' he declared rapturously as he sank to his knees on the floor next to the little terrier.

'Do be careful, Lucius,' Senovara warned. 'He doesn't know you yet and he might bite.'

But there didn't seem much chance of that. With that peculiar empathy which invariably exists between small boys and small dogs, the two of them immediately took to each other. The dog stopped barking and started to squirm on the floor ecstatically while Lucius tickled his tummy.

'Can I take him into the garden, Pater?'

'Please do, son!'

Lucius untied the rope and dog and boy galloped out of the kitchen door, nearly knocking Armea over as she carried Ertola into the house.

Quintus raised his eyebrows. 'Well, someone seems to be happy about our new acquisition,' he declared, taking Ertola from Armea's arms. 'What do you think about our new dog, Ertola?'

The child grinned at him, then squirmed to get down to follow her brother. Quintus set his daughter's feet on the floor and she ran out of the house. Senovara said soothingly, 'I'm sure the dog will calm down when he's been here a few days.'

'I hope so, otherwise he'll be driving my customers away. We'll have to put him in the *latrina* for tonight – there's nowhere else; I'll make a kennel in the garden for him tomorrow. By the way, Armea, do you know if he has a name?'

Armea shook her head. 'No. It's just a farm dog. Master Matugenus doesn't give them all names, just his favourites.'

Lucius came back into the kitchen, still with the dog in tow. 'Dog says he's hungry and I am too.'

'Armea, did you throw that lamb bone into the river or is it still in the pile outside the back door?'

'No, it should still be in the rubbish pile. I haven't been down to the river yet, Mistress.' She went outside and returned with the bone, which was liberally covered with mud and bits of onion skin.

'Don't give it to him in here. Take him back out into the garden, Lucius. You'll have to wait for your own meal.'

'That sounds like customers.' Quintus turned back to the shop. Senovara could hear voices but she was trying to gather her scattered thoughts and remember what she had planned to cook for dinner so she didn't take much notice. Then she realised that the voices were nearer. It sounded as though Quintus was showing people into the dining room. But who could be visiting unexpectedly who would be deemed worthy of the best room? They must be business friends of Quintus. Thankful that she and Armea had finished cleaning the room that morning and had lit the brazier to air the place, Senovara got out some beakers ready to provide refreshment if required.

Quintus stuck his head round the door. 'We have visitors.'

'So I hear. Do you want wine or beer?'

'Both, and you as well. It's the Pannonians whom Gaius wrote to us about!'

'What! But it can't be! Armea, take the wine, beer and water in to them while I get myself tidied up. We haven't any honey cakes left, have we?'

'No.' Armea shook her head. 'The children had the last ones yesterday for their supper.'

'Well, they'll have to make do with drinks. They'll probably think us mean and inhospitable, but there's nothing we can do about that,' she muttered, running into the bedroom, pulling the pins out of her hair.

She quickly re-coiled her hair into its bun and checked in the mirror that she had a clean face. There wasn't time to change her dress. She pulled the sleeves down and dusted herself off ineffectually with her hands. That would have to do. At least the best room was clean.

She sailed into the room, trying to look as though unexpected guests were a regular occurrence in the household.

'Ah, there you are.' Quintus turned as she entered the room. 'May I introduce my wife, Senovara, sir?'

A very tall man in centurion's undress uniform rose from one of the chairs and acknowledged Senovara. 'Hail, Madam. I must apologise for our unexpected visit to your home. We arrived very late last night and, having spent the day sorting out our new quarters, we decided to look around the settlement and get our bearings before it got dark. We found ourselves outside your shop, so called in to bring greetings from your brother-in-law, as instructed.'

Senovara stammered a welcome while taking in all the details of the stranger's appearance.

The man from Aquincum had an extraordinary face, an elongated triangle with a long chin above which his mouth was small yet full-lipped. His nose was large and fleshy and his eyes reminded Senovara of Jupiter's eagle: supercilious, flashing, authoritative. This was not a man who would suffer fools gladly, yet when she looked at his hands she was surprised to see that they were shapely, with sensitive fingers and well-kept nails; the eyes and the hands seemed to belong to different people. A complex man, this Veturius, son of Teutonus.

She became aware of two women dressed in grey cloaks sitting quietly on the couch, and smiled at them.

'May I present my wife, Adnamata, and my sister, Broginara?'

'Welcome to our home,' said Senovara. She moved across to sit on a stool by the side of the couch, settling herself down carefully, because the stool had a tendency to wobble, and inspected her new acquaintances with interest.

The younger woman, Adnamata, was short with dark hair, what could be seen of it under a white cap, which was pulled so tightly across her hair line and behind her ears that it made them stick out. Her eyes were also dark but with a slight squint.

Her skin showed the pockmarks of a spotty adolescence. She seemed very shy but when she smiled at Senovara her face lit up. She was no beauty, but Senovara could see what had attracted Veturius.

Her sister-in-law, Broginara, was a very different woman: she had her brother's height and dark hair but on her his long, triangular face became heart-shaped and the small mouth and full lips softer and more attractive. She seemed impatient of Adnamata's shyness, yet still protective of the younger woman. Senovara thought she looked very confident, but wondered why she had such sad eyes.

Becoming aware that she was staring, Senovara roused herself to make polite conversation. Had her guests had a comfortable journey from the north? she enquired.

'Not bad. We took our time and broke our journey at Vindomora and Cataractonium. We had all our belongings on the ox-cart, so it wasn't possible to travel fast. It was after dark when we arrived here last night.' Broginara's tones were low and attractive, with only an occasional slurring of her words to indicate that she wasn't a native Latin-speaker.

'And were your quarters ready for you?' Senovara had been in Eboracum long enough to know that centurions' quarters were not always properly prepared to receive their new incumbents on arrival.

'Yes, thank the Mothers! And they are quite spacious and clean, compared to some of those we've occupied before.' Broginara's voice held just that note of thankfulness mixed with complacency that Senovara had heard before in the women of army families who were used to moving regularly and making do with what they found at their journey's end.

'It hasn't taken long to get settled in today but we were lucky that the *medicus ordinarius*' wife had put some olive oil, bread and wine out for us, otherwise we'd have gone hungry last night and had to grope our way round in the dark.'

'Oh, that will be Basilia – she's an old friend of mine.' Senovara was pleased to find a link between her new and old friends.

'It was very kind of her.' Adnamata's voice was high-pitched and breathless and Senovara jumped. She had almost forgotten the younger woman was present.

'I'm sure you'll find that everyone in the fortress is very friendly; and in the settlement too. With many of the legionaries still up on the frontier, there aren't too many women here yet, so you'll soon get to know everyone.'

'There already seem to be many shops and stalls in the town. You have no idea how wonderful that seems to us after the limited choice we had in the *vicus* at Vercovicium.'

'We get produce brought in from all round the *territorium* and, of course, the ships bring all sorts of goods into the port from Germania and Gallia, for those who can afford them. But, surely, you could get almost anything you wanted up on the frontier? I've heard that Coria is now a large town with a great market.'

'True, but Coria is some distance from Vercovicium, and it's often difficult to get transport there and back, particularly in the winter. Veturius could sometimes be persuaded to bring back some supplies when he rode down to report to headquarters, but he always refused to shop for ribbons or our other essentials.'

'But we sometimes got visits from the travelling merchants, Broginara.' Again Adnamata's voice startled Senovara, such was the girl's stillness and silence while her sister-in-law was speaking.

'That's true. I don't know what we would have done without Salmanes' regular visits. He's a trader from Tyrus,' she explained to Senovara, 'who travels around the forts of the frontier selling trinkets.'

'Oh, I know Salmanes. He comes to Eboracum to meet his suppliers when the ships from the Mare Internum provinces dock at the quayside.'

This coincidence seemed to make a bond between the women and Senovara offered them more wine.

'No. We've disturbed you enough.' Veturius broke off from his discussion with Quintus of the worsening situation in Judaea and stood up. 'We'll leave you in peace and thank you for your hospitality.'

The Pannonian women stood up obediently, ready to say their farewells. Just then the door burst open and Lucius and the dog, with Ertola pressing behind, came into the room. Lucius stopped short at the sight of the strangers.

'Lucius, get that dog out of here!' thundered Quintus. The terrier started to bark at the sound of Quintus' voice and Lucius and Ertola disappeared behind their mother's skirts. Senovara grabbed the string round the dog's neck.

'This is my son, Lucius, and my daughter, Ertola,' Quintus explained to the visitors. 'The dog arrived from my brother-in-law's this afternoon and has already thrown the house into turmoil.'

Veturius laughed. 'I can well imagine.' He reached down, picked the barking dog up by the scruff of its neck and held it squirming in front of him. 'It looks as if it will be a good mouser. What do you call him, boy?' he asked Lucius, who was peeping out from behind Senovara.

'We haven't thought of a name yet, sir,' Senovara responded on behalf of her suddenly tongue-tied offspring.

'We'll have to think of something. Broginara, you're the intellectual of the family. What should this dog be called?'

She looked consideringly at the small beast, still dangling at the end of her brother's arm.

'Well, he seems a bit noisy. Why don't you call him Hylax? That was the name of the poet Virgil's dog,' she explained to the half-hidden Lucius, 'and it means "Barker".'

Quintus roared with laughter. 'Thank you, lady. That's an excellent name, both appropriate and literary.'

He looked at her approvingly and Senovara's heart sank. Quintus often expressed admiration for women who were well read and could entertain their husbands with witty conversation and with readings from the poets, but if his own wife spent all day reading rolls of poetry he'd soon get annoyed that his meals were not being cooked or the house cleaned. A well-educated wife was fine in theory but not practical for a shoemaker, she reassured herself.

'Please come and visit us soon, Senovara,' invited Broginara.

'I'd be pleased to,' Senovara replied as she and Quintus ushered their guests out through the shop. 'I'll try to call over the next few days.'

'Excellent. Just come to the *porta praetoria* and ask the guard on duty to direct you.'

'Farewell.'

Quintus and Senovara stood at the door of their shop and watched the tall centurion stride away, followed by his two womenfolk.

Quintus shot the bolts home on the shop door and turned to his wife. 'That was unexpected. What did you think of them?'

'I thought he was a bit frightening. So very tall and such piercing eyes! But Broginara and Adnamata seemed very pleasant. It will be fun getting to know them.'

'An oddly assorted pair, I thought, but Veturius was interesting, if wordy, and, despite his "piercing eyes", he wasn't as terrifying as some centurions I've known. What's for dinner?'

Senovara let out a shriek and headed for the kitchen – all thoughts of the evening meal had flown from her mind when the guests arrived.

A few days later, Senovara made her way towards the south-west gate of the fortress to visit her new acquaintances. She had dressed carefully in the newest of her four tunics, and was wearing her best jewellery, determined to counteract any adverse impression the Pannonians might have received during their visit. She had with her some fresh honey cakes in a basket as a house-warming present. She had also made sure that her own visit was not unannounced by sending one of Ursa's sons to the fortress to ask if a visit would be timely. The lad had been only too willing to go, as she knew he would be; any excuse to set foot in the fortress was fine by him.

The day was grey and still, and the smoke from hundreds of fires in homes and workshops mingled and hung in streaks over the low rooftops. The acrid smell of burning timber and charcoal was everywhere, overpowering the stench from the many rubbish heaps she passed. The streets were particularly busy that day and she found progress slow. Waggons taking supplies to the fortress seemed to be in every street and at one crossroads traffic had ground to a complete halt. A timber waggon trying to turn left had got jammed across the street. A large crowd was gathering, all offering advice, encouragement, and witticisms to the harassed waggoners as they tried to back up their team of six oxen. The noise was deafening with the shouts of the waggoners and the bellows of the oxen joining with the din of the crowd. Senovara watched with interest as chaos and order fought for precedence.

'Greetings, Senovara. Where are you off to?' The voice behind her made Senovara jump.

'Oh, hail, Basilia. I was heading your way, actually, to call on the wife and sister of your new centurion. I believe you've already met them.'

'Yes. They seem reasonable enough, though the wife is a bit quiet. I'll walk with you. Let's cut through behind here – we'll be here until the Rosalia if we wait for this waggon to be shifted.'

The women turned into an alleyway between two houses and made their way up a side street. They were soon at the south-west gate of the fortress.

Basilia greeted the two legionaries who were standing on guard duty. 'This lady is coming to visit the quarters of Veturius.'

The soldiers stepped back and indicated with a movement of their spears that Senovara was to go through.

'Where do I go when I get in, Basilia?' Senovara felt nervous at the thought of walking into the fortress alone. On the rare occasions when she had visited before, Quintus had always been with her.

'They're in the *praetentura*. Go straight up the Via Praetoria. Veturius is centurion of the third barrack block on your left.'

'Are you coming too, Basilia?'

'No, I have too many chores to do today to make social calls. I'll see you at the bathhouse tomorrow, no doubt. Farewell.'

Senovara headed through the gate into the fortress, looking about her in awe. Even though the fortress was not yet complete and only had a holding garrison, it still seemed very busy and noisy, with soldiers moving around purposefully and waggons being unloaded. Passing the whitewashed barrack blocks she could smell food cooking and see men sitting on the verandahs cleaning their kit and hanging their washing out on the railings. It all seemed very domestic. Then a small group of men marched past in full armour, carrying their great rectangular shields with the lightning bolts and eagles, symbols of Jupiter, painted on the red leather. No doubt they were just changing the guard at the gates but Senovara couldn't help but shudder as she looked at their long spears and sheathed swords. Even the sound of their hobnailed boots on the packed gravel of the road surface, the chinking of their apron mounts and swish of their tunics sounded menacing, and she hurried on.

At the third barrack block she turned left and made her way to the end of the row, where the centurion's quarters protruded beyond the front of the *contubernia*. She knocked on the door nervously, aware that she was being scrutinized by the soldiers on the verandah, and was relieved when Broginara opened it immediately.

'Hail, Senovara. Come in, and welcome.'

Senovara stepped over the threshold into a small entrance area, which seemed to be full of cloaks and baskets. She was ushered into a room to the right, noticing how thin the walls were; probably just wood, she thought, covered with a skim of plaster. The house would be cold in winter, even if they lit the brazier that stood in the corner of the room. She looked about the small living room with curiosity. Although Broginara had said that these quarters were bigger than the ones they had had at Vercovicium, the living room still seemed smaller than Senovara's own best room, which surprised her. But her new friends had made their new quarters homely by hanging drapes over the window that looked onto the barrack's verandah and by laying a woven rug on the floor.

She handed her basket, with its present of cakes made with honey from Matugenus' hives, to Adnamata who was waiting in the doorway of the adjoining room.

'Thank you, Senovara. And welcome to our new home. Let me take your cloak. Would you like to be shown round first or have some wine?'

Senovara, hearing the note of pride in Adnamata's voice, realised that her hostesses were as eager to show her their quarters as she was to see them. She had always wanted to see what a centurion's home looked like – she had questioned her sister-in-law on the one occasion they had met but had found it difficult to imagine the interiors from the description Flavia had given her. Now she would see for herself.

'You've seen the entrance, of course.' Broginara had constituted herself chief guide and led the way back into the lobby, where she hung Senovara's cloak on a wooden peg. 'It's very convenient having somewhere to keep our cloaks and other such things without having to have them cluttering up our living space.'

'And it keeps the draughts out, as well,' broke in Adnamata enthusiastically.

'This is our main room,' Broginara continued. 'Not very big, but this house has more rooms than we're used to.' She took them through the living room and out through another door and Senovara found herself in a good-sized kitchen with a stove built against the wall. The room looked rather empty, compared with Senovara's own kitchen with its bundles of herbs hanging from the rafters and its pots of preserves on the shelf, but then, she reflected, the Pannonians had not had time to lay in much in the way of supplies. There was a wooden screen cutting off one corner of the room, which she realised probably hid the large pot that did duty as a *latrina*.

She felt rather smug that her own house had a proper *latrina*. The main sewer from the fortress to the river ran just below the flagstones outside her kitchen door. Quintus had cut a hole into the side of the stone lining of the sewer and fitted a wooden pipe between it and the pit dug under the wooden bench in the room off the kitchen. It had taken him ages to enlarge a fault at the edge of one of the millstone grit slabs, but it had been worth it. Now they didn't have to keep carrying their pots to the open drain at the end of the street; all she had to do was throw some water down the hole in the bench every now and again to keep it smelling sweet. Senovara had often wondered if this arrangement was legal, and what would happen if the authorities found out, but Quintus told her several people had done it and no one would mind.

'Through here,' Broginara continued, 'is Veturius and Adnamata's bedroom and here is mine; small, I know, but we had one posting where I had to sleep in the kitchen, so this is great luxury.'

Senovara peered into the two rooms, admiring the fat pillows and mattresses on the beds.

'Those were part of my dowry,' whispered Adnamata. 'They're stuffed with feathers so they have to be turned every day.' Senovara was impressed. All her mattresses were filled with chaff and straw, though her pillows had feathers in them, courtesy of Matugenus' chickens.

Finally, she was shown a small room which led off the entrance hall. This, she was informed in respectful tones, was Veturius' room, where he conducted business and saw the soldiers who wanted to speak to him. The room itself didn't look particularly impressive, she thought, remembering Quintus' tales of being hauled up before the centurion when he was still serving. It was painted white all over in military fashion and the furniture was restricted to a plain table and two regulation-issue wooden stools. A shelf attached to one wall held neat piles of writing tablets, both the wax sort and written leaves, as well as rolls of papyrus, some loose, some in tubular cases. A bronze pen and a pottery inkwell lay on the table next to an iron stylus and a wooden box for wax. An iron candelabrum stood by the side of the table, placed at the right height to throw the maximum light over the work surface.

'Let us offer you some wine,' said Broginara when Senovara had expressed her delight with their living quarters and they were back in the living room. 'Please, do sit down.' Broginara indicated a group of four folding stools.

Senovara looked at them with interest. She had heard of these folding iron stools with their cushions supported on leather straps, but had not seen them before. They were a little fussy for her taste, with bright brass washers decorating the iron cross bracers, but they felt quite comfortable, even if there was nothing to lean back against. No doubt, she thought, for a family who had to keep moving house, folding furniture was only sensible.

Broginara came back into the room carrying two pottery jugs, one smaller than the other, followed by Adnamata carrying a circular wooden tray on which there were four beakers of the finest black ware from Gallia Senovara had ever seen and two small bowls. She set the tray down on a folding iron stand which Broginara placed ready while Senovara watched, fascinated. Everything seemed to be designed to fold up in this household.

'How do you like your wine, Senovara?

'Very weak, please.'

Adnamata handed her sister-in-law a beaker and Broginara, with great ceremony, proceeded to mix the wine to Senovara's taste.

'Do try an olive,' urged Adnamata, handing Senovara one of the small bowls. 'Veturius found a merchant ship in the docks this morning just unloading a new consignment. They've been packed in brine, so they should be quite fresh.'

Senovara hesitated. Although she cooked in olive oil occasionally, she had never really developed a taste for olives, but it would be rude to refuse. She popped one in her mouth, biting the flesh off the stone and swallowing it hurriedly before following it quickly with a sip of wine. She put the stone in the second bowl on the table indicated by Adnamata.

As her hostesses made themselves comfortable on their own stools Senovara looked at them with curiosity. When they had visited her and Quintus they had kept their cloaks on, so she hadn't realised that they didn't wear the layers of long,

T-shaped tunics that she and most of her friends wore. Now she saw that they wore the more complicated traditional clothing of the women of Pannonia, which she had never seen close to before. She thought it looked rather uncomfortable, with its tight bodice of fine wool with long fitted sleeves and turned-back cuffs and a tubular over-tunic fastened at both shoulders by bow brooches. She wondered how the women got into their bodices, until she noticed that the row of three circular brooches that each wore down the front was fastening an open seam. She also wasn't sure how comfortable the woollen girdles tied round the Pannonians' waists would be – she had never worn a belt or a girdle in her life and suspected that it might be very constricting. She had to admit the women looked colourful, though. Broginara's outfit consisted of a scarlet tunic over a light green bodice and underskirt, while Adnamata's tunic was bright blue with yellow undergarments. Senovara felt a little dowdy in her light blue woollen dress and cream linen shift. Even her best jewellery was put in the shade: as well as five brooches, each woman wore a large circular medallion over her breasts and gold ear-rings with pendant pearls; only Aqmat could have outshone the display.

Both women had removed the rather ugly white caps that they had worn as part of their outdoor wear and Senovara could see that Adnamata wore her long hair pulled into a complex bun worn high at the back of her head, with a plait running from the centre of her forehead across the crown. Broginara's shorter hair, on the other hand, was a riot of curls over her forehead, with the back hair held up by bone combs. All very fetching, thought Senovara enviously; she'd never been able to do much more with her own hair than twist it into an unruly bun.

As the women made polite conversation about Eboracum – which butcher provided the best meat, whether there was anyone in the town who sold medicines, which deities had already had temples built to them, and other matters, both important and trivial – Senovara longed to ask why such an attractive woman as Broginara had never marrried, and how Adnamata and her husband had met and married. Surely, if Veturius was from Aquincum he must have been stationed a long way from home by the time he was promoted to centurion and able to take a wife? Then Senovara recalled Quintus telling her that centurions were barred from marrying women from the province in which they were stationed, and that many returned home to find a wife. She wished she could ask if this had been the case for Adnamata and Veturius, but realised that the Pannonian women would think it very rude of her to ask such a personal question on so slight an acquaintance. She would have to curb her curiosity until she knew them better.

At that moment, Veturius strode into the room and all three women stood up, Senovara following her new friends' lead as the sheer force of the centurion's authority and personality drew her to her feet. He was in full uniform of white tunic and leather strip apron, with the chest of his mail shirt covered in honorary torcs and *phalerae*. His polished white metal helmet with its centurial crest of white horsehair running from ear to ear, and the silvered greaves protecting his shins, added to his splendour, while his sword, hanging on his left side, and his dagger on his right added a note of menace. He carried a vine stick in one hand and Senovara noticed for the first time that he wore a massive iron finger-ring set with a dark red intaglio. She found the full panoply altogether overwhelming at close quarters.

'Hail, Senovara,' he said. 'It is kind of you to call on my womenfolk. How is your husband?'

'He is well, thank you, sir. But I should be getting back now.' Senovara felt uncomfortable; the centurion's presence seemed to fill the small room and she realised, by the way they fussed around him helping him off with his helmet, that Adnamata and Broginara wanted to start preparing a meal for him. She also remembered her mother advising her that a first visit should always be short and avoid mealtimes, and she was keen not to appear gauche.

On the way home she reflected on the different attitudes women from the various provinces had to their men. In her tribe, and luckily in Quintus' Germanic upbringing as well, there was a tradition that men and women were equal partners in a marriage and that they should support each other in all their daily work. But she had been in Eboracum long enough to know that this was not an attitude shared by people from all the provinces. She had learned that in the eastern lands it was considered quite normal, even an indication of high status, for a man to have more than one wife. At the other extreme, she had heard stories that in the very far north of her own island of Britannia women sometimes had more than one husband. She grinned to herself as she imagined what Quintus would say if she announced she was going to take a second husband, like a Caledonian woman. She also laughed to think of any man being brave enough to marry more than one woman, especially if they were women of Enica's temperament, or one of the old feisty tribal queens such as Queen Cartimandua or Queen Boudica, both redoubtable women from what she had heard. British women were clearly very different to some of their sisters from the other provinces, thank the Mothers!

Women from Roma, itself, she had been shocked to discover, tended to be treated by their husbands as if they were children, to be guarded and cared for, admittedly, but not allowed a say on the way in which their children were brought up or even on how their own lives should be conducted. She believed this was the principle on which many Roman laws were based. Quintus, who had once visited Roma when he was in the army, had told her that this rule wasn't always adhered to among the plebeian families who had no property to worry about, but the only Italian women she had met or seen were officers' wives, drawn from the equestrian or senatorial classes, so she couldn't judge for herself how widespread it was. From Adnamata and Broginara's behaviour towards Veturius, she suspected that Pannonian women also considered their role in life was to look after their *pater familias*. Veturius had such a powerful personality, however, that she wondered if this was just the effect he had on everyone and if other Pannonian women were more independent. Quintus might know, she thought, as she picked her way round the puddles and animal droppings in her path. People were endlessly fascinating, she found, and coming to live in Eboracum had given her the chance to meet a wide variety of women from backgrounds she hadn't even been aware of growing up on a local farm.

The traffic had cleared while she was in the fortress and she made good progress getting home, turning into her street before she had had time to give serious consideration to what she had learned of her new friends and their way of life. Nearing the shop, she could see Ursa standing in the doorway of her own establishment next door, getting some air and watching the passers-by. Lurio, Ursa's husband, had been in the army with Quintus. On his retirement, a few years before Quintus, he had set himself up as a bronze-smith, making use of the skills he had learned during his service years when his special duty in the legion had been making military fittings from recycled copper alloy. Senovara privately thought it was just as well that the legions had to be self-sufficient, because it meant that the soldiers had to learn practical skills; she shuddered to think how disruptive the veterans would have been if all they had learned from military service was how to fight. Most of them, thankfully, could use their military training to make a useful contribution to the growing towns and settlements.

Like Quintus, Lurio was a German, from Moguntiacum, but Ursa was a Batavian, who had come to Britannia as the ward of her brother, who was serving up on the frontier with the First

Cohort of Batavians, currently stationed at Vindolanda. Lurio and Ursa had not waited for Lurio to retire before getting married, but had married according to Batavian custom. This had been much to the satisfaction of Ursa's brother, who was inclined to be a spendthrift and had been finding it hard keeping the two of them on an auxiliary's salary. Lurio, as a legionary, had earned three hundred *denarii* a year, as opposed to an auxiliary's salary of one hundred *denarii,* and had been of a saving habit all his working life, so was well able to provide for a wife and family. Unfortunately, he had forgotten to legalise his marriage after his retirement and Ursa had complained to Senovara several times about the legal complications they were now having to go through to legitimise their two sons. Only last year Quintus had had to go up to the fortress with Lurio to swear that Bassus and Canio, now strapping lads of nine and eleven, were, to the best of his knowledge, the legitimate issue of Lurio and Ursa, and that Lurio and Ursa had 'cohabited as man and wife for twelve years for the purpose of producing children'. Senovara thought this ridiculous. Anyone looking at the two boys with Ursa's brunette curls and Lurio's green eyes could hardly fail to recognise their parentage, but the family were still awaiting the final confirmation that their plea had been approved by the authorities and until it had been received the boys and Ursa would continue to be regarded by officialdom as non-existent.

'Hail, Ursa. Any news?'

'Nothing worth mentioning,' was the tired response. 'How's your new dog getting on? My boys have been nagging us for a dog ever since yours arrived.'

'Well, he's quietened down now he's got used to us. Quintus has made him a kennel in the garden, so we don't have to manoeuvre past him if we want to use the *latrina* in the middle of the night, but he does tend to bark at the slightest noise still. I hope he hasn't disturbed you?'

'No, I'm so exhausted these days it would take more than a small dog like Hylax to wake me once I'm asleep.'

Senovara made sympathetic noises. Her neighbour did indeed look tired, and she resolved to take Bassus and Canio off Ursa's hands one day soon so that the Batavian woman could rest. Just as she was about to make the offer, however, the noise of warfare came from the bronze-smith's.

'Oh, there they go again,' moaned Ursa. 'I love them dearly but when they start to fight I sometimes wish I had the legal privilege of disowning them like Lurio.'

She disappeared into the shop to break up the argument, which sounded as if it was being fought along the lines of gladiatorial combat rather than the more refined rules of a legionary battle.

Senovara laughed as she made her way down the alleyway to her own kitchen door, planning her evening's tasks. It was time she got on with her own life and stopped wondering about other people's.

Aprilis

T HE INVITATION TO Basilia's birthday party arrived early in the morning, while Senovara was washing clothes. It was delivered by one of the young boys who helped in the fortress hospital. He waited patiently while Senovara dried her hands and took the strip of wood from him.

On one side, written in ink, were the words *'To Senovara, wife of Quintus Flavius Candidus, from Basilia'*. On the other, *'Basilia to Senovara, greetings. On the Ides of Aprilis, for the celebration of my birthday, I give you a warm invitation that you come to us to make the day more enjoyable to me by your arrival. I shall expect you in the afternoon. Farewell, Senovara, my dearest soul, as I hope to prosper, and hail.'*

The boy stood by the door of the passage until Senovara had slowly read the careful handwriting and then said, 'Basilia told me to wait and take your answer back. There's no need to write it down.' Senovara thanked the Goddesses silently. She could write, of course, but finding a sheet of wood and preparing the ox-gall ink took ages and the writing itself didn't come easily.

She could, no doubt, have gone to the scribe's stall just outside the fortress gate; that was the approved thing to do and was, presumably, what Basilia had done, but by the time she had got as far as the scribe's she might just as well have carried on and told Basilia herself.

'Could you tell Basilia I would be delighted to come?' The lad nodded briskly and left.

Senovara considered the invitation. Birthday parties were something quite new to her. At home they had celebrated various feast days as a family but those had been religious events. Having a day which celebrated one's own birth had been unknown, largely because it hadn't been possible to record the precise day of a birth. Under the new Roman laws everyone had to be registered within thirty days of their birth, so no one had any excuse for not knowing when they were born, nor how old they were, because a person's age could be calculated from the year of the emperor reigning when they were registered. She herself had been registered according to the new law, but the idea of celebrating the day hadn't occurred to her or her family until she moved to Eboracum and found that it was quite common among people from the lands around the Mare Internum. Even Quintus was known to buy her a trinket on her birthday and she had quickly learned that she was expected to prepare a particularly special dinner on his.

A present! Of course, Basilia would expect a present. What could she take?

At that moment Quintus came into the kitchen and poured himself some beer. 'What did the lad want?'

'Oh, he brought me an invitation from Basilia. It's her birthday tomorrow, on the Feast of Jupiter Victor, and she's asked me to visit her.'

'That's the woman married to Marcus Anicius Ingenuus, the *medicus ordinarius*?' Senovara looked at him with exasperation;

they didn't know anyone else called Basilia. 'Yes, that's right, and she'll expect a present. What shall I take?'

'If you like you can take her some new shoelaces. I've just made some from the offcuts of that purple leather. She'll think them very elegant and if she tells everyone where she got them it will be a good advertisement for my wares.'

'Excellent idea. Thank you.'

'You might even get some for your birthday,' promised Quintus. Senovara smiled doubtfully. She still wasn't always sure when Quintus was teasing her.

'Have you had many customers today?' she asked, changing the subject.

'No. That's why I've had time to make shoelaces. Trade's very slow at the moment; if it goes on like this, you and Armea will have to start taking in washing, like Surilla, not just doing our own.'

Senovara laughed, surer of her ground now – this was Quintus' regular complaint, even when he was doing particularly well. 'Oh, I'm sure it will pick up when the rest of the legion return. It can't be very long now. Then there will be a new set of veterans wanting civilian clothing and all the young soldiers wanting to spend their savings. Not to mention all the wives, mothers and sisters coming down with them.'

'Well, it can't happen soon enough for me and the rest of the Eboracum *collegia* of merchants and traders, I can tell you.'

Quintus stumped moodily back to his workbench and Senovara got on with her washing, her mind busy with thoughts of the treat offered for the next day. She wondered who would be there. Ursa for sure, and Surilla and Pervica; possibly the widow Catia and the two Pannonians as well. Under normal circumstances these women, from very mixed backgrounds, would probably not have met socially, but, as Basilia said, they were all free women and there weren't so many women in the settlement that one could afford to be choosy about one's acquaintances; it wasn't as if any of them were barmaids or Egyptians! Senovara blushed to recall how long it had taken her before she had realised that by 'Egyptians' Basilia had meant prostitutes, and she still didn't fully understand why Basilia used the term; all the prostitutes she knew of were local girls and the furthest east any of them had ever been was Petuaria. Perhaps it was the kohl eyeliner they wore? As she puzzled over this conundrum she picked the linen shifts and underwear one by one out of the hot water in the cauldron, balancing each of them on the end of a long wooden spoon to avoid scalding herself, and placed them in cold water in the half-barrel sink to rinse. With the bowl of the spoon she prodded the material until it was cool enough to handle and then she started to rub each item through. When she was sure they were thoroughly rinsed and no dirty marks remained, she called to Armea to help her.

Between them, they wrung each piece of clothing as tightly as possible over the half-barrel and then stretched it back into shape. Senovara went outside and wiped the green boughs of the apple tree before Armea draped the clothes over them. The day was warm and clear and there was a light breeze blowing; the clothes shouldn't take long to dry, thought Senovara with relief. She was always thankful when the spring came, bringing with it good drying days. During the winter the house always seemed to be full of damp clothes! A fuller had recently set up business in Eboracum, so she could take her blankets and larger pieces of clothing to him but, as she only washed those once a year anyway, it didn't help with the regular laundry of the family's linen and the children's tunics. This still had to be tackled and often ended up being dried in the kitchen, much to Quintus' irritation. Today the washing was dry enough to be brought in by mid-afternoon, and the kitchen table was cleared, ready for Armea to smooth out the wrinkles in the material with the glass linen smoother. As she watched Armea strenuously rubbing out the creases in one of Ertola's under-tunics, Senovara decided this was definitely one of the benefits of having a slave. She hated linen smoothing. She had nothing against the smoother itself; indeed, she always thought the black glass ball, the size of a small apple, a pleasing and decorative item, and she liked seeing it sitting on the shelf in the kitchen. But using it was a different matter: rubbing the ball briskly up and down the material was hard work and by the time a whole pile of family laundry was done one's arms were aching. No, it was certainly good to have a slave to do the tasks one particularly disliked.

A knock on the kitchen door disturbed her thoughts. Outside stood a short, fat man in a very dirty tunic, carrying a large sack over his shoulder.

'Greetings, Senovara. I've brought your order of charcoal.'

'Would you leave it outside, Viducus? We've just taken the washing in and if we pour the charcoal into the basket now we'll get marks all over the clean linen. Charcoal dust gets everywhere.'

'True. But I have to take my sack. Good sacks don't grow on trees, you know. Bring your basket out here and I'll fill it up.'

Senovara would rather not have had to move the charcoal basket from its place under the stove while Armea was still smoothing – even the slightest disturbance of the charcoal store resulted in smuts all over the kitchen – but Viducus was inclined to be disobliging. He was perfectly capable of taking his charcoal away and the basket was already emptier than she liked it to be; if she didn't get this sackful she might be out of fuel by tomorrow evening. She rolled up her sleeves, lifted the basket carefully, carried it out of the back door and set it down on the flags.

Viducus shifted his sack, ready to pour out its contents.

'Wait!' Senovara screamed. She grabbed the door handle and slammed the door shut just as the black sticks shot into the basket in a rolling cloud of dust. She scowled at the charcoal burner in exasperation but he, oblivious of the fact that he might have caused offence, was rolling up his sack and whistling tunelessly.

'I'll go round and get the money from your husband, shall I?'

Senovara nodded and dusted herself down. Hopefully, she had got the door shut in time and her washing hadn't got covered in smuts. Viducus was so used to being covered in black grime that he failed to appreciate that other people might prefer to be clean.

The next day she and Armea took advantage of the continuing good weather to sow some vegetables in the garden. They had managed to get some rows of peas and beans in a few weeks ago, but it was important to get the onions, leeks and cabbages planted soon if they were to be sure of a decent crop.

The precious seeds had been stored over winter in little linen bags and, while Armea dug over the beds, Senovara sat at the kitchen table checking that the seeds were still good and that none had gone mouldy. Finding somewhere dry to store seeds was always a problem. Their house was drier than most, but with mists coming up from the river, the general wetness of the climate, and steam from cooking and washing, no house in Eboracum could escape being damp.

She poured the contents of each bag into a small black dish. Picking over the seeds, she noticed that some were already beginning to sprout, but she was pleased there were no signs of mould. With the help of the gods they should have a good harvest: she had made a special offering of olive oil at their household shrine that morning and made particular mention of the seed planting during the ritual.

In nine days' time it would be the spring planting festival, which the Romans called the Festival of Palilia. Quintus had told her that the Palilia was once a festival for shepherds and herdsmen in Italia but had now become the official day on which to celebrate the birthday of Roma. Senovara thought it rather ridiculous for a city to have a birthday but all the tradesmen and merchants felt that it was important to attend to show their loyalty to the Empire. She and Quintus always went

to the official ceremony held in the fields outside the settlement area, but Senovara considered that the sacrifice of a pregnant cow and the lighting of one bonfire, however large, was a pale imitation of the old native ritual of Beltine held around the first day of Maius.

She recalled, with a sense of nostalgia, the Beltine festivals at home when everyone on the farm had helped to build the two rows of bonfires. She and her brother and cousins had spent days roaming the woods around the farm, dragging brushwood and logs down to the compound, getting increasingly excited as the festival drew nearer. Invariably they had got into trouble for trying to add good wood to the bonfires – as soon as they had built a nice-sized bonfire someone would come along and take out some of the larger pieces to use in a domestic fire or to repair a fence. But eventually a satisfactory collection of pyres was built. Then the great moment came when the fires were lit and the cattle herd – all bellowing with fright – were driven down through the alleyway of flames and out to their summer pasture, encouraged by loud cheers from all the farmhands. After that there was a great feast when much beer was drunk and everyone joined in the dancing to encourage the fertility of the land – though she recalled wryly that she had usually been sent to bed before the party got too rowdy. One of her grandmother's regular jokes in her annual speech at the women's fire festival of Imbolc, in Februarius, had been to pronounce on the success of the previous Beltine festival; her criterion being not the quality of the harvest in the autumn, but the number of babies born in the district around the start of the year. Imbolc was rarely celebrated these days, sadly, but Senovara realised that the Roman Government was not particularly interested in festivals peculiar to women; such festivals had little political usefulness.

The Palilia, on the other hand, was the official birthday of Roma and as such was very political. Senovara always enjoyed looking at the faces of the crowd gathered for the ceremony because everyone there had a different reason for attending. Some local people, like herself, who had gardens or farmed the land around Eboracum, were hoping that the rites would result in good crops; most of the tradesmen were hoping for a profitable year in their workshops; others, who came from more eastern provinces, were there just to show their loyalty and would perform their own fertility rituals, as appropriate, on their own traditional feast days. The Palilia was one of those interesting days in the year when different religious beliefs were catered for by a single ceremony, even if it was a rather dull one by Senovara's standards.

She looked out of the door to where Armea was digging, using her right foot to push the iron rim of the wooden spade into the heavy soil.

'Do make sure you get all the roots out, Armea. Then dig in the ashes from that pile over there.'

Armea was a good worker, thought Senovara, willing and capable. Having her was making a great difference to the family's life. Senovara no longer felt completely worn out at the end of each day, which meant that she could give more attention to Quintus – so he considered the slave price of fifty *denarii* money well spent. The children got on well with Armea and were happy to stay with her when their mother went shopping or visited friends. Indeed, it would have been almost impossible for Senovara to have accepted Basilia's party invitation if they hadn't bought Armea; Quintus couldn't have looked after two small children all afternoon in the shop. Yes, it had certainly been a sensible idea of Quintus' to buy Armea.

Senovara shook herself. It was time she got ready for Basilia's party instead of sitting about. Ertola was having a nap and Lucius was now pestering Armea while she worked on the vegetable plot, so the house was quiet. Pouring some water into a bowl, Senovara cleaned her teeth with a twig before washing her hands and face, then, drying herself with a towel, she went into the bedroom and opened the cupboard by the bed. Pulling out her two newest dresses, she shook them out and laid them on the bed. She took a step back and looked at them critically. Neither was really new but both were still respectable. Which should she wear? The dark red or the blue? Quintus always said he liked her in the red dress so there was no point asking him, but she had a secret preference for the misty blue which could look almost mauve by the light of oil lamps. She held each tunic up against herself and peered down, sticking one foot out to try and judge the effect of the colour.

It was so difficult not knowing what one really looked like; mirrors could only show a tiny part at a time. If only she had a bigger mirror. She picked up the small one from the table and held it out at arm's length, trying to get an idea of what a full-length Senovara would look like. A small square of blue or red reflected back at her from the glass. A bronze mirror might have been better, as they were bigger, but they didn't reflect as well as the German glass mirrors, even though they were more expensive. She sighed, then brightened at a sudden idea. She propped the mirror on the floor in the corner of the room and stepped back – she could now see a bit more. Perhaps if she stood on something? She dragged a stool in from the kitchen and stood on it, twisting this way and that as she tried to see what she looked like.

A noise behind her made her look round. Quintus was standing at the door, gazing at her in astonishment.

'In the name of Apollo, what are you doing, woman?'

She reddened, embarrassed at being discovered in such a ridiculous position and feeling slightly guilty at the exposure of her vanity. She scrambled down off the stool in confusion.

'I'm deciding which dress to wear,' she replied, trying to imply that standing on a stool was a perfectly reasonable way to achieve this end. Quintus' left eyebrow lifted but he merely said, 'Wear the red – you always look fine in that.'

Senovara sighed again and nodded. As a compliment this lacked originality but it was the only advice she was going to get. 'Did you want something?' she enquired.

'Oh, I was just on my way to get some water. Shall I put the stool back?'

'Please.'

Quintus picked it up and went out, closing the door behind him. Senovara folded the blue dress up neatly and put it away in the cupboard. Undoing the brooches at her shoulders, she lifted the dress she was wearing over her head. As she emerged from the brown folds she caught sight of the left sleeve of her linen shift and groaned. She must have caught it in something when she was cooking: there was a large dirty mark by the cuff. It was lucky she had washed her other one the day before. She went into the kitchen, where Quintus was filling his jug with water from the barrel by the door. The laundry lay in a neat pile on the side table by the stove. She felt through the pile until she came to the shift and pulled it out. It was a little damp but it would do. She flapped it out through the kitchen door to shake out the creases.

'How long are you likely to be out?' asked Quintus.

'Not long. I expect I'll be back in plenty of time to prepare supper. Armea knows what to have ready, so it won't take long.'

Quintus nodded, then jerked his head as a voice called out in the shop. 'Customers!' he exclaimed, and he hurried out of the room.

Senovara went back into the bedroom and changed her shift. She pulled the red dress down over her head and adjusted it on her shoulders, then, reaching under the bed, she pulled out her jewellery box and looked inside for her best brooches which Quintus had bought her the first Diem Kalendarum after they had married. She stood up so that her dress folds hung properly, then unclipping the pins from their catchplates, pinned a brooch to each shoulder to hold the material in place. Picking up the mirror again she inspected each brooch and readjusted the chain that linked them together. They really were very pretty with their flared heads, some knobbly decoration around the bow and openwork catchplates. Quintus had been cross that he couldn't afford the enamelled type, but she preferred the plain bronze ones, which looked like gold if she kept them well polished.

She took out her bone hairpins and shook her hair loose. It took a while to get the small double-sided bone comb through her long hair, but eventually she had combed out all the tangles and had twisted her back hair into a neat bun, fixing it firmly in place with the pins. She checked in the mirror to see if she looked tidy, and put the comb back on top of the cupboard.

Turning back to the jewellery box she looked at the pairs of earrings lying in it. Should she leave in her plain bronze hoops or should she put in some fancier ones? What would the other women be wearing? She picked up each pair thoughtfully. Should she wear the spirals or were they too old-fashioned? Or the three-strand twisted hoops? Or even her very best silver hoops? She held up the mirror and placed the different earrings against an ear, one at a time. The three-strand twists looked best, she decided, and she hooked them into position. She selected two bracelets from the box and slipped one on each wrist. Holding her arms out in front of her, she contemplated the pattern made by the three strands of different yellow metals which had been twisted together to make the bracelets. The result was simple but very effective and, unlike Aqmat the Palmyrene, she was quite satisfied with only one on each wrist, just as she was content with the single plain iron ring which Quintus had placed on the second finger of her left hand on the occasion of their betrothal. Many women these days, she had noticed, were inclining more to the eastern habit of wearing lots of jewellery, particularly finger-rings, but she always felt overdressed wearing more than one finger-ring and she didn't like the jingling made by lots of bracelets worn together. She closed the lid of the jewellery box firmly on the rest of its contents and slid it back into its hiding place under the bed.

She picked up the mirror again and looked at her face critically. Her complexion was still good, she was pleased to see. A little too freckly for true beauty according to Roman precepts, but she had no need to apply halcyon cream to get rid of spots, or oyster-shell toner to improve the skin, or a bean-flower preparation to smooth out wrinkles. She was also blessed with good colour in her cheeks and lips – but perhaps nature could do with a helping hand? She opened the door and looked down the corridor towards the shop. The reassuring sound of Quintus talking to a customer came through the closed door. She fished out her jewellery box again and extracted a small pot which contained red wine lees mixed with lard. Quickly she dabbed a little on her lips and smoothed it in with a fingertip. She pressed her lips together and then checked the result in the mirror. Not too obvious; just a little redder than usual. Quintus would never notice. She put the incriminating little pot back in the jewellery box and hid it away again. She would never be able to persuade Quintus that respectable women, and even some men, wore cosmetics these days. If he had been Italian he might have expected his wife to wear make-up, or so she had been told, but the men of Germania tended to be very old-fashioned. She looked at her reflection again. Wetting a finger, she smoothed down some unruly hairs in her eyebrows, then briskly plucked out with tweezers a single hair which refused to lie down.

Right. She was almost ready. All she needed to do was change into a pair of dark red leather slippers and she could go. Then she remembered Basilia's present. Where had she put the purple shoe laces? She dashed into the kitchen and found them tied in a neat bundle lying on a shelf by the linen smoother. She put them in a small cloth wrist-bag and added her folding spoon and a knife – essential implements to take to a party. She also put in a small square of linen in case she needed a handkerchief or a napkin.

She looked into the children's room. Ertola was still asleep. Armea would have to wake her up soon or she wouldn't want to go to bed until late. She made her way to the back door and shouted for her slave.

Armea stuck the spade into the ground and came over to the back door, wiping her hands on the stout apron of sacking tied round her waist.

'I've sorted out the seeds,' Senovara said. 'Each bag holds a particular sort. The onions are in the first bag, the leeks in the second and the cabbage in the last.' She pointed to the table where she had arranged the bags in a line; Armea's reading had not yet got to the stage where it was helpful to label anything. 'If you can get in a row of each before dark, that will be good. You'll have to wake Ertola soon, though.'

'Yes, Mistress. The vegetable beds are ready for the seeds now. Ertola can sit on the path and watch me put them in.'

'Where have Lucius and Hylax gone?'

'Next door. They're playing with the lady Ursa's boys.'

'No wonder it's so quiet! I'm off. I shouldn't be too late, but if everyone gets hungry before I return, dish up the ham I cooked yesterday. There's a turnip on the shelf which could be cooked to go with it, but it's so old and woody that you'll need to cut it up quite small. If I'm back in time I'll make some dill sauce.'

She lifted her cloak off its hook on the back of the door and Armea arranged it round her shoulders and pinned it. It would have been more elegant to have worn a stole but the weather was still too cold to walk through Eboracum in so skimpy a garment. It would probably be safer to have her finery covered by a cloak, as well.

Senovara picked up her wrist-bag and said her farewells to Quintus as she passed through the shop. As she left she felt a sense of release and excitement. It was rare for her to escape from the housework for long, other than for her regular visit to the bathhouse. Going to a social event like a birthday party made her feel very much a Roman lady of leisure and, as she walked along, she decided she quite liked the feeling. Perhaps she should invite some friends round when it was her birthday. She resolved to observe how Basilia arranged her event. Basilia, after all, was one of her more cosmopolitan friends and would no doubt conduct a birthday party in the proper manner.

The streets leading to the fortress were quiet for once and Senovara wondered where everyone was. Then she remembered that it was the Feast of Jupiter Victor and that most of the soldiers would be occupied on the parade ground. Even the inns appeared to be short of custom, though they would probably fill up when the soldiers were released from their ceremonial activities.

By this time she had arrived at the house of the *medicus ordinarius*. She knocked firmly on the door. Immediately it was opened by Basilia's freedman, a sallow-faced boy of about twenty who doubled as Anicius Ingenuus' receptionist when the *medicus ordinarius* held his occasional surgeries for civilians. Basilia had explained that her husband was only acting as the fortress doctor while the bulk of the legion was still at the frontier. He would be replaced by higher-ranking medical staff when the legion returned, but had decided that when that happened he would retire and set himself up in civilian practice, calculating that the town would soon be big enough to support a doctor. That was why they had taken a house outside the fortress, rather than the official premises they had been offered in a wing of the *valetudinarium*, and why he held surgeries for the townspeople, joking that he needed the practice on women and children! Senovara couldn't imagine that the legion could have anyone better qualified than her friend's husband. He had been excellent when Quintus had had that terrible fever when Lucius was only two – Senovara had feared for her husband's life but Anicius Ingenuus had pulled him through. She had been pleased when Basilia had told her of her husband's plans; it was comforting to have someone so clever and capable nearby, even though her grandmother kept telling her that Roman medicine was just superstition and that she would be better served making her own traditional potions.

The servant took her cloak and showed her into Basilia's dining room. This was laid out in the Roman fashion, with three couches arranged in an open square round a low table. Senovara had heard that aristocratic Romans reclined on such couches when eating, but she had always thought this rather an uncomfortable habit and she was relieved to see that the couches were occupied by her friends, Surilla and Pervica, both of whom were sitting bolt upright.

Basilia rose from a stool by the head of one of the couches and welcomed her friend. 'Hail, Senovara. Thank you for coming.'

'Hail, Basilia. I hope you're having a happy day? I've brought you these as a small gift.' Senovara handed over the bundle of purple shoelaces.

'How grand! Purple shoelaces! I shall feel very elegant in these. Did Quintus cut them?'

Senovara admitted that he had and warned her that he hoped Basilia would tell everyone where they had come from, so his sales would increase.

A loud laugh came from Pervica. 'That's a cunning idea. A shrewd man your husband.'

'Come and sit down here, and let me pour you a glass of wine.' Basilia ushered Senovara to one of the couches and sat her next to Surilla. 'I'm expecting Adnamata and Broginara, as well as Ursa and Catia, and a Libyan woman called Vibia Pacata, whom I don't think you've met. She's married to another centurion of the Sixth and has just arrived in Eboracum.'

'The fortress is really beginning to fill up now,' commented Surilla. 'I'm already getting more laundry. I'm even thinking of taking on an assistant.'

Senovara was glad to hear it. She had often thought her friend's life must be hard and she was pleased that she was doing well.

'Were you thinking of buying a slave, then?' asked Basilia.

'No,' laughed Surilla. 'Taking in washing doesn't pay that well. I thought I'd put a notice outside my door and see if there's a widow who needs some work and would be interested in joining me.'

'There may well be women coming down with the troops who could do with a steady job. I don't know how some soldiers manage, even on a legionary's pay. I met a *librarius* the other day who had his mother, two sisters, and an aunt to support,' said Pervica. 'I can't remember when I've met a more henpecked man.'

The rest of the women grinned to themselves; Pervica's husband had had to fight a hard rearguard action over the years not to become henpecked himself.

The door opened and Basilia's servant announced Adnamata and Broginara, who were accompanied by a small, fine-boned woman with the very dark skin of someone from the southern provinces.

There was a flurry of welcomes and introductions before everyone got settled on the couches again. Senovara found herself sitting next to Vibia Pacata.

'How long have you been in Eboracum?' she asked rather nervously, hoping the stranger would understand her Latin.

'Only a few days. My husband, Verecundus, and I have just arrived from Lambaesis – he's been transferred to the Sixth Victrix from the Third Augusta. You wouldn't believe it, but we've been travelling since Ianuarius, because we came via Roma. We don't know yet, however, if we are to stay here or move on to the frontier.'

Not for the first time Senovara marvelled at the size of the Roman Empire and at the fact that by speaking Latin, albeit slowly and with a variety of accents, people from all the Roman provinces could communicate. She had no idea what the Libyan language sounded like but Vibia Pacata's Latin accent was pleasant and easy to understand.

The newcomer was a very attractive woman, dressed in a sleeveless cream tunic with a woollen wrap round her shoulders. Senovara was interested to notice that, unlike the other women, she wore no brooches, only earrings and a necklace of gold and white glass beads. She also wondered how long it would be before Vibia Pacata gave up on the dress of the southern provinces and started to wear the warmer northern dress. Having bare arms in Eboracum in Aprilis was rash, to say the least.

'Basilia mentioned that you are a Libyan?' she continued. 'Were you born in Lambaesis?'

'No. Lambaesis is in the province of Numidia. I was born at Lepcis Magna, which is in Tripolitania. Basilia, being Greek, calls everyone a Libyan if they come from lands to the west of Egypt, of course. I am descended from a desert people called the Garamantes, though.'

This was all very fascinating. Senovara had no idea why the fact that Basilia came from Athenae should result in her describing everyone from the southern provinces as Libyan. Several women from Mauretania had passed through Eboracum a few years ago but she couldn't remember Basilia calling them Libyans. Perhaps Mauretania was too far west of Egypt. Senovara's grasp of geography was limited to an awareness of where the tribal boundaries in Britannia were, and in this sort of conversation she was out of her depth, but politeness dictated that she should carry on.

'Is your husband from Lepcis Magna, too?'

'No, he is a Pannonian, like Broginara and Adnamata. He knew Veturius as a boy, so looked him up as soon as he learned that he was in Eboracum.'

Basilia started to hand round plates of delicacies. Senovara managed to avoid the olives this time but was happy to accept a portion of eggs in pine-nut sauce and some tiny sausages wrapped in bay leaves. She got her folding spoon out of her bag and tucked in, with her napkin ready to wipe her mouth. The guests' beakers were refilled with wine and water, and the conversation became more general.

'Is Catia coming?' Senovara asked Basilia as she accepted another sausage.

'Yes, but she said she'd be late.'

Pervica broke in. 'For the sake of Peace don't comment on her new hairstyle. Or if she's wearing a veil don't ask if she's in mourning or just come from the temple.'

'Why not?' Senovara was startled by this advice.

Pervica, Surilla and Basilia looked at each other and chuckled.

'Because she decided she wanted to curl her fringe the day before yesterday and borrowed some curling tongs from the maid who attends the wife of one of the tribunes at the fortress. Unfortunately, she left them too long heating in the fire and managed to set fire to her hair.'

'No!'

'It's true,' affirmed Surilla 'I heard her yells and ran in to find her flapping a towel at her head. She's not hurt, luckily—'

'Just her vanity!' interposed Pervica.

'—but she has a black frizzled patch which she's been trying to cover up by combing her hair across her forehead and wearing a veil.'

'But why did she suddenly decide to curl her fringe? She's never bothered much about her appearance before.'

'Ah, but she's never had any reason before. Now that Bonosius, the butcher, has started paying her attention she clearly feels she should make an effort.'

Senovara smiled. The elderly butcher's interest in the comfortable widow had been a source of endless amusement to the women for a couple of months. At first Catia had not even noticed Bonosius' interest. Then she had treated the whole idea as a huge joke. When she realised how determined Bonosius was, she had panicked and been very huffy and curt. That was the first hint that she might be warming to him.

'Unfortunately, having tried to titivate herself for Bonosius' benefit she now doesn't want him to see her until her hair has grown back, and the poor man can't work out what he has done to offend her, just when he thought he was beginning to make progress. She asked me if I'd get some meat for her tomorrow, otherwise she's threatened to live off vegetables for the next few days.'

'And, of course, it was all so unnecessary,' said Basilia. 'Bonosius wouldn't notice if she dyed her hair scarlet with whelks, he's so short-sighted.'

'As well as being after her money.' Pervica was her usual cynical self.

'No,' Senovara replied. 'I don't think it's only that. He's been very lonely since his wife died. Catia is a nice woman and a good cook – the fact that she has a bit of money put away is just the gilding on the statue.'

'Trust you to think kindly.'

'Well, I see no reason not to,' asserted Senovara stoutly. She turned to Vibia Pacata. 'You will like Catia, I'm sure. She's a very kind woman. She was married to a centurion of the legion who died almost immediately after he retired. She's not normally vain at all.'

'Perhaps I should offer her one of my caps,' suggested Broginara.

'That would confuse Bonosius even more. He—' Senovara broke off hurriedly as the subject of their discussion entered the room, wearing a fine linen veil over her head.

'Hail, everyone. I hope you haven't eaten all the goodies.'

'Hail, Catia!'

Everyone shuffled around to make room for the newcomer, while trying not to gaze at the frizzled area visible at her hairline. Even Vibia Pacata, Senovara noticed with amusement, kept her gaze firmly on Catia's face when they were introduced, although she managed a quick peek when Catia turned to take the wine beaker Basilia handed to her.

'So what's the news, other than the fact that I made a prize idiot of myself yesterday and am the laughing stock of Eboracum?' Catia grinned amiably at her friends.

They grinned back, amused by her self-mocking tone.

'Whatever were you thinking of, woman?' demanded Pervica.

'Well, I had a dream, you see.' The listening women stiffened. This was serious. No one with any sense would ignore a message given through a dream. Catia continued serenely, aware that she now had their full attention.

'In my dream, Venus appeared and told me I should try to make myself more attractive. Quite firm she was about it. Well, when I woke up I thought, there's not a lot I can do, really. My figure can best be described as being on the chunky side and my legs are so bowed I couldn't stop a pig in a passage. No amount of bean-flower would remove my wrinkles and a woman in her

114

fifty-fifth year can hardly start to wear cosmetics – at least, not enough to make any difference to my face. So that left my hair. I thought about dyeing it, but everyone is used to me being grey; if I suddenly started to use saffron or the German juices and appeared as a blonde or brunette, it would be a bit obvious. Even if I used Moguntiacum Soap it would scream "hair dye". So I decided to just give my fringe a bit of a curl. Lattio was going to do it for me, but her mistress wasn't well so she only had time to drop off the curling tongs before going back and I had to do it myself. Clearly it's trickier than I thought!'

Senovara was sympathetic to Catia's plight. If Venus appeared to her in a dream she too would feel obliged to obey, though she hoped that if she did have such a visitation the goddess would have something of more moment to relate than merely delivering a disparaging lecture on her appearance. But the story did explain why Catia, normally the most unselfconscious of women, should suddenly take it into her head to curl her hair.

The other women also seemed to feel that Catia had done the best she could in the circumstances, though there was some speculation as to why the goddess should have decided to take an interest in the life of an Eboracum army widow. The topic was discussed for some minutes, but the ways of deities were invariably obscure and no doubt, if Venus was determined to interfere, then there would be more dreams which might elucidate matters, so the conversation moved on.

'This is a very pretty room, Basilia. Was it already decorated like this when you moved in?' Broginara looked around, admiringly.

'The mosaic was already laid down. I believe this was one of the first houses in Eboracum to have a mosaic,' Basilia added proudly. Senovara looked down at the floor with its simple geometric design of small black and white stone tesserae. This was, in her eyes, the height of elegance. She knew there was a Gallic mosaicist who travelled around the region and had often hoped that one day she would be able to commission him to lay a mosaic in her own dining room, but it was likely to be years before Quintus was willing to spend money on that level of house decoration. His idea of interior design was based on the military tradition of painting white everything that didn't move! She had had a struggle to persuade him to paint the walls of their best room a fashionable dark red. At least she had stone flags in most of her rooms; many people had beaten earth, which sometimes turned to mud by the outside doors in winter and became very dusty in summer.

'It is a fine mosaic. You were lucky it was already installed,' commented Vibia Pacata. 'Such floors are very hard-wearing and stop the damp rising.'

'But you redecorated the walls, didn't you?' asked Surilla.

'Yes. The previous occupants moved before they had a chance to colour the walls. Anicius Ingenuus couldn't bear the plain white so he got the man who redecorated the Legate's quarters to come and do this room and the corridor. You have no idea the time it took him to decide on the colours! The poor painter came time and time again with strips of wood painted with the various colours and patterns. I thought it would never get done.'

'Didn't you have any say, then?' Pervica sounded surprised.

'No. He said that, as he was paying for it, he would choose. I couldn't argue with him. But I was quite pleased with the final effect.'

Her guests looked admiringly at the walls with their three wide bands of paint: the dado had a pink background with splodges of white and yellow, giving the appearance of marble; the much deeper central zone was dark red, divided into panels by black and yellow borders; and the zone around the ceiling was yellow. Senovara thought it looked very fine, but possibly a little impractical if there were young children in the house. Basilia's own two daughters had grown up and were now married in other provinces, so little hands were not likely to wreak havoc on the sophisticated wall paintings.

Senovara turned to Adnamata to ask her if she was planning to have the walls of her new accommodation painted, and saw to her alarm that the young Pannonian was looking faint.

'Are you all right, Adnamata?' she asked with concern.

'I'm afraid I'm feeling a little queasy. I've been like this for several days, but I felt quite well this morning and believed it had passed.'

'I thought you were very quiet,' Pervica commented. She looked shrewdly at Adnamata. 'Are you sure you're not pregnant?'

'I don't know,' admitted the young girl shyly.

'You don't know!' boomed the large Brigantian getting to her feet. 'Let's have a look at you.'

She took Adnamata by the chin and looked searchingly at her face. 'Yes. Definitely green around the eyes. You're pregnant all right. When did you last have a bleed?'

'Before the turn of the year.' Adnamata was beetroot red with embarrassment. 'But I've never been regular so I didn't think anything of it.'

'Well, we need to send Grata to you to help you prepare. She's the local midwife. She'll see you through. She looked after Senovara for both of hers, didn't she, Senovara?'

Senovara nodded. 'Yes. I can recommend Grata; she's very kind and will look after you well. She gave me a great deal of good advice when I had Lucius and didn't know what to expect.' She laughed. 'I remember having a terrific urge to nibble sticks of charcoal and thought I was losing my sanity. It was only when I talked to Grata that I learned that pregnant women often want to eat strange things. "Kissa", I think she called it.'

'It was sour apples with me when I was expecting my youngest,' Basilia admitted. 'I scoured the market looking for the smallest, greenest, hardest apples I could find.'

Surilla, Catia and Vibia Pacata were loud in their congratulations and the older women, with the light of baby lust in their eyes, bombarded Adnamata with advice on her diet over the coming months, while Broginara sat silently looking stunned.

'I never thought of her being pregnant when she complained of feeling sickly, Senovara,' she confided. 'I thought it was the result of our moving down from Vercovicium or that she had eaten something which didn't agree with her. What will my brother say?'

'He'll be thrilled. Men are always thrilled at the idea of becoming fathers to sons.'

'But it might not be a boy,' Broginara pointed out.

'True, but men never expect it will be a girl.' Senovara felt quite matronly offering these words of wisdom, even if they were a direct quote from her grandmother and not her own observations. 'But Adnamata must tell him soon. Now Pervica knows, everyone will know, and he should find out from her, not from someone else.'

Adnamata overheard this and got to her feet. 'Oh, yes. I must go home straight away!'

'There's no panic,' announced Pervica. 'You've got a few months yet. I reckon it will be about Augustus or September.'

'My husband tells me that a woman will give birth in the seventh, ninth or tenth month but never in the eighth,' said Basilia with the authority of a woman married to a medical practitioner.

'What does he know?' cried Pervica scornfully. 'Doctors know nothing about pregnancy. Always looking for problems and difficulties.'

'That's because they only get called in when something goes wrong,' said Surilla soothingly, noticing that Basilia was taking this slight on the medical profession personally. 'They never see the straightforward pregnancies or easy births.'

Even before the suggestion that something might go wrong, Adnamata had clearly been eager to go home; she now looked so alarmed that Senovara took pity on her.

'You get home and tell Veturius, and then go to bed with a soothing poppy draught,' she advised. 'In the morning I'll drop into Grata's on the way to the market and ask her to call on you.'

'Thank you very much, Senovara.' Broginara was back in control again. 'That's a very good notion. I'll see that she carries it out. Thank you for your hospitality, Basilia. Are you coming, Vibia?'

As Basilia showed the three women out, the others started to gather up their own belongings.

'I don't know what young girls are coming to these days,' grumbled Pervica. 'Not knowing she's pregnant! She must be at least three or four months gone.'

'It must be very difficult for these young centurions' wives,' Surilla mused. 'They're always so far from home and rarely have any older female relatives with them to advise them.'

'That's true,' agreed Catia. 'When my husband was alive we seemed to be moving all the time. It was hard to make close friends and find anyone to give you reliable advice. At least Adnamata has Broginara with her.'

Pervica snorted. 'She seems even less informed than Adnamata. But she'll probably be an efficient help to Grata when the time comes.' She looked slyly at Catia. 'At least when you and Bonosius get together you'll know when you get pregnant.'

'Pervica! Really, you get worse.' Catia threw a cushion at her friend. 'Venus will have to do more than give me advice on my appearance if I'm to become pregnant at fifty-five, even if Bonosius should honour me with a proposal of marriage.'

'An honour, is it? You've changed your tune. Only last month you were horrified at the thought of accepting a gift of pig's trotters from the poor man.'

Teasing each other with the good nature of old friends, the women said their farewells to Basilia and started off towards their homes. As they walked along, Pervica continued to twit Catia about her love life, while Surilla tried to curb her more ribald remarks.

Senovara, however, was lost in her own thoughts. She was remembering the day when she told Quintus she was expecting their first child. She had made his favourite meal of chicken in green sauce and taken special pains with her appearance, though quite why she had felt all this to be necessary she couldn't now recall. She had told him her news when he had finished eating and was relaxing over a last beaker of wine. He was so silent for a few minutes that she began to worry in case he thought they should have waited longer before starting a family, but she needn't have been concerned. He was merely speechless with pride at the thought of becoming a father. They had talked long into the night, making plans for their future child, with her sitting on his knee in front of the glowing brazier. She had known early in her pregnancy that she was carrying a boy; both Pervica and her grandmother had told her so. When she asked Grata for her opinion, the old midwife had just looked at her and said, 'Likely it is.'

She hadn't told Quintus, though; her grandmother had told her to keep it to herself 'in case it turned'. The only time he had ever got drunk during their married life was the night Lucius was born, though Senovara had never been sure if this was through worry about her or pride in having a son; she had been too sleepy to notice. To be fair, he had been pleased when Ertola was born, too; quite content to have a daughter. 'A good pair of shoes needs a left and a right,' he'd said, 'so I reckon a happy family needs a son and a daughter.' And they were a happy family. The only cloud was that Ertola was not talking yet, but no doubt she would any day now, Senovara told herself. There was no point in being impatient.

By this time the women had turned into their street.

'Farewell, ladies,' called Pervica as she turned down the alleyway which led to her back door.

'Farewell,' they replied as they reached their own doors.

Senovara went on to her house, still lost in her memories. Yes, the Mother Goddesses were to be thanked for keeping her family safe and happy; she had much to be grateful for. She stopped at the threshold of the shop with her hand on the latch as her husband's voice came loudly through the open window.

'And did it not strike you that it might not be a good idea to let Hylax loose in the garden when Armea was planting seeds, you stupid child? Wait until your mother gets back and finds out the mess you've made between you!'

He sounded more exasperated than cross and Senovara hurried in to find out what was going on. Even in a happy family, she reflected, moments of discord were never far away.

Maius

As SENOVARA OPENED the door of the bathhouse, she was met by a blast of noise and heat, accompanied by a strong smell of damp linen, bath oil, wet human bodies and mould. She handed her lead admission token to the attendant who was sitting in a booth just inside the door and looked about her, searching for Ursa among the chattering women scattered about the great changing room in various stages of undress. She hated arriving on her own. The sheer size of the *apodyterium* always took her breath away, leaving her feeling small and insignificant. From the stone floor the pale blue and green walls seemed to rise for ever towards the domed ceiling. She looked round eagerly, hoping to see Ursa or anyone else she knew.

A watery light came through the green glass of the small rectangular windows set high in the walls. Extra illumination was provided by flaming torches in iron sconces, but their flickering seemed to create more shadows than light, particularly around the figure of the goddess Fortuna, whose stone statue sat in a niche against the far wall, surrounded by offerings.

A brisk trade was going on at the various stalls within the room. Senovara recalled wryly that when she had first visited the bathhouse all that a customer could buy in the *apodyterium* was a drink of water. Now any service one required was provided. It would soon be difficult for the bathers to find room to get undressed! Quintus had told her that on men-only days bathers could even have their teeth pulled out by a dentist and that a quack doctor sold nostrums to those seeking cures for their ills, from the common cold to impotence. Even on the four days in the month when the bathhouse was open to women, there was a girl selling beer, wine and water, and another selling chicken legs, lamb chops and other snacks. If she wished, a client could now have clothes repaired while she bathed, have a massage, or hire a gaming board and dice to while away the time. A woman from southern Gallia had recently set up a booth in which a client could have the hairs on her legs or under her arms professionally plucked; so far this had not caught on with many of Senovara's friends but there were now enough women from the more easterly provinces living in Eboracum for the beautician to be making a reasonable income. As she went by the booth, Senovara could hear the yelps and swift intakes of breath which indicated that a client was submitting to this torture for beauty's sake. She shuddered; plucking one's eyebrows was one thing, plucking the hair from the rest of one's body was too painful to contemplate, as was the use of depilatory creams, which burned the skin. And why bother? thought Senovara. It might be worthwhile in Roma, where women wore the sleeveless *stola*, made from cloth so fine that hairy legs would be noticeable, but in chilly Britannia it was usually only husbands who saw their wives' legs or underarms outside the bathhouse.

Through the crowded gloom Senovara saw a figure waving at her from a corner niche and pointing to a space beside her on the stone bench running round the walls. It was Ursa, almost unrecognisable with a cloth tied round her hair and just a towel round her body. Senovara hurried over.

'There you are! I was beginning to wonder if you were coming.'

'I'm sorry. I got held up at home. Lucius fell over in the yard just as I was about to leave. It took a while to clean him up and quiet him down.'

She put her belongings on the bench beside her friend and took a towel out of her linen bag. She made her way to the centre of the room, where a large stone bowl on a plinth stood, filled with water for the bathers to wash their hands and faces before taking off their clothes. She washed quickly, then made her way back to Ursa as she dried the back of her neck.

'There's no hurry,' said Ursa. 'There's a big group of soldiers' women in the *frigidarium*. If we wait a few minutes they'll have moved on to the *tepidarium* and there'll be more room. How are the family?'

'Well, thank you, bar Lucius' grazed knee. I can't tell you how wonderful it is to be able to come out and leave them like this. Before I had Armea I always had to ask you or another neighbour to look after them while I went for a bath, or leave Quintus to mind them. There were times when I wondered whether it was worth the bother and I should just stick to sponging myself down.'

'How is the slave girl getting on?'

'She's so quiet it's difficult to tell.' Senovara wondered if Armea was missing the farm but supposed it would be odd if she wasn't feeling homesick. She could remember how strange everything had felt when she first moved to Eboracum herself.

'She seems reliable,' she continued. 'I don't feel worried about leaving her alone with the children. After all, Lucius has just proved that he's as capable of injuring himself when I'm there as when I'm not.'

'I haven't seen your neighbour Aqmat for a while. Is she ill?' asked Ursa.

'No. She's gone up to the frontier with her husband, Hairan. She gets very lonely when he's away and as he was planning to be away for some months, visiting all the new forts to get orders for his flags and standards, she decided to go with him. If she thought Eboracum was cold, damp and foggy, she's not going to like the frontier. My brother-in-law, in his letters, is always saying that the fog sometimes doesn't lift at Vercovicium for days.'

Senovara wrapped her linen towel round her and looped the drawstring of her bag over her wrist. 'I'm ready. Shall we go through?'

'Why not? It looks as if the Female Cohort has moved on to the *tepidarium*. I've tipped the attendant to look after our belongings, but I'd put your bath slippers on straight away, if I were you; Lollia, two doors down from me, cut her feet badly last week treading on some pieces of broken bath-flask in here.'

Senovara took a pair of thick wooden sandals from her bag and slipped her toes between the leather thongs. The two women moved through into the next room, where there was a cold plunge bath and a water tank.

'Do you want a plunge?' enquired Ursa.

Senovara looked doubtfully at the film of oil on the surface of the water in the plunge bath, among which strange green blobs of depilatory cream were floating. 'I'll wait until later. I'll just use the dipper.'

Senovara unwrapped her towel and picked up one of the small bronze bowls from the shelf by the water tank. Dipping the bowl in, she poured the cold water over her shoulders and down her legs, briskly rubbing it over the rest of her body.

'I've got some new scented oil – try some.' Ursa took a small, fat, green glass bottle out of her wrist-bag and took the bone plug out of its narrow neck. She waved the open bottle under

Senovara's nose. A pleasant smell of lavender and bergamot wafted through the air.

'Oh, that's lovely. Much nicer than the oil I've got with me. Did you make it up yourself?'

'No. There was a travelling pedlar selling it in the market a few days ago. You had to take your own bottle and he filled it for an *as*.'

Senovara tipped a little on her hand and started to smooth it over her arms. Both women gently massaged the oil over their torsos and legs.

'Here – I'll do your back if you'll do mine,' Ursa offered, as she poured a little oil in the palm of her right hand.

Senovara turned her back and began to relax as she submitted to Ursa's gentle massage, appreciating the smell of the perfumed oil.

'Many thanks, Ursa. That was lovely. Your turn now,' said Senovara as Ursa finished with a sweeping flourish up Senovara's backbone.

Ursa shivered when Senovara's cold, oily hands touched her back.

'Sorry,' Senovara laughed. 'It takes a while for my hands to warm up, even in the bathhouse.'

'At least your hands aren't as rough as Pervica's. She nearly had the skin off my back the other day.'

Senovara applied the oil in long, smooth strokes, then put the bottle on the bench beside them and finished rubbing Ursa's back. Ursa put the plug firmly back into the bottle and put the oil away in her wrist-bag. Picking up their belongings, the two women moved through the doorway into the *tepidarium* and found a place among the women sitting gossiping on the benches around the room. They made themselves comfortable and Senovara felt the oil and the heat start to soak into her skin.

'Of all the new things I've discovered since I came to live here, this is the most civilised,' Senovara grinned. 'But I always get told off by my grandmother when she asks if I've visited the bathhouse. She considers bathing an insanitary, newfangled invention of the decadent Romans and part of an imperial plot to soften us all up. According to her, washing one's face and hands every morning and having a top-and-tail wipe-down every three or four days is quite enough. Apparently, there was nearly a riot when Matugenus suggested getting a bath-house installed at the farm.'

'I'm all for it, personally,' said Ursa. 'A bit of imperial decadence is what we all need to set us up.'

'What's this about imperial decadence?' Basilia came into the *tepidarium* with her hair pinned up on top of her head and a fetching pale yellow towel round her ample person.

'Hail, Basilia. We were just saying how civilised this is. Makes us feel like ladies of leisure for a while.'

'It's good to get away from the chores for a few hours and have a good gossip without being interrupted by our men,' agreed Basilia. 'But not everything imperial is so good. Have you heard about the attempted rape by a soldier from the fortress last night?'

Senovara and Ursa looked at her in horror. Surely such a terrible thing could not have happened in Eboracum?

Basilia nodded. 'Yes. Marcus told me. They caught the soldier immediately, Apollo be praised, and have him imprisoned at the fortress.'

'But what happened?'

'Well, from what I understand, this soldier was in the drinking den by the blacksmith's. You know, the one with the yellow cockerel painted on its sign?' The others nodded. 'The inn-owner has a daughter, quite young, about fifteen, and turning into a beauty. Ridiculous of her father to have got her serving drink to soldiers, but some men have no sense. If her mother was still alive it might have been different but she died of the summer fever a few years back. Anyway, the soldier had been drinking steadily since he came off duty in the afternoon, and not watering it either, from all accounts. The inn-owner threw him out after an argument about a dice game, and presumed he had gone back to his barracks, if he thought about it at all. Just as it was getting dark he sent his daughter to the trough to get more water, and the soldier jumped her as she went down between the inn and the blacksmith's. Luckily, one of the drinkers had come outside to relieve himself in the pot at the end of the alley, and he pulled the soldier off the girl before he had got very far. Her screams and the yelling of the two men brought other people out into the street, and between them they dragged the soldier back to the fortress. Marcus was asked to go and check on the girl but he says she was just bruised and shocked.'

'So what happens now?'

'I asked Marcus that and he reckons the soldier is lucky he was pulled off in time. If he'd raped the girl he'd have been put to death. As it is, he still might be – the Emperor is known to have no time for such behaviour – but Marcus thinks he'll just have his nose cut off.'

Ursa snorted. 'His nose! That isn't the offending part.'

'I agree, but that's what the law says.'

'And what about the girl?' asked Senovara.

'Well, because she wasn't raped she probably won't get any compensation, though I doubt if that drunk has any property for her father to claim; probably drinks away his salary. There's bound to be talk, though, which won't improve her marriage chances – but then as the daughter of an innkeeper she wouldn't be considered much of a catch anyway.'

'Surely no one will blame her for being attacked by a drunken soldier!' Senovara was aghast.

'Don't you believe it,' retorted Basilia. 'People are already starting to say she made an assignation with him or that she was being too friendly with the drinkers.'

'But she's so young.'

'Maybe she is to us but the Legate's very aristocratic, and you know the senatorial families marry girls as young as twelve—'

'I've heard as young as seven if the man doesn't want to be tied down to domestic life,' interposed Ursa. Senovara's eyes widened; in most tribes of the northern provinces it was considered improper for a girl to marry before she was twenty-one, though she knew that even in Britannia girls were getting married earlier these days as their families followed Roman practice. But seven years old was appalling.

'Precisely,' Basilia went on. 'So Minicius Natalis may not consider her too young at all, though whether that tells for or against the soldier is anyone's guess.'

'Well, I hope the Legate deals harshly with him,' Senovara said stoutly. 'We don't want Eboracum getting to be like Camulodunum in the old days. Look what happened there.'

'I can't see any of our local tribesmen rebelling nowadays,' Ursa laughed, 'though I can just see your grandmother standing on a farm waggon, leading the men into battle like Queen Boudica.'

They all grinned and then, as the image of Enica standing on a farm cart, shouting war cries with her grey plaits flying in the wind, caught their imagination, they started to giggle until they were all helpless with laughter.

'Can I sell you ladies any ribbons?' An old woman had come over to them, unnoticed. She had a selection of coloured braids in a box and began to pull them out one by one, holding them up to the light from the flickering torches so that her potential customers could appreciate the colours.

'No, thank you.' The three women shook their heads; they preferred to buy their ribbons by daylight rather than in the murky gloom of a bathhouse. The pedlar moved on in search of other prey.

Silence fell as the warmth began to work on their bodies. Looking about her, Senovara noticed some bathers were making braids with bone weaving-tablets or mending clothes, but she disliked sewing in the bathhouse because the material ended up limp and creased. Two women were playing *duodecim scripta* on a folding wooden board table, watched and advised by two others; the click and roll of the three dice made a gentle background noise to the subdued hubbub of talk which reached them from the *apodyterium*. Senovara felt very lazy just sitting, but the air of the bathhouse always sapped her energy – doing anything useful or which required thought seemed like too much effort.

She could feel herself begin to sweat gently. This was the part of the ritual that she enjoyed the most; the next stage was more uncomfortable and she groaned when Ursa pulled her to her feet.

'Time to move on. You look as if you're falling asleep!'

In the *caldarium* there was little gossiping; everyone was too hot, and the only sound was the scraping of the hooked bronze strigils against flesh, as bathers removed the oil and dirt on their bodies. Occasionally there were splashes, as one by one the women slipped into the hot water in the tank in the apse. Once again Senovara and her friends found space on the benches and leaned back against the warm walls. Senovara felt sweat break out on her forehead and begin to trickle down her face. She knew her hair was wreathing into wild tendrils but wearing a towel around her head like Basilia or Ursa made her hair go flat and sticky and she preferred to leave it uncovered. A drip of sweat fell from the end of her nose and ran down between her breasts and she rubbed it absent-mindedly with her towel.

Time in the bathhouse meant time to think, and Senovara had a great deal to think about. Ertola was now two and a half and, although she cried and laughed like other children, she had never said a word and Senovara was beginning to get very worried. It was all very well her grandmother saying that some children learned to talk later than others, but surely by now Ertola should have been saying simple words? At the beginning of the year Quintus had agreed with Enica and had been inclined to scoff at Senovara's worries, but recently she had found him watching his daughter with a frown on his face as she played silently with her doll or ran around the garden throwing a leather ball to her brother. The previous evening he had tried again to teach Ertola to say her own name but had got nowhere. Tears prickled in Senovara's eyes as she remembered how patient he had been with his daughter and the look of despair on his face when he had to give up when it was time for the children to go to bed. Later that night, lying in their own bed, they had discussed what to do. Clearly, the gods were displeased for some reason and needed to be propitiated, but which god or goddess had they offended? Senovara was sure she had been assiduous in her duties to their household deities, keeping the *lararium* clean and tidy, providing offerings of bread or fresh flowers every morning. On their birthdays, and on the anniversaries of her parents' and in-laws' deaths, she and Quintus went through all the necessary rituals; surely their family deities were content? The situation called for more serious measures, and for several hours the two of them had debated their next step. Senovara was inclined to blame witchcraft for their daughter's silence and wanted to try amulets and charms, but Quintus was less superstitious and pointed out that, as far as they knew, they had no human enemies malicious enough to inflict such misery on them. Eventually, his determination to ask for the help of the Mother Goddesses prevailed. It was decided that he would go to the shrine of the Matres as soon as he had a spare hour, and ask the priestess whether they could make a sacrifice on behalf of his daughter. As Senovara sat quietly in the *caldarium,* she worried about how much this would cost and if it would work. Without Quintus' knowledge she had brought a small flask of olive oil with her with the intention of pouring it as an offering to Fortuna before she left the bathhouse – as extra insurance.

Beside her, Ursa and Basilia were starting to stir. Senovara came out of her reverie, and found Ursa handing her one of the bronze strigils the bath authorities provided for their customers' use. Senovara wiped the edge of the blade with her linen towel to remove the traces of its previous user and started to scrape down her arms, removing a creamy mixture of oil, sweat and dirt from her skin. She knocked the strigil against the rim of the stone bowl in the centre of the room to clean the blade then started to scrape her legs. Undoing her towel and holding it at both ends she dried her back vigorously then rubbed down the front of her body. Naked, she made her way cautiously to the hot pool in its apse, wary of the sheen of oil and water which made even the rough pink *opus signinum* floor slippery, and lowered herself into the steaming water beside Basilia and Ursa.

'The water isn't very hot today,' grumbled Basilia as she splashed around.

'That's because we're later than usual and more people have been in before us,' explained Ursa.

'This bathhouse is too small to cope with all the people in Eboracum these days.' Basilia was still disgruntled. 'Either they let us women in more than four days a month or they'll have to build another bathhouse. The attendant was telling me that nearly a hundred women had a bath in here last time – it's a good thing we were early that day. There must have been more oil than water in the hot plunge by the time they closed.'

'Quintus was at a meeting of the *cives Romani consistentes* yesterday and heard that two more bathhouses are being planned for the settlement on the other side of the Abus.'

'About time too! When the rest of the legion get back it will be impossible to move in here for soldiers' women – I reckon the military should provide soldiers' families with their own bathhouse.' Ursa sounded indignant.

'Why should they? They don't provide the families with anything else. Marcus says the army have cleared some land on the other side of the Abus for the families to park their carts when they arrive, but he hasn't heard if the Legate plans to mark out the ground for them to build houses in an orderly fashion or intends to let them fight it out between them.' Basilia shook her head in despair. 'It's the mothers I feel sorry for. Most of the wives and sisters are tough young women who are used to fending for themselves, but some of the soldiers' mothers haven't followed the army before, and how much help they get depends on their sons' duties. Or even on the sons,' she added, darkly.

Senovara felt unable to contribute much to this conversation. Although she had lived in Eboracum for six years, the bulk of the legion had been away during that time and, as Quintus had already retired when they married, she had no experience of being an army dependant. She had met a few women who had come to Eboracum to live with their sons or brothers when their *pater familias* died but had never thought much about the lives and difficulties of those women whose new *pater familias* was a serving soldier. Now she wondered how they coped with being uprooted and dumped outside a new fort or fortress and expected to provide their own shelter. No doubt some soldiers made sure their womenfolk were made comfortable as soon as possible but, looking at Ursa and remembering the feckless brother who had been Ursa's only protection before she met the steady Lurio, she was suddenly aware of how hard her friend's life must have been before she married.

'Did you have to build your own shelter when you joined your brother at Vindolanda?' she asked.

'No,' laughed Ursa. 'I'm no builder. Luckily, the fort at Vindolanda was well established when I got there and Crotus found me lodgings with a centurion's widow in the *vicus*. There were six of us girls living with Flavia Baetica, two to a room, and she kept us firmly under control, I can tell you. She had her husband's vine staff on the wall in the living room and I used to wonder if she'd rap us on the knuckles with it if we misbehaved. But she provided a safe haven for us among all those soldiers; I wouldn't have fancied living on my own in that *vicus*. As it was, Lurio used to complain that it was easier to break into the fort strongroom than visit me when we were courting, Flavia was that strict.'

'Are you three going to stay in there all day? Other people are trying to have a bath,' said a strident voice, and the three women looked up to see a large, matronly female glaring down at them.

They climbed out of the bath hurriedly. As they wrapped clean towels round themselves, Senovara caught Basilia's eye and they looked back at the bath, where the water was rising rapidly up to the rim as the matron lowered her bulk into its hot depths. They bit their lips and tried not to laugh – the woman took up so much room in the bath there was no space for anyone else. No wonder she had wanted them to get out. They hurried out through the *tepidarium* to the *frigidarium* before they disgraced themselves.

Senovara was glad to see that one of the bath attendants had skimmed the debris from the top of the cold plunge bath while they had been sweating. Dropping her towel on the floor, she leaped into the water, gasping as the cold struck her warm, naked body. She jumped up and down a few times and then clambered out thankfully and dried herself quickly.

Back in the *apodyterium* the women got dressed without delay, resisting the blandishments of the girls selling food and drink.

'Are you planning to go to the cemetery for the Rosalia?' asked Basilia.

'No, there's no point,' Senovara replied. 'Both my parents are buried at the farm and Quintus' parents are buried in Germania. We have none of our family in the Eboracum cemeteries.'

'Nor have we,' responded Basilia, 'but Marcus and I always go to pay our respects to some of his old patients. It would seem odd to me not to go to a cemetery during the Rosalia, so we've sort of adopted some of the soldiers who died here a long way from home. Their relatives can't visit them, so we do instead.'

Senovara was touched by this kindly gesture. She tried to think of anyone she had known who was buried in one of the local cemeteries and who would not be receiving a visit from a relative during the next five days. She couldn't think of anyone, but Basilia's remark reminded her that that evening was the first night of the Lemuria and Quintus might wish to perform the midnight ceremony from Italia, designed to bring divine protection to families and stop ghosts walking. It might help Ertola. She would remind him when she got back.

'I believe Bonosius has offered to accompany Catia to the cemetery during the Rosalia. Her husband's ashes are buried there, you know. She hasn't decided whether to let him, though,' announced Ursa, as she tucked a wool scarf into the neckline of her dress.

Basilia and Senovara smiled at her news. The romance between the butcher and their widowed friend was on again, now that Catia's hair had grown back, but it was making slow progress. Taking Bonosius with her to visit her husband's grave during the family festival of the Rosalia would be a serious declaration of intent on Catia's part, and Senovara could quite see why she was in two minds about it.

'I'll call in on her on my way home,' said Basilia, picking up her bags to leave. 'Find out if she's decided yet.'

'Are you ready to go, Senovara?' enquired Ursa.

'No. You go on ahead. I want to dedicate to Fortuna before I go.'

Her two friends said their farewells and left, both still rosy pink from their bath. Senovara folded her two towels and put them in her bag with her bath sandals. She threw her cloak round her shoulders and brought the hood up over her head. She took a small glass phial from her bag, and made her way over to the statue of Fortuna. Bowing her head, she quietly asked Fortuna to help Ertola find her voice, and offered her olive oil as a gift in return. A sensation of peace came over her, which she took as a sign that the goddess had heard her plea. She poured the oil over the statue's feet and made her way out of the bathhouse, feeling comforted.

When she got home, as soon as she entered their shop, she realised that something important had happened. Quintus was sitting on his bench looking stunned with his legs dangling down and the surviving ruff of his hair standing on end as if he had been running his fingers through it.

'What's happened?' she asked anxiously. 'It's not Ertola or Lucius, is it? They're not ill, are they? There hasn't been an accident?'

'No, no, nothing like that. I've just had a message from the fortress. The Legate, Lucius Minicius Natalis himself, wants me to make him a pair of boots. He intends to come here in person to discuss it.'

Senovara sat down with a jolt on the customer's stool, her eyes wide in amazement. 'But surely he gets his boots from Roma or Londinium? Why does he need a new pair from a bootmaker in Eboracum?'

'I don't know. All the message says is that Lucius Minicius Quadronius Verus Natalis, Legate of the Sixth Legion Victrix, presents his compliments and wishes to visit tomorrow to arrange for a new pair of boots to be made.' He waved a rectangle of wood, on which she could see the words written in a clear, beautifully neat hand.

'Tomorrow!' Senovara looked around her in horror. 'But look at the mess this place is in! We must tidy up.' She bustled out of the room calling for Armea.

All the rest of the day the entire family brushed and scrubbed and tidied until the workshop gleamed. Even Ertola trotted back and forth with brushes and dusters, while her mother directed the operation like a military campaign.

'I'll never find anything again,' groaned Quintus.

'Just make sure you know where to find the tools you'll need during the visit. Anything else we'll find after the Legate has gone.' Senovara looked at her husband proudly. It was a great honour to be asked to make boots for someone as important as the commanding officer of a legionary fortress, especially someone known to be as particular about his appearance as Minicius Natalis. But it was time to do something about an evening meal; Quintus wouldn't be able to cope with the visit if he wasn't properly fed.

She was cooking sausages that evening. Some lengths of pigs' intestines had been soaking in cold water for three days, waiting to take their mixture of pork and boiled spelt grits. Senovara poured water over a handful of spelt in a pan and set it on the stove to heat. She took her mortarium down from the shelf and put in a few pieces of chopped pork. Grasping her stone pestle in her right hand, she ground the meat against the sharp quartz set in the walls of the bowl. As she worked, she gradually added the rest of the pork, transferring the ground meat into another bowl when the mortarium got too full. She added some pine kernels and ground those as well; then, taking the wooden bung out of one of the amphorae set into the floor of the kitchen, she ladled out a small quantity of liquamen, wrinkling her nose at the smell. She mixed the pork, pine kernels, liquamen and boiled spelt together, added some salt and pepper, then started to stuff the sausage skins. This was a fiddly job and it was useful to have Armea to hold the skins open, but it was also quite a satisfying task as the skins began to plump up. She twisted the skins with a practised hand as each sausage reached the right length and eventually she had a plateful ready. She put them to one side of the table but, catching sight of Hylax's concentrated gaze as he sat on the kitchen floor watching her every move, occasionally shifting his weight from one front leg to the other as he vainly anticipated a sausage dropping to the flags, Senovara moved the plate to a high shelf out of harm's way.

Armea had already peeled some turnips so it didn't take long to prepare the meal. As the family sat down to boiled sausages with turnips in a mustard sauce, Senovara remembered that she had meant to speak to Quintus about the Lemuria. She had forgotten all about it in the excitement about the Legate's visit.

'Quintus, today is the first night of the Lemuria. I know it's not a tradition in either of our families but I thought you might wish to follow the ritual tonight.'

He looked at her in surprise, then, following her eyes to their daughter, who was tucking happily into her sausages, he nodded. 'You're right. We can't afford to ignore anything which might help.'

That night she and Quintus lay in bed waiting for the fortress horn to blow the middle hour. As soon as the single note reached them, Quintus got out of bed, spat out the black beans he had been holding in his mouth, and made the *fica* sign with his right thumb between his first two fingers. He climbed back into bed.

'You have to do that again the day after tomorrow and then two days later,' Senovara reminded him.

'I know, woman. But whether it works or not is in the gift of the gods. It seems more like superstition than proper worship. Perhaps I should make an offering at the Feast of Mercury next week?' He looked solemn and Senovara knew that, despite his scoffing words, he was taking the ritual seriously.

The next morning they were both up before dawn, unable to rest with the impending visit of the Legate before them. They dressed in their newest tunics and spent longer at their morning toilet than they would normally have done. Armea was given strict instructions that both children must be kept out of the way until the Legate had gone.

'Should I bring some wine in, do you think?' Senovara asked anxiously.

'Well, we can offer him some, but I doubt if he'll want to drink the sort of wine we can afford. He only drinks the best Falernian, I expect.'

All morning Senovara wandered between the house and the shop, unable to settle to anything and she realised from the number of times that Quintus came into the kitchen for a drink of water that he was just as nervous. At last, as the fortress horn signalled the fifth hour the sound of horses' hoofs were heard at the end of the street.

'That will be them, I reckon,' said Quintus, smoothing down the hair on the back of his head and tweaking the neckline of his tunic. Senovara looked around the shop to check that all was in order, and plumped up one of the leather cushions from the best room which she had placed on the usually bare customer's stool.

Through the open shutter she saw a group of horses stop outside their door and a groom run to hold the head of a big bay. She moved back to the door leading into the house, not wishing to be noticed but keen not to miss anything. The door opened and a legionary stepped in.

'Quintus Flavius Candidus?' he asked.

'Yes, that's me,' replied Quintus.

The soldier held the door open and stiffened to attention as a clean-shaven man in the polished breastplate of a legate stepped into the room, stooping to avoid the low lintel. Senovara caught her breath as she took in every detail of his magnificent appearance. His brown hair was cut in the latest fashion and shone with pomade. His olive-coloured skin was as smooth and soft as a woman's. Round his neck and wrists he wore a number of gold amulets; Senovara wondered if he had been subject to much misfortune in his life to need so many protections against the Evil Eye. When he advanced into the room she could smell his perfume and she noticed that his eyebrows had been plucked to shape.

He was followed by three other men, one an ordinary soldier who joined his colleague on guard just inside the door, the others a *beneficiarius*, who appeared to act as the Legate's secretary or aide, and a good-looking young tribune in his late twenties or early thirties who looked around the workshop with interest.

'Hail, Quintus Flavius Candidus.'

'Hail, my lord.' Quintus' arm shot out and up in an army salute as he automatically responded to the Legate's greeting.

Minicius Natalis laughed. 'Relax, man. You're retired now.'

Quintus grinned sheepishly, and ushered his distingushed customer to the stool.

'Now, Flavius Candidus, I want to know if you can make me a pair of boots like these.' He snapped his fingers and the secretary stepped forward, taking a pair of boots out of the leather bag he carried in his right hand.

'As you can see, they're damaged. One of my horses stamped his hoof on one of them – you can see where it has scraped all down one side and split the back and laces. Made a pretty bruise on my foot, too, I can tell you. Can you make another pair like these? I must have a pair of purple boots – can't go round in these red ones all the time. I'd provide the gold leaf, of course.'

Quintus took the boots from him and studied them. Senovara craned her neck to see what they looked like. As far as she could make out, they were of purple leather with an openwork pattern cut out of the instep and gold leaf motifs applied round the heel and the tops. She had never seen such magnificent boots before. She looked anxiously at Quintus, wondering if he would be up to the task.

'Yes, sir. I can make you another pair like this but, if you prefer it I could repair this damaged one or just replace it – I think I've got some purple leather which will nearly match this to make up the pair.'

The Legate looked appalled. 'Wear repaired boots?' he exclaimed pettishly. 'You must be joking. I will only wear new boots – and matching ones at that. If you can't do it, I'll have to send to Londinium for a bootmaker. I haven't got time to go down myself.'

'No, my lord, there's no need to do that. I have purple leather and can make you another pair, if you wish,' Quintus hastened to reassure the Legate, worried he might have lost the sale through his tactlessness.

'Good. Get on with it then.'

Quintus picked up a piece of thick hide from his bench and placed it on the floor.

'If I might ask your lordship to stand on this?' he invited.

Minicius Natalis grunted. The *beneficiarius* stepped forward and, bending down, removed his superior's boots, revealing fine, cream woollen socks. The Legate stood up and placed his feet firmly on the strip of hide. Quintus knelt down and swiftly cut round both feet to make the pattern for the boots' soles. Then, indicating respectfully that his customer could sit down again, he reached for some strips of linen and proceeded to measure round the Legate's ankles and his instep. When he had finished, the *beneficiarius* put the Legate's boots back on and Minicius Natalis stood up.

'I'll send someone down with the gold leaf tomorrow. Send the boots up to the fortress when you have finished. Ask for Marcus Pontius Sabinus here.' He indicated the tribune, who smiled amiably at Quintus before following the Legate as he swept out of the room.

'Oh, Quintus!' wailed Senovara. 'You didn't offer him any wine!'

'No I didn't,' admitted her husband, looking horrified. 'But I made a bigger fool of myself by suggesting that I repair his old boots. Catch him wearing anything but the best and latest thing. Have you seen these?' Senovara went over to the bench where the offending footwear had been abandoned by its owner. She stretched out a hand nervously and touched the gold design on the heel. 'Can you really make boots like these?'

'I reckon so. Not that there's much call for such round here but I have the right leather, thank Jupiter, and I can do openwork. The gold leaf has me a bit worried, though. I did some decoration on shield faces when I was serving but that's a while ago now. I hope I haven't lost the knack. You can't make any mistakes with gold leaf.'

'I'm sure you haven't,' his wife said stoutly. 'Didn't he look fine?' she continued more thoughtfully.

'Got a bit of a reputation for being fussy about his appearance, but don't you be fooled by that. Lucius Minicius Natalis isn't as effeminate as he looks or sounds. He won the four-horse chariot race in the Olympic Games the year before he took command here – that's only four years ago.'

Senovara's eyes widened. She knew enough about horses to know that handling four at once in a chariot race was not a game for the fainthearted. Watching the Legate fussing about his boots, she had got the impression of a man too concerned with his manicure to risk breaking his nails handling reins.

'He wore a lot of amulets,' she mused.

Quintus laughed. 'That's his other reputation. Full of superstitions. Spends huge amounts of money dedicating altars and erecting statues to the gods, the more exotic and obscure, the better. Always worried that he's missed a deity out. But he can afford it. As rich as Croesus he is. He'll pay a good sum for these boots and not quibble about it, either.'

Senovara was relieved. Neither Quintus nor his customer had mentioned a price, which was unusual. Most of his customers haggled for ages before commissioning new boots or shoes, but she supposed that it would not have been seemly for the commanding officer of a legion to do so.

Quintus suddenly gave her a quick slap on the rump. 'Come on, my dove,' he exclaimed. 'We may have forgotten to offer our distinguished guest a drink, but I could surely do with one myself. Get in that kitchen and start pouring. Your husband is about to become a wealthy man and should be properly looked after.'

'You've got to make the boots first. You won't be wealthy until you've finished them and by that time I might have spent the money.' Senovara ran laughing into the kitchen before Quintus could grab her. She was flushed with the excitement of having had the Legate himself in their shop and bursting with pride that it was her husband who had been chosen to make the new boots. She would certainly have a tale to tell her friends when she next met them in the market.

As she got the wine jug down off the shelf, her son's firm voice came to her from the garden, bringing her concerns flooding back.

'No, Ertola! You need to do it this way.'

Senovara looked outside. Lucius was showing his sister how to make his new bone top spin on the flagstones by the back door. Behind him, Armea was hoeing between the tidy rows of green shoots in the vegetable plot. It was a peaceful scene. Armea was working silently, taking advantage of the children's absorption in their new toy to get on with the gardening. As she watched, Quintus came into the kitchen and joined her by the door. They stood with their arms around each other's waists. Ertola chortled as the bone top spun round on its axis, and her parents smiled.

'It's just as well that we may soon have some spare *denarii*,' said Quintus soberly. 'We don't know how much it's going to cost to get her speaking. The gods are demanding, and dedications and offerings are expensive.'

'She seems happy enough,' Senovara said quietly. 'Not speaking doesn't seem to bother her; she can always make herself understood.'

'True, but that's just with us. Eventually she'll need to communicate with other people. To get by these days, even girls have to be able to read and write; how will we teach her if she can't speak?'

Senovara had a sudden vision of their daughter growing up silent in a noisy world, and buried her head in her husband's shoulder.

'Here, this will never do,' Quintus said in alarm. 'We should be celebrating our good fortune, not getting miserable about the future. One of the gods will help us, don't you worry. Now let's have that beaker of wine.'

Senovara sniffed and wiped her eyes with the back of her hand. She gave a watery smile and moved back into the kitchen. He was right. There were so many gods; surely one of them would take pity on a small child.

Iunius

IN THE GAPS between the houses the clouds were rushing across the sky, grey and angry, with rims of bright yellow towards the late afternoon sun. The air was filled with the sound of shutters, gates and doors banging and crashing. There were also booming noises, as if a great god was amusing himself by blowing across the neck of a wine jug. Straw, leaves and twigs whipped through the air, striking passers-by in the face as they struggled along the streets. With a loud ripping, a thick linen blind was wrenched from where it had been protecting a shop doorway and immediately disappeared over the rooftops. The shopkeeper rushed out, wringing his hands in despair. In moments a strong wind had become a tempest, funnelling down the narrow streets; he had had no time to realise the gravity of the situation and take his blind down.

An empty barrel, which had been left out to dry, rolled down the street, fetching up against the pillars of the whetstone shop. Merchants who still had their wares displayed in the street rushed in and out of their doors salvaging baskets, boxes and barrels, while others wrestled to cover open windows with wooden shutters.

Senovara held her shawl more tightly round her head and hung on to her basket as the wind buffeted her this way and that. She was not in the best of tempers, and being pummelled by the wind was not making her feel any happier.

Her grandmother had decided that it was time she paid her annual visit to Eboracum, and Matugenus had sent a message via the carter that Senovara was to expect the old woman the next day. Enica's grandson – Senovara's cousin Amatus – was intending to visit Eboracum from his farm near Petuaria to buy some tools, and had arranged to break his journey from the coast at his old home; his grandmother had jumped at the chance to accompany him to Eboracum. The message warned Senovara that Enica was determined to spend several days visiting her great-grandchildren and had ordered Matugenus to collect her when he came in to deliver produce to the market.

Senovara's feelings had been mixed at hearing this. She loved her grandmother dearly but had to admit that she was a demanding guest, quick to disparage anything which suggested that her granddaughter had taken to Roman ways. She was also eagle-eyed when it came to any hint of slovenly housekeeping – Senovara and Armea had been running around all day dusting, sweeping and cleaning but Senovara was only too aware that they had probably missed some corner which Enica would discover within minutes of entering the house. After hours of frantic effort Senovara had decided that she would have to stop and concentrate on the evening meal before it was too late. She had bought some thrushes in the market earlier that day and Armea had plucked and cleaned them for her. All she had to do was brown them in the frying pan and then put them in a cooking pot with onions, coriander and lovage to stew slowly. An easy and cheap meal to cook, once the messy task of plucking and cleaning had been finished, and one she always enjoyed, especially as she planned to serve the stew with the first new broad beans of the season.

Disaster had struck when she had pulled the frying pan out of the cupboard and unfolded its handle. As she set it on the fire the iron hinge-pin dropped out onto the floor and the handle fell off. With a cry she dropped to her knees to search for the small rod, calling to Armea to be careful where she put her feet in case she accidentally kicked it into an inaccessible corner. After some frantic scrabbling she had finally found the elusive pin, but then realised that she hadn't taken the pan off the fire during her search and it was now red hot. Cursing, she knocked the pan off the flame with the poker and poured some cold water into it to cool it. When she could eventually pick it up, she had taken it in to Quintus to ask him if he could repair it but he had been busy with a customer and simply told her to take it to Sudrenus, the blacksmith. It had taken Sudrenus only a few moments to put the pin back in place and hammer the ends to secure it, but Senovara was irritated that the incident had not only left her behind schedule but also meant that she was now out in the street with a storm blowing up.

She screwed up her eyes as dust blew into them and turned her back to avoid a flurry of debris hurtling towards her. Thankfully it was not yet raining but when she chanced a look skywards she saw that the racing clouds were darkening and realised that a deluge was not far away. She hurried along, keeping close to the front of the buildings, hoping for some protection. A low rumble of thunder seemed to pursue her as she turned the corner into their street.

As she neared the shop she saw Quintus outside, struggling with one of the wooden window shutters. She hastened to help him, dropping her basket with the frying pan safely inside the door before grasping the edge of the shutter.

'You go inside and be ready to slip the bar into place,' directed Quintus. 'I'll get this shut and the front bolts into position, but I don't think they'll hold on their own in this wind.'

With her skirts flapping wildly round her legs, as if trying to impede her progress, Senovara rushed inside. Already small scraps of leather were flying about the workshop in the draught from the window and hobnails were rolling off the bench. Her right foot slipped on a hobnail and she had to steady herself by grabbing onto the bench. She picked up the wooden shutter bar from where it leaned under the window, and held it ready as her husband strove to hold the shutters closed long enough to get the iron front bolts into position. At last the room went dark when both shutters submitted to his efforts and Senovara quickly slotted the bar into place. She watched anxiously while the shutters strained to escape from their fetters but the stout oak bar held firm. As Quintus came into the shop the door whipped out of his grasp and slammed shut behind him.

'Wild weather this. Jupiter is enjoying himself by the sound of it,' he said when another rumble of thunder was heard, ominously close.

'Come through into the kitchen and light a candle,' suggested Senovara, picking up her basket. 'Some hobnails have dropped on the floor; you'll never find them in this gloom.'

She led the way into the kitchen and took off her shawl. Armea was there, huddled together with the children and all three pairs of eyes were full of fear. A sudden flash of lightning filled the room.

'Come on, you two,' Quintus directed Lucius and Ertola. 'You can help me find my hobnails. We'll leave Armea and your mother to their cooking.' He held out a hand and both children ran to clutch at his fingers. They followed him out of the room, guided by a lighted candle which Quintus held aloft in his other hand. Senovara was relieved. She didn't like thunder and lightning any more than anyone else – they implied too strongly that the gods were angry – and she sympathised with the children's fears, but she wouldn't have been able to get on with the meal with them both clinging to her skirts. Seeing Armea jump at a very loud crash of thunder, she realised that as the mistress of the house she would have to show an unconcerned calm or the young girl would be panicking.

'Right, Armea. Let's start this meal again.'

She pulled the frying pan out of the basket and put it firmly back on the stove, pleased to see that Armea had had the sense to keep the fire going while her mistress was at the blacksmith's. She scraped some beef dripping out of a small bowl and dropped it into the pan; it ran melting around the iron base and she placed the plucked thrushes on top. While Armea chopped the onions, Senovara kept up a steady stream of cheerful conversation to keep the girl's mind off the storm raging outside.

'When my grandmother comes tomorrow,' she mused, 'I think she'd better have Lucius' bed. We'll put a pallet down in the front storeroom for him; he'll think it a great adventure. If my cousin wishes to stay as well, he'll have to make do with the floor.'

Armea looked grateful when she realised that she was not expected to vacate her own small bed in the kitchen pantry.

'By tomorrow, this storm will have passed and the weather should be quiet enough for us to light the oven outside. While my grandmother is here we'll have to bake our own bread; I'll never hear the last of it if we offer her shop bread. So first thing tomorrow I shall want you to grind some flour so that I can make some loaves – I'm presuming they will be here by the sixth hour and will need something to eat. We can keep the oven going and roast a leg of lamb for our evening meal.

Bonosius has promised to keep me a joint, so you can collect it after the flour is ground.'

She bustled around the kitchen, her mind racing through the next few days, calculating what she should cook and what she would need to buy. She knew it would be no good setting Roman meals on the table – her grandmother would eat only stews and roast meat served in the traditional way. Not for her the carrots and leeks or the new spices and sauces that the Romans had introduced into Britannia. She was, however, at a disadvantage in that her teeth were very worn down through a lifetime of eating coarsely ground flour and hard meat; these days there was a limit to what she could chew comfortably. Senovara sighed. It looked as if they were in for a week of plain stews. She wondered if the leg of lamb was altogether wise, but knew her grandmother would expect roast meat on the evening of her arrival. She hoped Bonosius had found her a tender joint. She would steep it in vinegar water and smear plenty of honey on it just in case.

The braised thrushes were ready and she called down the corridor into the shop to fetch her family to the table. Lucius and Ertola ran into the kitchen, their fear of the thunder and lightning forgotten in the excitement of hunting for hobnails.

'Oh no you don't!' Senovara exclaimed as they clambered up onto their stools. 'Look at the state of you. Come here and wash your hands. What your great-grandmother will think of your manners when she arrives tomorrow, I dread to think.'

The children's faces fell and Senovara grinned ruefully. They had, no doubt, forgotten that Enica's visit would mean they would be continually told to sit up straight, to wash their hands, and to mind their manners, not by Enica but by their mother. Senovara always swore that she would not let her strong-minded relation make her feel inadequate, but had to admit to herself that she always did. Enica hadn't even arrived and already she was fussing about the children's behaviour. Senovara plunged their hands into a bowl of water and rubbed vigorously. 'You must also remember, Lucius, that your great-grandmother speaks very little Latin and gets very cross when she doesn't understand what people are saying. You'll have to speak my language to her.'

Lucius scowled as he made his way back to his stool, but said nothing.

Senovara set the pan on the table and fished out the birds by their feet, putting two each in three of the bowls for the adults and Armea. She chopped up the meat of two more into small pieces for Lucius and Ertola to share, then ladled some sauce into all the bowls. The broad beans were already on the table, glistening with olive oil and liquamen.

'Enjoy the beans,' she encouraged her family. 'They're the first from the garden so they'll be sweet and tender.'

'And I presume that from tomorrow all our vegetables will be plain boiled?' enquired Quintus, helping himself to a chunk of bread.

'I'm afraid so. There's no point in giving Grandmother a reason to complain about our "fancy cooking habits".'

Lucius looked up from his plate with interest. 'Do we have fancy cooking habits, Mater?' he asked.

'According to your great-grandmother we have. She prefers her food cooked in the old Parisian way, which means no liquamen, no spices, no olive oil, no wine.'

'At least cooking her way you can taste what it is you're eating,' commented Quintus.

Senovara raised her eyebrows quizzically, not sure if this was a slight to her own cooking, and he hastened to explain.

'At the Guild Feast on the Festival of Mercury last month we were served a *patina* which, if Sacer hadn't told me, I wouldn't have known was made of fish, there were so many herbs and spices in it. Felicius Simplex, who fancies himself an intellectual, quoted something from some play about hot spices being like screech owls, eating out the guts of dinner guests.'

Senovara grinned but before she could say anything Lucius spluttered with laughter at his father's story and she had to slap the child's back as he choked on his food.

All evening and most of the night the storm raged, battering the front of the building, but by the first hour of the day it had died away, leaving a calm morning with the promise of heat. Everyone in the house was up early to check for signs of storm damage and to prepare for the invasion of relatives. After making sure the front of his shop was intact and that the roof was still in good repair, Quintus took Lucius and Ertola into the garden to gather up the twigs and boughs scattered by the wind; such a bounty of usable firewood could not be ignored just because visitors were coming. Senovara had decided that, with more people in the house, they were bound to need more water than usual so, as soon as they had broken their own fast, she and Armea collected all the buckets in the house and went off to the trough. It was some time since Senovara had been to the water trough, because that was now one of Armea's daily tasks. When they got closer, and Senovara saw several of her friends gathered around waiting their turn, she realised she had quite missed the daily gossip and jokes which were an invariable but enjoyable part of the chore. If there were more than three people wanting water, everyone had to wait while the trough refilled and this gave them all a chance to catch up on the latest news.

'Hail, Senovara,' called Pervica. 'We haven't seen you here for a while.'

'I know, but with Enica and my cousin due this morning I thought we'd need more water than usual. What's the news?'

'Oh, the usual. My old man's still having problems with his sciatica and one of the boys had me up all night complaining of an earache. What with preparing a potion of wild chicory in wine for Bruccius' aching back and pouring warm bull's gall in leek juice down Trenico's ear, I'm beginning to think I should become a *seplasarius* and at least get paid for my efforts. Don't men make a fuss when they have the slightest thing wrong with them? They should try suffering all that we women have to put up with bringing them into the world and see how they like it.'

Surilla laughed at her friend's look of disgust. 'Talking of bringing men into the world, Senovara, how's Adnamata?'

'Fine, I think. I haven't seen either her or Broginara for a while and, as I've been having my monthly bleed, I wasn't able to go to the bathhouse to find out from Basilia how everyone up at the fortress is getting on. When Enica has gone I must try to make time to pay a call on Adnamata. By the way, does any of you know how the great romance is getting on?'

'You mean Catia and Bonosius?' asked Pervica. 'Well, she managed to avoid him accompanying her to the Rosalia in Maius – but you knew that, didn't you?'

Senovara nodded, smiling. Catia's tale of rising at dawn and nipping off to the cemetery before Bonosius appeared had made them all laugh. Catia's poor deceased husband had got scant attention that morning as his widow rushed through the rites at great speed, worried that her portly suitor would suddenly appear.

'I think he was quite hurt about that,' said Surilla, 'but she was quite right. The Rosalia is a family ceremony and Bonosius being there would have made his attachment to Catia official. He seems to have taken the hint, though, and has been less assiduous in his attentions these last few weeks.'

Pervica trawled her bucket through the water in the trough. 'Right. That's me fixed up for the morning. I must be off to see how my invalids are getting on. Farewell.' She strode off, holding the wooden stave bucket on her head, her back as straight as a spear.

'I don't know why she bothers to make her concoctions. I presume she could just bully those men into feeling better, if she wanted to.' Ursa had arrived at the trough in time to hear Pervica's comments about her family's ailments.

'Oh, Pervica's like our dog, Hylax. Lots of barking in public but as soft as a sponge when it comes to her family's comfort, no matter how much she shouts at them. How are you today, Ursa?'

'Full of news. Guess what I just saw as I came along? A waggon of travelling actors.'

'Really?' This was news, indeed.

'I asked them if they were planning to put on a performance and they said they'd be setting up on the other side of the Abus for at least seven days. They intend to put on a show twice a day.'

'What sort of show?' asked Senovara, her eyes shining with excitement.

'I asked that, too, and they said that they do a mixture of plays and music and that one of them was a juggler, so it should be good.'

'We must go,' decided Senovara. 'Have you ever seen actors, Armea?'

'No, Mistress.' Armea's face was bright pink at the thought of being included in the treat. Then she looked doubtful. 'Will we be able to go, with the old mistress visiting?'

'I don't see why not,' replied Senovara. 'A travelling troupe came to the farm once, when I was a little girl, and Grandmother let them set up camp down by the stream. I remember they put on a play especially for us. I can't remember what it was called but it was all about an old man who had to buy prisoners to exchange for his son who was a prisoner of war, and then he found that one of these prisoners was another son of his who had been kidnapped as a child. It was all very confusing and exciting but very funny as well. We talked about it for months afterwards. I expect Enica will be just as keen as the rest of us to go. But we must get back; there's still a lot to do this morning.'

She said goodbye to her friends and, picking up both her buckets, set off down the street, followed by Armea, equally laden.

When they got back to the house, Senovara fished the old stone quern out from under the kitchen table. 'Do you prefer to use this thing on the table or on the floor, Armea?'

'On the floor, please.'

Senovara thought for a moment, then spread a sack on the flags – that would stop flour and husks getting trampled everywhere. It was the mess, as well as the work involved, which always persuaded her to buy her bread from the baker's rather than grind her own flour. She heaved the base stone onto the sack and then slotted the top stone into place. Armea scooped a bowlful of grain out of the big pottery bin in the corner and squatted down on the floor next to the quern. Grasping the wooden handle, she slotted it into the hole in the side of the top stone and started to move it vigorously back and forth while she slowly poured grain into the central hopper. White flour started to appear between the edges of the stones.

Senovara put a small wooden barrel down by the slave. 'Put the flour in that. You'll need to fill it if I'm to make enough loaves for everyone. Get more grain from the bin when you need it.'

Armea nodded, not taking her gaze away from the grain in the hopper. As she worked, the ring of flour increased slowly round the quern.

While Armea was preparing the flour, Senovara went outside to the domed clay oven built in the corner between the back of the house and the garden wall. Taking the iron cover off the door, she got down on her hands and knees and raked out the ashes and unburned pieces of wood onto the ground. It was so long since she had used the oven that she had decided to light a fire inside it the night before in order to dry it out and check for cracks. Sorting through the debris, she picked out some of the bigger pieces; they would be nice and dry. She put them back in, placing them in the centre of the circular space around some dry leaves and curls of wood which Quintus had prepared. He often sat in the kitchen after his evening meal, shaving thin curls from the ends of sticks with a sharp knife to keep for tinder. They had an old sack in the corner of the kitchen, between the wall and the stove, in which wood shavings, dry leaves and other suitable kindling was kept ready to hand for lighting the fire or the oven.

Senovara climbed to her feet and went back into the kitchen, carrying the oven door. The charcoal on the top of the stove was glowing cheerfully. Using the iron tongs she picked out some of the hotter pieces and put them on the door. Then, blowing on the charcoal to keep it going, she went back to the oven and shot the fuel inside. She moved the lit and unlit fuel together with the ends of the tongs and blew gently until the tinder caught. She added some new charcoal, then, after waiting for a few minutes to make sure that the fire had really caught, went back into the house.

Armea by this time had ground enough flour for the first batch of bread. Rolling up her sleeves, Senovara used a beaker to measure flour into a large bowl, then added a little of the beer yeast in warm water that had been waiting by the side of the stove. Making a small well in the flour, she started to mix everything together with her hands. When she had a ball of dough mixed to her satisfaction, she set the bowl on the edge of the stove and went out to check how the oven was getting on. Peering into its depths, she saw that the small amount of fuel she had set alight was going well and more wood could be added. She added several short lengths and replaced the oven door, propping it open at the bottom with a couple of small stones so that there was just the right amount of draught.

When she returned to the kitchen, she saw that Armea had finished milling another quantity of grain.

'That should be enough for the time being, Armea. You'd better go and get that leg of lamb from Bonosius. I'll clear up in here.'

She removed the top stone of the quern and dusted its adhering flour into the little barrel. She scraped off the surface and edges of the bottom stone and added this further handful to the barrel, then lifted the two quern stones off the sack and pushed them back into their resting place under the kitchen table. She picked up the sack by the corners and directed the rest of the flour into the barrel. Still holding it by the corners, she carried the sack out into the garden and shook it briskly to clean it. As she came back past the oven she bent down to check how the fire was going. A good glow could be seen through the gap under the door and she adjusted the amount of draught by changing the props for some smaller pebbles.

Back in the kitchen, she sat down on a stool, feeling hot and bothered and wondering what else needed to be done. The children were next door, playing with Ursa's boys: Senovara could hear shouts and the crash of wood as they fought with their toy swords. She hoped Ertola was keeping out of the way; the boys tended to get excited when they played at being legionaries fighting barbarians. She got to her feet. She mustn't forget to make up Lucius' bed for Enica and to arrange some bedding in the shop storeroom for Lucius.

By the time the fortress horn had blown the sixth hour, Senovara had baked several round loaves and was putting the leg of lamb into the cleared hot oven. Quintus stuck his head round the back door. 'They've arrived,' he announced.

Senovara jammed the oven door into position and slapped a little wet clay round the edges to seal it. She ran into the kitchen and quickly washed her hands, drying them on her skirts before making her way through the shop to the street. When she reached the shop door she saw her grandmother's upright figure sitting on top of an old farm cart, and her cousin

157

Amatus stretching up his hands to help the old lady down. Senovara ran round and waited until Enica was standing on the road dusting her skirts before hugging her.

'Welcome to you both,' she cried. 'How are you, Grandmother?'

'Fine, now Amatus has stopped jolting me about in that ramshackle cart of his.' Enica's brown wrinkled face and shrewd eyes looked tired and cross but she returned her granddaughter's hug with vigour. Her head came only up to Senovara's shoulder, and more than ever Senovara thought that the old lady, in her dark green tunic and brown cloak, looked like an inquisitive walnut.

'Come on inside where you can be comfortable.' Senovara ushered her grandmother in through the shop, but her efforts to direct her into the best room were of no avail. The old lady made her way firmly into the kitchen.

'Where are my great-grandchildren?'

'Playing next door. Armea will go and fetch them.'

'Wait,' ordered Enica. 'Let me have a look at you, Armea.' She looked searchingly at the girl. 'How are they treating you?'

'Well, thank you, Mistress.'

'I'm not your mistress any more, girl,' grumbled Enica. 'It wasn't my idea to send you off to Eboracum. You should be back at the farm where you belong.'

By this time Armea seemed thoroughly confused over whether or not she should go and collect the children. Trying not to laugh, Senovara nodded towards Ursa's house and put her hand on her grandmother's arm.

'Armea will go and get the children,' she repeated, 'while you take your cloak off and I pour you some beer. You must be thirsty after your journey.'

By the time Senovara had got Enica settled with a wooden mug of beer in front of her, Quintus and Amatus had brought in a variety of leather bags and sacks.

'Hail, Quintus. I trust I find you well?' Enica enquired of her grandson-in-law.

'Very well, Enica, thank you,' he responded in the local dialect, in which he had become proficient since his retirement.

'What's all this, Grandmother?' asked Senovara as she took in the quantity of luggage. 'You seem to have brought most of the farm with you.'

'She has,' commented Amatus ruefully as he greeted his cousin. 'Grandmother was convinced she'd starve in Eboracum so she brought some provisions with her. It's good to see you, young Senovara.'

'And you too, Amatus. How are Oconea and the children?'

'Fine and blooming, thank you. They send their love.'

During this exchange, Enica had been rummaging in her bags. 'Amatus has become very rude since he married. I didn't think I'd starve, but I did think you might like some provisions. Nothing in Eboracum is fresh, in my opinion. I've brought some eggs, some honey, a few bags of dock leaves, sow thistle and elder stalks and, of course, some hawthorn buds, picked just this morning.' She placed several packages on the table.

Senovara gave Enica a hug. 'Oh, I do miss hawthorn buds,' she cried. 'There are so few hawthorn bushes in Eboracum and no one ever seems to sell them in the market. I'll make a *patina* with them to go with the lamb tonight.'

Lucius and Ertola trotted into the kitchen to greet their great-grandmother, who swept them both into her arms, her two long grey plaits lashing out as she did so, threatening to knock everything off the tables. Lucius responded amiably enough but Ertola looked a little scared and Senovara recalled that she had been hardly more than a small baby when she last saw her redoubtable old relative.

Enica crooned endearments to the children, then sat down with Ertola on her knee and Lucius held tightly by her side. Getting over her initial shyness, Ertola started to play with one of the old lady's plaits and Enica laughed.

'Still not talking, then?' she asked the child.

Quintus and Senovara looked at each other. They had made a sacrifice at the shrine of the Mother Goddesses at the end of the previous month, as they had planned, as well as offerings to Fortuna, Mercury and their household gods, but Ertola had still not spoken.

'Never mind, little one. You will one day,' continued Enica. 'Why don't you take me to see this dog I've heard about. Is that him barking in the garden?'

Ertola nodded, then, jumping down from Enica's knee, took her great-grandmother's hand and dragged her off through the kitchen door, followed by Lucius, who was making up for Ertola's silence by giving the old woman a lively description of Hylax's perfections.

Senovara, Quintus and Amatus all gave a great sigh of relief and burst out laughing.

'She doesn't change, does she?' asked Amatus. 'Still as bossy as when we were children.'

'How old is she?' asked Quintus.

'No one knows,' he replied. 'Children didn't have to be registered in those days. She reckons that the Emperor Claudius was still alive when she was born and Cartimandua was still Queen of the Brigantes, so she must be in her eighties. But she still runs round the farm like a young girl. Gives poor Ahteha a terrible life, as far as I can see, but you probably see more of Matugenus than I do and know more about how they get on.'

'Have you heard from Bodenius?'

'We had a letter only a few days ago. Just to say he had arrived at Aquincum and was well. He never says much.'

'We've recently met a family from Aquincum,' Senovara informed him. 'A new centurion at the fortress comes from there. He has his wife and sister with him and they tell me Aquincum is much larger than Eboracum but is otherwise quite similar, lying on a plain next to a great river.'

'It sounds as if there'll be opportunities for Bodenius to do well there, which is the main thing,' put in Quintus, looking at the situation from the military point of view.

'He's certainly done well, so far,' said his brother proudly. 'Already an *optio*. But I sometimes wish he wasn't so far away. It would be nice to see his ugly face once in a while.'

'Are you planning to stay the night?' asked Senovara, not wanting to consider that none of them might ever see Bodenius again.

'If I may. I've got a lot to do in Eboracum and, although I could spend tonight with Matugenus and Ahteha, I wouldn't get to them until very late. It would probably be safer to leave tomorrow morning and just stop off for a midday meal with them. I can then get home by early evening if I time it right.'

'Talking about a midday meal, I had better get on with today's, otherwise Grandmother will have just cause to complain about being starved.'

After their meal of freshly baked bread and vegetable soup, Senovara showed her grandmother where she was to sleep while Amatus headed off to the market and Quintus went back into his workshop. Senovara had hoped that the old lady would want a nap after her long journey, but Enica scorned the suggestion in favour of a tour round the house. No corner escaped her notice and her granddaughter had an exhausting afternoon defending her housekeeping. Senovara was also questioned closely about the children's health, where her neighbours came from, how various acquaintances were, and what life was like in Eboracum, while she tried to carry on her usual daily tasks and keep an eye on the roasting lamb. By the time Amatus returned after a successful foray to the market, Senovara's head was pounding. In desperation she told Armea to ask Enica's advice about the vegetable garden, and fled to her bedroom to rub her forehead with a mixture of ivy leaves boiled in vinegar and rose oil. She lay on the bed for a few minutes to let the headache cure work and to gather her scattered senses. Having her grandmother for several days was going to be even more of a strain than she had feared.

Senovara groaned and got to her feet. Only empresses could take to their beds; she had too much to do. It was just as well she had decided to stick to a traditional roast for the evening meal, as this involved little final preparation. Hopefully, Amatus' need for an early start would encourage her grandmother to go to bed at a reasonable hour.

When the family gathered that evening round the kitchen table, on which the leg of lamb had pride of place, Enica started to question Quintus about how his business was doing.

'Oh, work comes in steadily, Enica. I'm earning enough to keep your granddaughter and great-grandchildren fed and watered.'

'He was chosen to make some boots for the Legate last month,' broke in Senovara proudly. 'Purple ones decorated with gold leaf.'

Enica snorted. 'These Romans make fools of themselves with their fancy ways. Purple boots! Whatever next?'

'Hopefully, more purple boots,' teased Quintus. 'I was paid more for that pair than I can get for six pairs of plain ones, and just think of the extra trade I might get from people who hear where the Legate got them. He might even order some more himself – he seemed very pleased with my work.'

Senovara had been thrilled to hear, when Quintus returned home from delivering the boots to the *praetorium* a few days before, that the Legate had been there himself. She had presumed that he would simply leave the boots with the young tribune, as instructed, and had been relieved that he was wearing his newest tunic. Quintus had been stiff with pride as he told her that he had presented himself in Marcus Pontius Sabinus' office, only to be told to wait, because the Legate wished to see him. He had been offered a stool but had hardly had time to get seated before he heard a bell being rung behind a door and was shown in to the Legate's presence. He had slipped the new boots onto the Legate's feet himself and watched as Minicius Natalis paraded up and down the room, testing his new footwear.

'And did he like them?' Senovara had asked breathlessly, hardly able to bear the tension.

'He declared them to be excellent,' Quintus replied, grinning from ear to ear. 'And, what was even better, he paid for them in silver *denarii* then and there. That will swell our savings nicely.'

'Are you expecting trade to increase when the legion returns from the frontier?' said Amatus, breaking into Senovara's thoughts.

'I hope so,' responded Quintus, 'but I heard today that the Governor, Sextus Julius Severus, is to be transferred to Judaea to put down the revolt. It wouldn't surprise me if he took some of the troops from Britain with him. It would be just our luck to find that the whole of the Sixth ends up in the east, leaving Eboracum as a ghost town.'

Senovara felt a cold chill grip her at this news. Eboracum only existed because of the fortress. If the army left, most of the civilian population would have to leave too if they were to make a reasonable living. There would be few people remaining who would need or could afford new footwear. Quintus might even decide that they needed to move as well.

'Is it likely that the Sixth will go?' she asked nervously.

'No, probably not. Britannia isn't all that settled and needs its three legions. It's not that long ago that they transferred the Ninth across to Novio Magus. I doubt if they'd shift another legion out of the province so soon, but the ways of the authorities have always been a mystery to me; when I was serving I often wondered where they got the information on which they based their decisions – they didn't seem to listen much to the *exploratores*.'

'Have you heard who'll replace Sextus Julius Severus as

Governor?' asked Amatus.

'No one seems to know that. It may be that his successor hasn't been chosen yet.'

'Well, it probably won't affect us, whoever is Governor, unless he introduces new taxes. Have you noticed that they never decide to cut the taxes but always increase them?' grumbled Amatus.

Quintus laughed. 'At least I can pay my taxes here. Do you have to go into Petuaria to pay yours?'

'No, that would be too easy. I have to go to Derventio, of all places. A complete waste of a day it is too.'

As the meal continued Senovara suddenly remembered that she had not told Quintus about the actors.

'When Armea and I were fetching water this morning Ursa told us that a troupe of actors has arrived and is setting up on the other side of the Abus. Shall we go and see one of their performances, Quintus? They're here for several days.'

'Actors! I haven't seen a play for years. When I was with the Sixth on the frontier, there were people who travelled from fort to fort entertaining the soldiers and I saw many plays, but they don't usually come this far south. Yes, of course we'll go. They don't start tonight, do they?'

Senovara shook her head. 'I don't think so; they were just arriving when Ursa saw them so they probably won't be ready yet.'

'That's a shame. It looks as though you are to be robbed of a cultural treat, Amatus.'

'Not so,' his cousin-in-law responded. 'The latest gossip from Petuaria is that they're planning to build a real theatre there, with a proper stage and seats and everything. We'll be able to go to the theatre whenever we like and pity you poor people in Eboracum.'

'Ridiculous!' Enica had been quite quiet up to this point, concentrating on chewing her lamb. Now she had finished she was ready to denounce all things Roman again. 'When we had travelling players at the farm they performed perfectly well without lots of scenery and a big building. All these great public buildings going up all over the place are unnecessary and costly – that's what all your taxes are paying for, young Amatus.'

'Well, if we get entertaining plays out of the taxes, I won't mind so much,' said her grandson with a smile.

'Will you come with us to see the actors, Enica?' asked Quintus.

'I certainly will. I enjoyed the last play I saw, as I recall, although that must be over fifteen years ago. Do you remember it, Senovara?'

'I do. I was telling the girls at the trough this morning. I'll find out when the first performance is to be and we'll all go.'

The next morning, Amatus brought his mule round from the garden, where it had been tethered overnight to the apple tree, and harnessed it to the cart. He piled his purchases onto the cart.

'Did you get everything you wanted?' asked Senovara, handing him the two leather balls, stuffed with chicken feathers, which she had bought as presents for his two children.

'I think so. Sudrenus was able to supply me with most of the ironwork I needed, thank the Mothers. I've also got an amphora of liquamen for Oconea – for some reason she thinks the liquamen from Eboracum is better than the stuff we get from Petuaria, though I keep telling her that it's exactly the same. I've bought her a necklace as well; do you think she'll like it?'

He reached into his leather satchel and pulled out a necklace of dark blue glass beads strung on a fine bronze chain.

'Oh, that's lovely!' exclaimed Senovara. 'It will go beautifully with her blue eyes. She'll be delighted, I know.'

Amatus looked pleased and carefully stowed the necklace away. 'Thank you for your hospitality, Quintus. I hope to see you on a visit to us one day soon.'

Quintus smiled, but neither man thought such a visit likely; Petuaria was a long day's ride away and Quintus had no reason to go there.

'Goodbye, Grandmother,' called Amatus, climbing up onto his cart. 'Goodbye, Senovara. Goodbye, children.' He waved gaily, clicked his tongue to the mule and set off down the street.

After they had seen him turn the corner, the family went back indoors to continue with their own day.

'I'm going to hoe your vegetable plot,' announced Enica firmly.

'But you're a guest,' protested Quintus. 'You don't have to work while you're here.'

Senovara pulled a face at him behind her grandmother's back. If Enica wanted to garden, she wasn't going to put her off. It would keep her from interfering with the housework, and Senovara had some washing to do.

'I wasn't made to sit around and do nothing like these Roman women. But first you must show me where you empty your pots, Senovara.'

'But we have a *latrina*, Grandmother. You don't need to use a pot. You didn't bring one with you, did you?'

'I certainly did. Catch me using a *latrina*. Nasty, smelly, unhygienic places. A pot is good enough for me if there are no fields handy.'

'Well, just leave it in your room and Armea will empty it each morning,' said Senovara despairingly.

As Enica marched off to get a hoe from the storeroom, Senovara turned to Armea.

'Just pour the contents of Enica's pot down the *latrina*,' she said, 'and swill it out with some water. There's no point arguing with her.'

'She won't use the one at the farm, either, Mistress. Master Matugenus gets very cross.'

Later that day Senovara and her grandmother sallied forth to do some shopping, not without a certain amount of trepidation on Senovara's part. Enica had told her that one of the reasons for her visit was to buy some woollen material for new tunics. Senovara was surprised by this, because Enica had always spun the wool, and dyed and woven the cloth for the family's needs, herself. Enica had explained that she had at last agreed with Matugenus that, since he could get a good price for the wool he produced on the farm, it was more sensible to sell it and buy just what was needed. 'My old hands find it difficult to spin wool evenly these days,' she had admitted, 'and I've heard that you can get many more colours if you buy the cloth ready woven.'

Senovara recalled that, when she was young, everyone on the farm had invariably been dressed in the same colour, as her grandmother could produce dyes of only a few shades and tended to colour whole batches of cloth together to save time. The idea that the family and labourers were to become multi-coloured was fascinating. She had shown Enica her own tunics the previous evening before they went to bed and had been amused by the old woman's enthusiasm. There had been no snide comments about 'Roman ways' in this context. Several merchants had set up shop to sell both woollen and linen material on the other side of the Abus, so Senovara had no fears that they would be unable to find some suitable fabric, but no doubt Enica would find much to criticise on the way. Senovara anticipated an exhausting few hours.

They made their way down the street, their progress hindered by several of Senovara's friends who stopped to greet her and Enica. Eventually they turned right at the south-west corner of the fortress and walked towards the wooden bridge that spanned the river separating the fortress from the newest part of the civilian settlement.

As they crossed the bridge Senovara saw a small group of covered carts on the flat land on the south bank of the river.

'Look, Grandmother, that must be the actors. We must find out when they're starting their performances.'

This was not difficult. Everyone was talking about the troupe, and Senovara was delighted to learn that there was to be a performance that night. If they could get their shopping done quickly, she calculated, they would be back in plenty of time to get the family ready.

Luckily, the Fates were on her side. The first cloth shop they arrived at had plenty of choice and the merchant was charm itself. He produced wooden chairs with cushions for them, and while they sat in comfort he brought out roll after roll of fabric of every colour in the rainbow: greens, blues, reds, yellows, purples were all there, as both plain and patterned cloth. There was also a bewildering range of weaves. Enica's eyes shone when she felt the quality of the textiles, although Senovara was amused to hear her disparage the material as she attempted to bring the price down. The merchant's eyes also shone when he realised that the old matriarch was buying in bulk.

'Hold that dark red up to the light again,' Enica directed the merchant. 'Do you think that would suit Ahteha?' she asked Senovara.

'Indeed it would. And that pale blue would look lovely on you, Grandmother.'

After some lively discussion it was decided that Enica would order enough green and brown wool of the second quality to supply the farm workers with the new tunics they needed, and some lengths of red and blue wool of the first quality for herself and Ahteha.

The merchant agreed to deliver the material to the shoemaker's the following day. 'Good,' declared Enica. 'I'll see about some linen for undertunics tomorrow. Let's go back and see if Quintus is willing to go to the play tonight.'

Somewhat amazed by this enthusiasm and the success of the

shopping expedition, Senovara followed as the old lady strode energetically across the bridge.

On their return they found that Quintus had already heard of the opening night and needed no persuading to attend. It seemed only minutes after their return that, having served up the remains of the previous night's lamb, Senovara found herself walking back across the bridge with her whole household. As they made their way to the riverbank they met many friends and acquaintances who were heading in the same direction. The whole of Eboracum seemed to be there, both military and civilian, all wearing their best clothes and eager for the unexpected treat.

The actors had travelled in wooden carriages, like huts on wheels with a seat in the front for the driver and a door in the side so that people could get in and out. The carriages were arranged so as to make three sides of a square; the space between them was to do duty as a stage. Rows of benches for the audience had been provided across the open end of the square by placing planks of wood across sections of tree trunk. As Quintus led his family towards these rickety seats, one large matron was deposited unceremoniously on the ground when the other people sharing her plank stood up to let someone past, and the air was filled with her cries and curses.

The whole scene was illuminated by flaming torches in iron holders attached to the sides of the carriages. Mingling with the throng were vendors of snacks and drinks, all calling their wares and happily making money.

Quintus paid the attendant and they made their way to one of the benches. It was a good thing they had got there early, thought Senovara, as more and more people continued to arrive. Soon all the seats were full and people were standing at the back and at the sides. Quintus handed Ertola to her and pulled Lucius onto his knee to make room for his friend Sacer, who had just arrived.

'Many thanks, Quintus. I didn't think there'd be so many people, otherwise I'd have come earlier – it must be all this fine weather encouraging people to come out. Hail, Senovara. Hail, Enica,' he added, catching sight of the old lady.

He was shushed by the rest of the audience as a man dressed in a toga, and with a carved wooden mask covering his face, appeared in front of them.

'He'll be the Prologue,' Quintus whispered to Senovara.

'I am Lar Familiaris, the guardian spirit of the house – that house from which I have just come,' announced the actor in a loud, clear voice, pointing to one of the carriages. Some soldiers in the audience laughed and he quelled them with a gesture before continuing to summarize the plot. Senovara listened, enthralled, as he explained that a miser had buried a large sum of money in the house and had refused to tell his son where it was buried before he died. Now he, the Lar, was going to reveal the hiding place to the miser's grandson, whose name was Euclio, in the hope that the heroine, Phaedra, Euclio's daughter, would then be able to marry her lover, Lyconides.

It all sounded very confusing but as the play unfolded the audience roared its approval at every twist and turn. When Euclio, finding that he had lost his pot of gold, turned in apparent despair to a member of the audience and asked for his help, saying: 'What do you say, sir? I'll believe you – I can see you've an honest face,' the crowd erupted with cheers and catcalls.

'By Jupiter! He's chosen that centurion who rumour has it is skimming off the profits from the supplies going through Cataractonium. What a good person to choose,' Quintus chortled.

The actor rounded on the audience. 'What's that? You're all laughing at me, are you? I know you lot; I know this town is full of thieves. Look at you all sitting there, so respectable in your nice clean clothes. I bet one of you has my pot of gold.'

This reduced his audience to tears of laughter, and Senovara was quite glad when the scene ended and the actor's place was taken by a juggler, because her sides were aching. Even Enica had tears streaming down her face.

The evening was a huge success. The play kept everyone laughing, and the jugglers and singers who came on between the scenes were applauded loudly. But eventually it came to an end and the audience, reluctantly, had to leave.

Ertola had fallen asleep on her mother's knee early in the evening and Senovara handed her over to Quintus to carry home while she took Lucius' hand. The family made their way back across the bridge, eagerly discussing the evening's entertainment.

'That juggler was clever,' declared Lucius. 'I'm going to see if I can do that when I get home.'

'I used to be able to juggle with apples when I was a girl,' announced his great-grandmother. The whole family stopped in their tracks and stared at her in amazement; being able to juggle apples seemed a remarkably skittish accomplishment for such a stern old lady.

'Oh, yes, I was quite good at it. Tomorrow morning, young Lucius, you find all your leather balls and we'll see if I can still juggle.'

Quintus opened his mouth to say something then, thinking better of it, set off again.

'Did you enjoy the play, Armea?' asked Senovara.

'I did.' Armea's eyes were shining. 'But I thought the singing was the best bit.'

'You weren't sitting next to Sacer,' Quintus commented acidly. 'He kept joining in with the songs he knew and he's no nightingale, I can tell you. I'm just about deafened in my left ear.'

'I only wish the actors had camped a bit further from the river,' said Senovara, scratching her head. 'I kept being bitten by mosquitoes. I'm going to be covered in bites tomorrow morning. We should have taken some mint with us.'

Her grandmother snorted. 'Mosquitoes never bother me. You're getting soft, Senovara.'

'That's how I like her,' said Quintus roundly, as he unlocked the front door.

Senovara smiled at the compliment, and led the way through into the house. Quintus had clearly enjoyed the evening. It would be lovely if Eboracum built a proper theatre, as Amatus had told them Petuaria planned to do, she thought, as she put her sleepy daughter and excited son to bed; then they could go to see plays regularly. Having a night out seemed to do her hardworking husband good but it was too rare an event for her liking. Perhaps the town council would discuss building a theatre at their next meeting; most of the *quaestors* had been in the audience and would probably be keen on the idea. Perhaps a rich merchant would pay for it? Then she recalled what Quintus had said about the possible transfer of the legion. No one would want to pay for a theatre if there was to be no audience left, she thought dismally. She shook herself. There was no point in worrying about what might never happen; the lives of men were in the hands of the gods, anyway. It was time to go to bed and dream about all the events of a busy day.

Iulius

SENOVARA LET HERSELF out of the garden gate, with Hylax jumping around her feet at the end of his rope lead. She looked down at him and frowned. Taking him with her had not seemed a good idea, but Quintus had insisted when she mentioned that she intended to cross the river to gather some dandelions and ground elder to supplement their vegetable supply.

'Take Hylax with you. It's getting to be like a siege camp over there these days. He'll see off anyone trying to accost you.'

She had agreed, but grudgingly; Hylax had a tendency to be a lively and unpredictable companion. She still blushed when she remembered the occasion when she had taken him to the market and he had dragged her across the street and buried his nose up an *optio*'s tunic. The *optio*'s look of outraged surprise when he turned round would remain in her memory until the day she died. Quintus had roared with laughter when she had recounted this embarrassing incident, and had patted Hylax.

'Good dog,' he had declared in an encouraging tone, much to her disgust.

Today, however, she acknowledged that taking Hylax might be a reasonable precaution. For several days there had been a constant stream of carts and waggons rolling through the streets as several cohorts of the legion returned to Eboracum. At first, led by officers on horseback, there had been the columns of soldiers marching in time, with their immediate belongings hanging from the pole that each man carried over his shoulder. Then there had been the official waggons, the spare horses and the supply carts. These had all disappeared into the fortress before, slowly at first, but increasing to a steady stream, the waggons of the soldiers' dependants had started to arrive and had been directed to some cleared land on the south side of the River Abus, where a group of civilians were already established. As well as the children and womenfolk, there had also been a host of merchants and traders and others who had to follow the soldiers to make their living. Senovara had seen some of them when doing her shopping and had been shocked by the number of prostitutes and other camp followers who were planning to set up in Eboracum.

Ursa hailed her across the fence from her garden, breaking into Senovara's thoughts. 'Where are you off to?'

'I thought I'd go and gather some greens from the grasslands on the other side of the river. We've had so little rain recently that my vegetables aren't growing as fast as they might.'

'Same here. I sent the boys to the trough the other day for some water to pour over my seedlings – they weren't pleased, I can tell you. There was a lot of grumbling about "women's work" until I pointed out that no water meant no food, which meant hungry boys. That seemed to do the trick.'

Senovara laughed. 'I'll let you know if there is much to gather on the grasslands. Quintus reckons the incomers will have picked the place clean already, but I'm hoping they haven't had time to find the best areas yet.'

'They've already stripped the market – there was hardly anything left when I went to get some bread this morning. If the army doesn't organise some extra supplies soon, I can see us all going hungry. I saw more waggons coming through while I was out. There must be hundreds of new people here already and a scruffy lot some of them are, too.'

'After five days on the road I suppose we'd not look our best,' commented Senovara charitably, 'but it's worrying that they don't seem to have brought supplies with them. The Eboracum traders can't be expected to provide enough food for so many more people just like that. Luckily, I've got plenty of grain and Matugenus brought me a side of bacon and some eggs when he collected Grandmother. It's just vegetables I seem to be low on.'

She took leave of her neighbour and continued on her way. It was good to get out on her own for a while. Her grandmother's visit had left Senovara feeling like an old rag which had been wrung out and left to dry. Since Enica's departure, Lucius and Ertola had been particularly noisy and difficult, probably pleased that they were no longer being constantly told to be good, and taking advantage of their mother's weariness.

Lucius, bored with his new juggling skills, had rediscovered his old friend the hedgehog, and there had been several tearful arguments when he was again banned from bringing it into the house. A bit of peace and quiet was much to be desired, thought Senovara ruefully.

She made her way round the corner of the fortress, with Hylax still leaping about with excitement. Progress was slow, because he wanted to cock his leg at every street corner or passing cart and was keen to investigate every interesting smell, but Senovara was in no hurry and waited patiently while he completed his self-appointed tasks. In the alleyways between the buildings there were few people about and the noises of the traffic and the street traders were subdued, as if they were a long way away. A determined line of ants attracted Hylax's attention and he barked, breaking the silence. For a moment Senovara watched the ants as they carried bits of leaves and twigs across her path. She was struck by their similarity to the soldiers who had marched into the fortress two days before; there was the same air of purpose and organisation; the same sense of an important plan of which each individual knew little other than that they were essential to its success.

Eventually Senovara and Hylax reached the bridge, only to find it choked with waggons. A column of soldiers on horseback was trying to get across the bridge, back to their base; the officer in charge was purple in the face with fury as he shouted at the traffic to make way. For a moment no one could move forward or back. Then a soldier forced his way to the north end of the bridge and stopped more traffic joining the chaos. To avoid being squashed, Senovara had to step back onto the riverbank as the waggons already on the bridge were driven over, before the horsemen going the other way could trot across. When all was clear she joined the line of pedestrians and waggons going south and walked across the Abus, only to find her way hindered once more by the press of waggons waiting their turn to get onto the camping ground. A group of harassed soldiers was trying to direct people to vacant spaces but some of the waggon drivers were not very expert at getting round tight corners and there was much cursing as the newcomers crashed into the belongings of those who had arrived earlier.

Senovara's eyes widened as she took in the busy scene. Wherever she looked there were waggons – a number were just carts with luggage piled on top of them but some had wooden superstructures, like the waggons the actors had travelled in. When she walked past, she could see that the interiors of these were laid out like miniature rooms. At least the occupants of the better waggons had some comfort and a roof over their heads

– those travelling with plain carts either appeared to be sleeping under them or else had fastened strips of material or hide along one side of their cart platforms, pinning the other edge to the ground to form simple, one-sided tents.

All the newcomers were cooking on open fires and the smell of food surrounded Senovara as she picked her way through the camp. Some cauldrons held plain stews, others offered up unusual spicy smells which made her nostrils twitch and hinted that their owners hailed from the eastern or southern provinces. The carcasses of animals and birds of all sizes rotated on spits, suggesting that the invaders had begun to take their toll on the animal population of the area.

Children ran about everywhere, apparently unconcerned by their sudden move from the frontier and protected by some benign deity from being run over by the traffic as they darted about the camp. There were children in clean, neat tunics with good leather sandals; others in torn, dirty clothes with filthy bare feet. Some played with balls, like those she had given her cousin to take home for his children; others sat on the ground playing games with pebbles on boards scratched in the dirt. The majority were chasing each other, shrieking with laughter or arguing with loud yells and screams. Every now and again an adult shouted at them to be quiet, or rushed out to separate a wrestling match, but mostly they were left to entertain themselves and Senovara wondered if anyone ever tried to teach them to read or write.

The women seemed to be from all walks of life and from all over the world. Senovara was fascinated to see a very tall black-skinned woman, her dark complexion contrasting with her white, sleeveless tunic. As she watched the woman chiding two unrepentant children with cheeky smiles, Senovara wondered if she was a Nubian or an Aethiopian and wished she had the nerve to talk to her and find out. A few moments later, Senovara passed a young girl with the whitest skin and palest blonde hair she had ever seen. She had heard of the 'silver women' who came from the tribes north of Germania and assumed that this must be one of them. She looked around avidly, hoping to see one of the Arimaspians who were reported to only have a single eye in the middle of their foreheads; she had always imagined that these people, who were said to live near the cave of the North-East Wind, existed only in travellers' tales but looking at the wide range of people around her, with their different colours of skin and hair, she began to wonder if the tales might not be true after all.

Not all the women were young. There were respectable matrons who sailed through the camp like boats through water; there were incredibly old women with scrawny necks and faces which bore witness to a lifetime of experience and toil – each wrinkle a record of an event in their lives; there were slatternly women with wild hair and harassed expressions, who could have been either older or younger than they looked. Senovara's heart went out to a couple of elderly women who just sat on the steps of their waggons looking bewildered. One blind woman was being fed by a young boy, while another was using a triangular walking frame of wood, with a small wheel at each corner, in order to get about.

The noise of singing and laughter from a group of tents set slightly apart from the others indicated that some of the working women had wasted no time establishing themselves. A small but constant stream of off-duty soldiers making their way to and from these tents made their purpose only too clear, but Senovara also noticed that there were just as many men working in the camp, starting to build more substantial shelters for their womenfolk. The sawing and hammering, added to the cries of the children, the barking of dogs and the laughter and curses of the women, made more noise than Senovara had ever heard; even the din of the market seemed a gentle murmur by contrast.

It took Senovara quite a while to get through the camp and she felt relieved when she eventually emerged onto a reasonably empty road. Hylax had kept close to her heels, only jumping out once or twice to bark at some of the many dogs that scavenged around the carts and tents. Even he had seemed cowed by the noise and bustle of the camp, and Senovara wondered doubtfully just how much help he would have been if she had got into trouble.

When she arrived at the grasslands, she realised that Quintus had been accurate in his prediction that the incomers would have picked the area clean of anything edible. She kept walking through a small wood to an open glade which she hoped would have escaped their notice. Here, to her delight, she found a small patch of wild strawberries and enough ground elder and dandelion leaves to fill her basket and make her effort worthwhile.

She let Hylax off his lead while she picked her potherbs and he scurried back and forth, sniffing the ground, his stiff little tail wagging frantically at the wonderful variety of new smells. Every now and again he gave a yelp and set off in pursuit of a trail but he always came back despondent having caught nothing. When she had filled her basket, Senovara picked up a stick and threw it to him, laughing as he returned it to her in triumph. She tried to take it from him to throw again, but he hung on and the two of them sidled round, each tugging at the stick, Hylax growling amiably.

'I'm sorry, Hylax,' Senovara said eventually. 'I can't spend all day playing with you. We're going to have to go home; there's a meal to cook and these greens are beginning to wilt already.'

She grabbed him by the scruff of his neck and tied the rope round it, then, picking up her basket, set off back towards the encampment.

More soldiers had come off duty and had walked over from the fortress to see how their families fared. Their reception seemed to be as mixed as their womenfolk, Senovara noted with amusement. Some were greeted with cries of affection, their children rushing to welcome them and be swept up into loving arms, their wives, mothers or sisters kissing them as they arrived. Others were clearly in disfavour: loud arguments could be heard from several of the waggons, and Senovara had to bite her lip in an effort not to laugh as she hurried past one waggon where a soldier was having his ears soundly boxed by a tiny little woman who had to stand on tiptoe to get a good aim. Senovara wondered what he had done to deserve this greeting; his look of shamefaced guilt suggested that he knew his punishment was deserved.

With Hylax in tow, she stepped off the bridge and turned towards home. Their way led through the military tile fields where row upon row of red, mould-made clay tiles had been laid out in the sun to dry before firing. There were hundreds of them: flat, square building tiles, curved *imbrices*, and big roofing *tegulae*, all needed for the building work at the fortress. Throughout the field, small groups of soldiers, their tunics rolled down to their waists, carried wooden litters of dried tiles to the kiln to be fired, or brought freshly moulded ones down to dry.

Senovara was by now preoccupied with plans for the evening meal and hardly took in her surroundings until Hylax gave a yelp and began to pull at his lead. She looked down to see what was wrong, and he suddenly took off, barking excitedly as he saw a black rat emerge from behind one of the litters. She struggled to hold him back until a sudden lunge pulled the rope from her hand and he made off across the tile field in close pursuit of the startled rat. There were furious cries from the tilers as he and his quarry stampeded across the damp tiles, leaving a trail of impressed footprints. Senovara picked up her skirts and ran after him, avoiding the tiles herself, until she arrived, panting, at the spot where Hylax had the rat cornered behind a pile of fired roof tiles awaiting shipment. A soldier made a grab for Hylax's lead, pulled him away, and brought him over to Senovara.

'Here you are, lady. This is yours, I believe.'

'I'm afraid he is. I am so sorry – I hope he hasn't done too much damage?'

'No. A few footprints aren't a problem. Lucky he landed on the flat *tegulae*, though. If he'd trodden on the *imbrices* we would have had something to say.'

Senovara took the lead and made her way back to the road, mortified by her pet's behaviour. This was the last time she would allow herself to be persuaded to take him anywhere. A stout stick was a less troublesome form of protection. She resolved to tell Quintus so when she got home; but when she entered the shop she found Armea in charge.

'Where's Quintus?' Senovara asked anxiously.

'He's in the best room. The centurion Veturius is visiting.'

Senovara took her basket into the kitchen and pulled off her shawl, wondering whether she should look into the best room to greet Veturius or if he and Quintus were happy discussing old campaigns and wouldn't want to be interrupted. She let Hylax out into the back garden and poured herself some water to get the taste of road dust out of her mouth.

'Senovara, is that you? Veturius is here and wants to talk to you.' Her husband's voice rang down the corridor. Senovara tucked a stray hair behind her ear and went into the best room to see why she was wanted. As she entered, Veturius put his beaker of wine on the table, stood up politely and greeted her with a broad smile.

'Hail, Veturius,' she responded warmly. 'I hope I find you well? How are Adnamata and Broginara these days? I haven't seen any of you for some time.'

'Broginara and I are well, thank you, but Adnamata is giving us cause for worry. She's become very fretful recently – she's convinced herself that the baby will be born with something wrong with it and nothing Broginara or I can do or say will persuade her otherwise. I wish you'd come and talk to her, and calm her down if you can.'

Senovara heard this plea with concern. Pregnant women often fell prey to worries and fears about what might go wrong but they usually had experienced friends around them with whom they could discuss their problems. Adnamata had few friends in Eboracum to put her worries into perspective.

'Of course I'll come and see her. I'll call tomorrow morning. But hasn't she seen Grata, the midwife?'

'Yes, as soon as you suggested she should, but only the once. I don't think she expected to see her again until just before the birth.'

'It would be better if she spoke to Grata if she has any particular worries. Grata knows what she is talking about and is very reassuring. I'll call on her on my way to the fortress and suggest she might drop in on Adnamata in the next few days.'

'Good. I'll tell my women to expect you tomorrow and Grata some time soon. Thank you. But Quintus tells me you've been on the other side of the river. How is it over there?'

'Chaotic. I've never heard so much noise nor seen so many people. Is it always like that when a legion moves?'

Quintus and Veturius looked at each other in amusement.

'Oh, that's nothing. You should see what it's like when the whole legion moves in one go. This was just a few cohorts.'

'Well, I hope when the whole legion shifts base the army plans the supplies for the civilians better. Ursa tells me they have stripped the market like a plague of locusts, and they've taken most of the herbs and greens from the grasslands – yes, you were right, Quintus,' she added, as a smug, I-told-you-so expression flitted across her husband's face. 'Just be grateful that Matugenus brought us that side of bacon and that we have the garden. Some families will be going hungry in Eboracum in the next few days unless more supplies are brought in.'

'Oh, you'll be surprised how quickly things settle down,' Veturius assured her. 'But, be warned, prices will probably go up. The traders will make sure more food is brought in as quickly as possible, but they'll take advantage of the extra demand and raise their prices. It always happens, I regret to say.'

Senovara was outraged at this, but realised that the two men had lived through this sort of upheaval many times and took the resulting misery as an unavoidable state of affairs. She changed the subject and told them of Hylax's misdemeanours in the tile field.

'His footprints will soon be on the rooftops of one of the new fortress buildings,' declared Veturius. 'A splendid record of a splendid little dog.' Having been involved in naming Hylax, he had remained a great supporter of the little terrier and always enjoyed hearing of his exploits.

'I remember my century being sent a consignment of tiles when I was up north,' said Quintus. 'They'd been trampled over by a herd of cows, and every single tile had a hoof print – some had several. When it was finished the building looked as though one of the gods had driven his herd over it. Whenever it rained the water gathered in the depressions and glittered. It looked very strange, I can tell you.'

'We had a similar situation some years ago when a legate, who will remain nameless, got so excited hunting a wild boar that he chased it across a military tile field on his horse with his pack of dogs in full cry. Completely destroyed a whole day's output of tiles. I thought we were going to have open mutiny from the men, especially as the boar got away.' Veturius snorted with derision. 'But I must get back to my duties. Thank you for your hospitality, Quintus, and thank you, Senovara, for agreeing to visit my wife; we will expect you tomorrow.'

Senovara said her farewells and left Quintus to see their guest out while she went back to her kitchen to prepare her afternoon's harvest for supper; mixed with eggs and baked, the leaves would make a good meal.

The next morning she hurried through those of her daily tasks which could not be avoided, then, leaving the children in Armea's charge, set off for the fortress. On the way she made a short detour to the tiny, one-roomed cottage in which Grata lived. The door was open: the midwife was in.

Senovara knocked on the wooden door-post and when a voice called to her to enter she ducked her head and stepped down into the dark interior. This was one of the first civilian buildings to be put up after the Roman army made Eboracum their base in the area; the road had been resurfaced several times since then and each successive layer had resulted in the floor of the cottage retreating further into the ground until it now looked like part of the earth itself.

As Senovara's eyes became accustomed to the gloom, she made out the low bed that doubled as a consulting couch and Grata's sleeping quarters. In the corner there was a stone and clay stove on which a copper cauldron sat, its contents simmering gently and emitting a pungent herbal smell. The squat figure of the midwife stood behind the wooden table in the centre of the room, grinding up some herbs in a mortarium.

'Hail, Senovara. What can I do for you? Not expecting again, are you?' The midwife's low chuckle reverberated round the room.

'No,' laughed Senovara. 'I've followed your instructions and use a plug of wool soaked in olive oil every time and I always wash myself with vinegar afterwards. Two are enough for me. I'm here not for myself but for Adnamata, the Pannonian centurion's wife.'

'Is she not doing well? She seemed a strong, healthy girl when I saw her; a bit immature but quite old enough to have a child. I didn't expect her to have any problems. I reckon she's due about the beginning of September so I was planning to check up on her later this month.' The old midwife emerged from the gloom and pulled a couple of stools out from under the table, indicating that Senovara should make herself comfortable. She reached for a large pottery jug and poured them both a beaker of beer.

'I don't think there's anything wrong with her really,' said Senovara, 'but her husband says she's fretting and has convinced herself that the baby will be born with something wrong with it. I'm just off to see her and try to cheer her up, but it would be a kindness if you could call in to reassure her. You'll be able to check if there is anything truly wrong and set her mind at rest if she has nothing to worry about.'

'Of course I will. These young military wives are always the ones who get in a panic. I suppose it's being so far from home, and their husbands are usually no help at all. They may be able to understand the men under their command, but present them with a pregnant woman and they seem to lose all common sense. But isn't Adnamata's sister-in-law with her? She seemed a sensible sort of girl.'

'Yes she is, but Broginara has never been married herself and hasn't had any experience of helping a pregnant woman, so I can imagine that she's limited in what she can do to help.'

'Well, try to find out what the problem is. If you're worried come straight back here and I'll go up to the fortress immediately, but I'm waiting for a message from Sangus. His wife is due to give birth any day now – in fact, she's greatly overdue by my reckoning – so I don't want to be out when she starts. Check that Adnamata is eating properly and is taking a reasonable amount of exercise. It may be that the Pannonian tradition is for mothers-to-be to spend hours in bed – some of these provincials have some curious ideas about pregnancy, I've found, and women who lie in bed all day give themselves too much time to imagine horrors. But if there's anything wrong, one remedy which covers all problems is a veined amulet. I've got some here; you can take one along with you.'

Grata got up from her stool and started to rummage around on a shelf crowded with glass flasks, pottery jugs and wooden boxes, for Grata supplied medicines to help women conceive, stop them conceiving, or to induce a miscarriage, depending on their needs. The beams of the cottage were festooned with bunches of herbs used in these medicines and their smell filled the room with a cloying scent. Most of the women of Eboracum had made their way to this tiny cottage at some time in their lives, and there was little that Grata did not know about what ailed women or the remedies to correct matters.

Senovara gazed fondly at the round little figure as she searched for the amulets. Grata had proved a great friend and support when she had had Lucius and Ertola. When she had first told her grandmother that she was pregnant, Enica had announced that she would come and stay when the time for the birth came near and would assist. Quintus had looked less than keen on this idea, declaring that he might as well move out for the duration as he would, no doubt, be made to feel thoroughly in the way. As it was, Lucius had arrived earlier than anyone had expected, and Grata had had to cope on her own; by the time Enica was fetched from the farm, her great-grandson was already screaming the house down and generally making his presence felt. Enica had not been pleased at missing such an important event as the birth of her first great-grandchild and when Senovara discovered that she was pregnant again, she had had great difficulty in dissuading her grandmother from moving in for the whole length of the pregnancy. Enica had still turned up a full month before the birth but by that time a heavily pregnant Senovara was so tired looking after a lively three-year-old that she had been only too pleased to pass the housekeeping to her grandmother. She had been rather worried about how Enica and Grata would get on, but the two old women had both officiated at too many births not to be able to work together efficiently. In fact, there had been times during her labour when Senovara had felt that her ideas about how things should be done were of no importance at all and that it was Grata and Enica who were the main characters in her small drama.

Grata gave a triumphant cry. 'Here they are. I knew they were around somewhere.' She came back to the table carrying a small wooden box from which she pulled out a small egg-shaped stone whose dark red surface was covered with black and white veins.

'Give this to Adnamata. Tell her to carry it around with her at all times, and whenever she becomes anxious she should roll it round in her hand. It will give her the protection of the gods.'

Senovara took it nervously, feeling the cold smoothness of the stone, aware of the power it might hold. She placed it in her basket, wedging it beside some of the bacon she had cut to give to Adnamata.

'Now, young Senovara, you can tell me what is worrying you as well.' Senovara looked startled. As far as she knew she didn't appear worried and she thought she had kept her fears about Ertola's lack of speech to herself. But you couldn't hide anything from Grata. Senovara had often wondered if the midwife's ferociously crossed eyes meant that she saw things other people didn't. When she first met Grata, Senovara had been concerned about those eyes, having been brought up in the belief that the owners of crossed eyes brought bad luck to all they met. She had rapidly revised this idea; indeed, had found the eyes a comfort: when Grata was examining a patient it was impossible to be embarrassed at what she was looking at because you could never be sure what it was she was looking at. But Senovara still couldn't rid herself of the idea that the crossed eyes gave Grata special powers. She found herself telling the wise old woman all about Ertola and how she and Quintus had made special sacrifices to several deities but so far to no avail.

Grata listened quietly, asking no questions. When Senovara had finished her story, the midwife took her right hand and shook it gently.

'I doubt if you need worry unduly. Whenever I've seen Ertola she's been perfectly happy. She doesn't have that anxious look children have when they can't hear or can't understand what is going on. She probably just sees no need to speak, if you all know what she wants all the time. Keep asking her questions, or deliberately misunderstand her sometimes – exasperation can lead to speech as fast as the will of the gods. But an amber amulet might help; they're excellent for affections of the throat if Ertola does have something wrong with her.'

She rummaged once more in the little box and brought out a tiny phallus carved in amber. A small hole had been drilled through it to take a cord. 'Tie that round Ertola's neck so that it rests at her throat. Not too tight – you don't need to throttle her – but not so loose that it dangles away from her skin when she plays. You can bring it back when she speaks.'

Senovara looked at the tiny symbol as it rested on her hand. She ran a finger over its honey-coloured surface, feeling a slight tingle as she did so. She felt quite frightened of it and placed it on the cuff of her dress, turning the material over a few times to trap the amulet securely against her wrist so that it wasn't lost before she got home.

She was about to thank Grata when a small boy rushed through the door.

'Grata, Sangus sent me. You're to come immediately.'

Grata grabbed a large leather bag from a hook on the wall, moved the bubbling cauldron off the fire, and patted Senovara on the head as she passed.

'I must be off. Come and see me again if you're still worried or if you think Adnamata needs me urgently.'

She bustled Senovara out of the door and slammed it shut behind them. She waved her hand, then set off after the boy at a steady pace, her capacious bag swinging purposefully at her side.

Senovara turned down by the side of the cottage and made her way to the fortress gate. She felt no nervousness about visiting on her own now – she had called on the Pannonians several times and on Vibia Pacata as well, so she was familiar with the military security arrangements and the layout of the fortress. She nodded at the soldiers on duty at the gate and told them where she was going, then carried on to the centurion's quarters.

This door was also open to let in the warm summer breezes and she called out as she stepped over the threshold.

'Anyone at home?'

Broginara appeared from the centurion's office at the sound of her voice, a duster in her hand. 'Hail, Senovara. Veturius told us to expect you. Adnamata's in here.' She ushered Senovara through into the living room, where Adnamata was sitting on one of the folding stools, podding peas into a bowl on the floor. The stools might be ideal for a family who moved house often but they didn't strike Senovara as being very comfortable for a pregnant woman, and when Adnamata stood up to greet her guest it became clear that she was very big with child. Senovara wondered if the girl was further along with her pregnancy than they had calculated.

She kissed both women with affection and handed over Matugenus' bacon, pointing out that it came from a local farm and had been properly cured so would do no harm, even if it was now Iulius. Several people she knew would not eat pig meat in the summer, and she herself avoided fresh pork, but she never felt any concern about the farm bacon.

As she settled herself on a stool she looked closely at Adnamata, searching for signs that all was not going well, but could see nothing to alarm her.

'How are you feeling, Adnamata?' she asked.

'Tired. And constipated,' came the cheerful reply.

Senovara laughed. 'I remember it well. Have you tried a broth of beetroot and leeks? I found that worked well.'

'Broginara keeps trying to make me drink elm-bark water but it just makes me feel sick. Beetroot and leek broth sounds more palatable.'

'If you're going to make rude comments about my elm-bark water I shall leave you two married women to it,' retorted Broginara. 'I'm going to the market to see if there's anything left.' She tactfully withdrew.

After she had gone, Senovara questioned Adnamata more fully about her pregnancy. 'You are keeping occupied, aren't you?' she said. 'It's important to have plenty to do; some people swear by walking, reading aloud and singing during the last months of pregnancy. I always found I had enough housework to keep me occupied without deafening my neighbours.'

Adnamata agreed that she had enough to do, though Broginara and Veturius kept trying to stop her doing too much. She submitted to a searching enquiry as to her diet. No, she wasn't trying to 'eat for two', nor was she eating very spicy foods; she was sticking to plain boiled spelt and the breast meat from small birds, as Grata had advised. Altogether, she felt very well, despite the constipation. 'I'm just worried that the baby won't be perfect. The other day I was out shopping and I saw the most pitiful child, whose head was all misshapen, and another one with a harelip. Then coming home I passed a dwarf. What if there's something wrong with my child?'

'Why should there be?' said Senovara stoutly. 'You're doing everything you're supposed to do, and you dedicate to your household gods every day, don't you?'

Adnamata nodded.

'Can you feel the baby moving?'

'Moving! He kicks like an onager.'

'Well, that sounds as if everything is working properly. But Grata thought you might like to have this amulet for extra reassurance.' Senovara fished in her basket and brought out the small red egg. 'She says you're to carry it with you at all times and roll it around in your hand whenever you feel anxious. She also said she'll come to see you in the next few days. You need to start thinking about preparing all you need for the birth, and she'll be able to advise you about what you should have ready; you know, like olive oil, pieces of wool and bandages.'

'Bandages!' Adnamata sounded alarmed and Senovara hastened to reassure her.

'To swaddle the baby in, of course, after he's been washed and sprinkled with salt.'

Adnamata relaxed. 'I'd forgotten about swaddling. Grata will have to give me a list of everything we need, or I'll forget something vital. It was kind of her to send me the amulet, though.'

She held it up to the light from the unshuttered window. The dark red stone glowed and seemed to have a life of its own. Senovara thought it looked frightening and reassuring at the same time.

'Do you think I'm carrying a boy or a girl?' asked Adnamata suddenly.

'Well, I'd guess a boy. You've got a good colour in your face, and, if it's kicking well, that also tends to point to a boy. Grata will be better able to judge, though. I've never known her to get it wrong. Do you have a preference?'

'I haven't – I just want it to arrive safely. But Veturius wants a boy. I suppose he feels that he's spent most of his adult life looking after females, first with Broginara and then with me, so he'd like a boy to bring up.' Senovara looked puzzled, so Adnamata added, 'You knew he was my guardian before we married, didn't you?'

Senovara hadn't and wanted to learn more.

'Well, my father died when I was fourteen. My mother had already died when I was a small child and my father used to worry about what would happen to me if I was left alone – both my parents were single children, you see. So he asked Veturius if he would take over as my *pater familias* if the need arose. Pater and Veturius had joined the army together and served in the same unit for many years, until they both were promoted to centurial rank. Then Pater was killed during manoeuvres. Veturius was stationed at another fort by then, but he got special leave of absence and came straight away. He took me back with him as soon as the funeral rites were completed. I was so young then that he didn't think there would be any problem – Broginara was already living with him and he presumed I'd marry one day, but I suppose I wasn't a very attractive young woman and no one asked. When I got to the age of twenty he began to worry that people would start to talk, so he decided to marry me himself. We'd become quite fond of each other over the years – he's an easy man to be proud of – so I was quite happy to agree.'

Senovara was rather shocked by this matter-of-fact attitude to marriage, but on reflection thought the story explained a great deal that had puzzled her about the Pannonians: the difference in age between Veturius and his wife, the way Adnamata treated him more like a father than a husband, and, probably, why Broginara had been so stunned to learn that her sister-in-law was pregnant.

There was a great difference in age between Quintus and herself, of course, but their story had been much more satisfactory, in her opinion. She had often accompanied her father on his trips to Eboracum, so it had been only a matter of time before she had visited Quintus' shop to buy shoes. The first time it was her father, Totius, who had needed a pair of boots. Quintus had just retired from the army and set up his workshop in one of the wooden huts outside the fortress gates. She had been sixteen, as skinny as a *pilum*, with long brown plaits which hung down over her shoulders. Quintus had offered her a stool to sit on, just as if she were an important customer, and she had sat watching enthralled as her father stood on the leather and had his measurements taken. She blushed to recall how fascinated she had been by her future husband during that first meeting. He had been so kind, so strong and so efficient in his work, though hardly a romantic figure, as she'd be the first to admit. When her father returned to collect his boots, Senovara had not been able to go along, as her mother had wanted her to help with the beehives, so it was a while before she had seen the bootmaker again.

The second time it had been she and the boys who needed some sandals. Her father was pleased with his boots so had decided that when the rest of his family needed new sandals they should go back to Quintus. It had been a great outing – the last they had had together before her cousin Bodenius had joined the army. She, Matugenus, Bodenius and Amatus had sung songs and told jokes all the way to Eboracum until her father cried out for some peace and quiet while he negotiated his way through the narrow streets that had sprung up in the settlement. It had taken quite a time for them all to have their feet measured and Quintus, with great good nature, had entertained the boys by telling them stories of his army life. Her father had declared him to be not only a good bootmaker but a decent, sensible man, and had developed a habit of visiting the shop for a gossip and a tankard of ale whenever he was in Eboracum.

Senovara had never known for sure when he decided that Quintus was the man for his daughter; her father had never said and, being a sensible man himself, had allowed the two of them to get to know each other without any hint that he had matrimonial plans for them. She had often wondered if Quintus had said anything to Totius about being interested in her during one of those visits, but he would never say. Just teased her about how skinny she had been and how he'd waited, for his own comfort, to see if she would round out. But when she turned twenty he had come to the farm, wearing his best clothes, to ask for a betrothal ceremony with the stated aim of marrying her the following year, after he had moved his home and business from his first wooden workshop to the premises they now lived in. Her father had asked her if she was willing, according to the custom, and she had said yes immediately, having no doubts by that time.

Senovara looked at her Pannonian friend and asked if she had had a betrothal ceremony.

'No. There was no point. Veturius already had all my worldly goods under his control; he'd been holding my dowry in trust. We just went to Veturius' legate and got our marriage registered. I don't even have a marriage contract.'

'But doesn't that mean you could have trouble proving your marriage is legal?' Senovara thought of Ursa's problems.

'Oh, there should be no difficulty. Veturius has a copy of the registration and we will, of course, register our child's birth, which will be further proof.'

Senovara was not convinced. As a young bride she had been excited about the preparations for her betrothal ceremony but had felt the legal negotiations to be an unnecessary fuss. Since moving to Eboracum, however, she had met a number of women who, like Ursa, could not prove that their children were legitimate, and others whose husbands had suddenly repudiated their marriage vows on the grounds that they had signed nothing. The knowledge that Quintus' friend Sacer had a copy of their marriage contract in his care now seemed very comforting.

Not that she had ever worried that Quintus would divorce her; their marriage was a success, even though they came from different provinces and there was nearly thirty years' difference in their ages. It was rare that these differences made themselves felt. There had been the argument about what metal her betrothal ring should be made from, but that had mostly been an argument between Quintus and himself. As a Roman citizen he felt that a betrothal ring should be of iron, but his German upbringing kept telling him that an iron finger-ring was a symbol of slavery. It was this same upbringing that made him firm in the belief that a man and his wife should be equals, and he had worried about this contradiction for weeks until she had told him that she would prefer an iron ring because her mother's ring had been of iron.

There had also been the tricky question of the dowry. Quintus had stated that in his tribe the husband traditionally brought his future in-laws oxen, a horse with a bridle, and a shield with a spear and a sword, while the bride gave her betrothed weapons; but neither family needed weapons and Totius had enough oxen and horses for his needs already. They had compromised eventually on a sum of money and an amphora of wine for the betrothal feast, and Senovara had bought Quintus a fine knife with a carved bone handle.

After all the excitement of the betrothal, the marriage ceremony had been a bit of an anticlimax. By then Senovara was eager to start married life and had seen no need to wait any longer. The whole family had ridden into Eboracum to meet Quintus and his brother at the fortress, where they all witnessed the marriage contract being signed in front of the Legate; then they all went back to the shop to a simple meal and a great number of toasts to their health and happiness. It had been a happy family day and Senovara felt sorry that Adnamata had been denied such an occasion. Having that family support had been important. Senovara remembered feeling both happy and sad as she had waved her relatives off when they left to return to the farm without her. Happy that she was now a properly married woman with a good husband; sad that she was no longer her father's responsibility. Yet, even as she had stood in the street waving, she had known that she could go back whenever she wanted; that she had a family who would worry about her and who would make sure that Quintus kept to his marriage contract. Adnamata and many women like her had no such support. If anything happened to their husbands or if their marriages failed they were on their own, their families either too far away to help or no longer able to.

Senovara shook herself. This would never do. She had come to cheer Adnamata up, not worry about the insecurity of marriage.

'Have you seen anything of Vibia Pacata?' she asked.

'She's called several times but I believe she and her husband aren't expecting to be here much longer. He's to be transferred up to the frontier to take command of a century of auxiliaries.'

Senovara was sorry to hear it. She had enjoyed talking to the woman from Lepcis Magna, whose two children were of similar ages to Lucius and Ertola, but, despite a couple of visits to each other and meetings in the houses of friends, they had had little real opportunity to get to know each other. The women in the fortress didn't go to the water troughs in the civilian settlement and had less need to shop in the marketplace, because their husbands drew military rations and they usually had slaves to shop for them. They rarely stayed long, in Senovara's experience. The legates and tribunes usually had three-year postings, while the centurions seemed to be constantly on the move. Possibly when the legions had left the frontier in the control of the auxiliary units everyone would settle down and there would be less movement, but at the moment no one attached to the military knew from one day to the next where they would be.

'Veturius isn't likely to be moved back north, is he?'

'Not that he has told me. I hope not. Vercovicium was a horrible place. I was always expecting that we'd be attacked by the northern tribes, and it constantly seemed to be raining. I was glad to leave. Even with the mists from the rivers, Eboracum is much nicer.'

Senovara was startled. 'Were you ever attacked? Quintus' brother has never said anything in his letters about raids on the frontier.'

'No. Veturius used to tell me I was being silly; that the most rebellious tribes were too far to the north to be able to reach Vercovicium without our army getting plenty of warning. I heard of a few night raids by the Novantae on the coast near Alauna, but he used to shrug those off as being merely by cattle rustlers. I was never very comfortable about it, though, despite his assurances.'

Listening to Adnamata's high-pitched, breathy voice, Senovara realised that here was a woman who would always worry about everything that happened around her; who would never be relaxed about the world she lived in. Her worries about her pregnancy were part of her general attitude to life, but then, her experiences to date had reduced her certainty to her husband and her sister-in-law; everything else had proved transitory. Senovara hoped she would have an easy time of it in childbirth and that the child would be born healthy. She was glad she had brought Grata's amulet and, as she made her farewells, she reminded Adnamata to keep the stone egg with her at all times. Having something to hold on to might give the Pannonian girl the strength she so obviously needed.

On her return home she showed Quintus the tiny amber amulet Grata had given her.

He looked at it with interest. 'I've never handled amber before,' he said. 'I've seen it occasionally but never felt it. One of my old army messmates used to call it "lynx urine", but I've also heard it called "the snatcher", because it picks up leaves and pieces of straw. It gives you a strange sensation when you rub it, doesn't it?'

Senovara felt that this was what made it so powerful and proved its link to the gods.

'It's odd to think how far this has travelled,' Quintus continued. 'Merchants trading with the islands in the Northern Ocean bring it back, you know?'

Senovara wasn't particularly interested in where it came from, only that it would help her daughter. 'The hole isn't very big, Quintus. Do you have a strip of leather fine enough?'

'Leather that fine would just snap. You'd be better off using woollen thread.'

Senovara went through to their bedroom and looked in the cupboard where she kept her tunics. At one side she had a few balls of wool for mending clothes; one ball of cream wool looked fine enough. She carried it through to the kitchen and cut off a length with a knife; then, licking her thumb and forefinger, she rubbed the cut end to make a point and threaded it through the amulet.

She stuck her head out of the back door and saw Ertola and Lucius chasing each other round the apple tree.

'Ertola, come here. I've got something for you.'

The little girl trotted up the garden on her short, sturdy legs, the sun picking out the red highlights in her fair curls and a look of pleased anticipation on her round rosy face.

'Here you are, little one,' said Senovara, tying the wool round her daughter's neck. 'Here is a pretty amber bead to keep you safe. You mustn't take it off,' she added warningly as Ertola pulled at the amulet. 'It's very important that you keep it on all the time.'

She looked consideringly at the warm yellow bead as it lay at Ertola's throat. Would it work? she wondered. Ertola said nothing.

Augustus

S ENOVARA HAD BEEN up since dawn, panicking. Had she thought of everything she and the children would need while they were away? Would Quintus be able to cope on his own?

Quintus watched her in amusement. 'You aren't going to Cappadocia,' he said, 'only to your brother's. He has, as I recall, a perfectly civilised home with food and water and all the modern amenities.'

'I know, I know. You needn't scoff. I realise I'm fussing but I just know I'll forget something vital.'

At this moment Lucius trotted into the kitchen. 'Can I take the hedgehog to Uncle's?' he asked.

'No!' his parents barked in unison.

'There'll be other hedgehogs at the farm,' Senovara put in quickly, seeing on Lucius' face the mulish look that usually preceded a temper tantrum.

'There'll also be sheep and ducks and hens and cows and pigs,' added Quintus consolingly.

Lucius brightened up. 'And dogs?'

'And dogs,' affirmed Senovara. 'Hylax will stay here to look after your father and make sure he isn't lonely.'

Quintus' eyebrows rose at this but he didn't interrupt.

'And you can make friends with the farm dogs,' Senovara continued, 'but don't forget to take Borysthenes. Aunt Ahteha will want to see him.'

Lucius ran off to find his wooden horse and his parents gave a sigh of relief at another tantrum avoided.

'I've left a cooked leg of lamb for you to slice for your meals. Make sure you keep it out of Hylax's way and covered with a cloth to keep the flies off—'

'Stop fussing, woman. I looked after myself for many years before I met you. Aye, and took my turn cooking for my messmates. We didn't starve and I didn't poison anyone. I'll be fine.'

Senovara smiled sheepishly. She knew he was perfectly capable of looking after himself, but she couldn't help worrying. The point of the visit to her brother's farm was to get the children out of the disease-ridden settlement, but her husband would still be in danger.

The weather had got hotter and hotter throughout Iulius, with no rain to flush through the sewers. At first people had welcomed the warmth and sunshine; welcomed the long days when they could work into the evening or sit outside their front doors in rare moments of relaxation; but it hadn't been long before they started to complain that this was the worst drought Eboracum had ever had, and to worry that the settlement must have offended the gods. Every unusual event over the past few months was now identified by the gossipers in the market or the bathhouse as a sign of the gods' anger. The new star which some said had appeared in the sky in Februarius and the lunar eclipse in Maius were considered to have been particularly bad omens, which should have been heeded at the time. The authorities had eventually stepped in and conducted a series of official sacrifices in order to placate the gods, but to no avail.

By the end of Iulius the river had shrunk so low that the ships could no longer get near the quay and had to lie out beyond a bank of grey, fetid mud. The sailors had to lay boards down so that they could get across to their ships without sinking into the mud but there were times during the day when the smell and the flies meant that no one could venture near the riverbank. The worst area was where the main sewer from the fortress reached the river; the retreat of the water had left the stone arch of the outfall high and dry, and all day long the air was filled with the sound of flies feasting on the human waste left marooned on the surface of the mud.

As the heat continued and still the rain did not come, the smell in the stagnant air became overpowering, particularly in those streets where there were gaps between the flagstones over the drains. And everywhere there were the flies – small, biting flies which filled the air in a haze as they swarmed over the dried-up water troughs; big, fat, black flies which crawled sluggishly over anything which might provide food. Senovara shuddered as she remembered finding Ertola lying asleep in her cot one afternoon with dozens of flies crawling over her mouth and eyes. When she had snatched the child up, brushing away the flies, she had found in the bedding a half-eaten honey cake which Ertola had been sucking when she fell asleep. That had been the deciding factor for Senovara and she had started to nag at Quintus to let her take the children out to her brother's farm.

Quintus was at first unhappy about it. 'There are flies in the country,' he pointed out. 'The animals attract them.'

But even he had started to worry when people began to fall ill. He had seen this sort of contagion strike armies on campaign. Some people were struck down with a high fever and lay on their beds, rolling their heads from side to side, whimpering as they fought off the demons. Not everyone who got the fever died; the people who had the diarrhoea and sickness, however, were all fated and the wails of the mourners added to the more usual sounds of the town.

At first the contagion had been confined to the oldest parts of the settlement closest to the quayside. Then it spread to the encampment on the other bank of the river before spreading away from the Abus. When the eight-year-old daughter of the barber in the next street died, after a sickness which lasted just one day, Quintus had immediately sent a message to Matugenus via a carter who passed the farm regularly. The next evening had brought the welcome news that Matugenus would take Senovara and the children back with him the following day when he came in to the market. His message included the warning that he intended to arrive in Eboracum early, travelling in the cool of the morning, but would be leaving at midday. With so much illness in the town he had no intention of staying to talk to friends; he would just sell his goods and leave as quickly as possible.

As she bustled about gathering what she needed for the journey, Senovara was not bothered about why disease had come to the town, which deity was displeased with the people, or what the authorities should do about it. She just wanted to get her children away. She would feel safe in the familiar surroundings of the farm where the old gods would protect her.

There was a shout out in the street, and Quintus stuck his head round the door. 'Matugenus is here.'

Senovara was suddenly afraid to go. This would be the first time she and Quintus had been separated since they had married, and she felt guilty that she was leaving him to face the forces of the malign gods alone.

Quintus, interpreting her look accurately, took her in his arms and hugged her. 'Don't worry. I'm a tough old veteran, remember? If the Dacians and the Caledonians couldn't finish me off, the gods of disease won't manage it.'

Silently, Senovara asked the gods to forgive him for daring to tempt their anger. He had once told her that disease had killed more of his comrades than had fallen in battle. In particular, she was trying to keep from her mind his story of a time in the east when strapping young men had succumbed and perished, tent by tent. Even now he sometimes woke at night sweating with the memory of the survivor's set faces as they cremated their colleagues – he said the stench of burned flesh had hung over the camp for days. Everyone in Eboracum had been aware of that smell a few times over the last few days, and Senovara knew it had revived her husband's memory of that old campaign and lay behind his decision to send his family away.

He put her away from him gently. 'Everything will be fine. Get your bags now; Matugenus will want to be off.'

She wiped her eyes with her sleeve and smiled damply as Lucius pounded into the room, dragging his uncle behind him.

'Come on, Mater,' he demanded. 'Uncle Matugenus is ready to go.'

'But I've only just got here,' protested Matugenus as he hugged his sister.

'I'm sure you've got time to have a beaker of wine or a tankard of beer before you set off,' invited Quintus, slapping his brother-in-law on the back. 'If I know anything about it, there'll be several false starts to this journey. Senovara has been packing and unpacking all morning so something vital is bound to be forgotten.'

'Some beer will take the taste of the market out of my mouth,' agreed Matugenus, 'but I don't want to delay too long.'

'Have you eaten?' asked his sister.

'No, but I was going to suggest that you brought some food with you. We could stop on the road somewhere, like we used

to when Father brought us in to the market.' He picked up
Ertola and waved her above his head. 'Hello, young lady.'

Ertola cooed at him and pulled his long moustache. He
laughed and held her on his knee as he sat down to drink the
beer that Armea handed him.

While the men drank and exchanged gossip, Senovara and
Armea wrapped some bread and slices of meat in a cloth and
made up a jug of water and vinegar, stoppering it firmly with
a clay bung covered with cloth, before putting everything in a
basket. Lucius hopped from foot to foot in impatience, annoyed
at having his adventure delayed.

At last Quintus drained his cup and stood up. 'Are you taking
Ertola's cot?'

'If there's room in the cart.' Senovara looked at her brother
enquiringly.

'Plenty of room. Why don't we put the cot on board and
then pile your bags on top of it? We can tie the cot down with
rope to stop it sliding about.'

Quintus went into the children's room, picked up the wooden
cot and carried it outside to where a dusty mule and its cart stood
patiently waiting, tied to a window shutter. The cart already had
a number of baskets on it but by moving these about room was
made for the cot. Quintus' old leather army bag and a couple of
bundles tied in sacking were squashed on top.

'In you get, Lucius,' said his uncle, hoisting the squirming
child on to the seat. 'You sit next to me at the front, and when
we get out of the town and the road is quiet you can take
the reins.'

Lucius' eyes shone and he bounced about on the wooden
seat in anticipation. Quintus patted Senovara's shoulder as
he helped her up beside her son. He would never dream of
showing open affection to his wife in public, and she had
ceased to expect it. The cart was high, and she had to use
the hub of the eight-spoked wheel as a step so that she could

climb over the side. She settled herself as comfortably as she could on the low bench at the front of the cart, gathering as much of her dress and cloak fabric as possible under her bottom to cushion the jolting of the iron-clad wheels on the hard road surface and to stop her skirts flying up in the wind – Matugenus was unlikely to be able to rouse the mule to anything faster than a trot and there was not a breath of wind, but she had learned that it was better to plan for modesty than to be caught unawares.

Armea handed Ertola up to Senovara and then clambered unassisted into the back of the cart, fitting herself among the luggage.

'Hold on tight,' Quintus told his son firmly, 'and look after your mother and sister for me.'

Lucius reddened, clearly overwhelmed by this new responsibility.

'We'll send messages back with one of the carters,' Matugenus said as he climbed up onto his seat. 'If you decide to come as well, just turn up.'

The men's eyes met in silent understanding. If the rains didn't come in a few days and the pestilence got worse, Quintus might well wish to join his family. Senovara was too busy making sure her children were safely secured on the cart to be fully aware of the exchange, but when the mule started to move off she turned to gaze at her husband, fighting back her tears, until they turned the corner of the street.

Beyond the huddle of the houses the road ran between rows of graves. The cemetery had been quite small until a few weeks ago, but now there were fresh mounds on both sides of the road and eddies of smoke filled the air from the funeral pyres of those whose native tradition demanded cremation. Few of the rectangular burial mounds or the circular cremation graves had tombstones. The stonemasons were going to be busy later in the year, but people were too concerned with their health and trying to keep their businesses going through this frightening summer to spend time and money on tombstones. Cynics said it was wiser to wait until the disease was over, so that you knew how many people could be included in the inscription on a single tombstone, rather than face the expense of several memorials.

As the cart ambled along, Senovara heard pipes and horns to her left and turned her head to see a funeral procession making its way towards a newly dug grave. The bier, which held a plain wooden coffin, was carried by six men led by a hired group of wailing mourners, all with their heads covered. The members of the family followed behind, carrying flagons of wine and oil or baskets of food, ready to pour libations and serve the funerary feast. The lack of decoration on the bier and the plainness of the coffin indicated that this was not a wealthy family. Senovara hoped they were not burying their breadwinner.

Beyond the procession, she could see a funeral pyre waiting for another victim, its builders stacking the logs in neat rows, first one way, then placing the next layer at right angles across the first. Some families followed the Roman custom of conducting their funerary rites at night but Senovara had noticed that, such was the fear of the pestilence, many were burying their dead as soon as was decently possible. She was, however, interested to see one small huddled group sitting round a grave sharing a meal – it would appear that some people were determined to accord their relatives the rite of the *cena novendialis*, the ritual meal held at the graveside on the ninth day, despite the dangers.

Eventually the mule cart left the town and its cemetery behind and the air freshened perceptibly. The sight of the fields and woods that she had passed so often as a young girl calmed her, and she started to point out items of interest to the children: a sparrowhawk hunting its prey fascinated Lucius while Ertola crowed with delight at the sight of a hare sitting up in the middle of a meadow. A few times she was worried that Lucius was going to fall out of the cart as he tried to take everything in, even though he was firmly wedged between her and Matugenus.

As they crossed the main river to the east, a hilly ridge could be seen in the far distance, blue in the haze.

'Look, Senovara. There's the hill at the back of the farm, can you see?' Matugenus pointed at the horizon.

Senovara's eyes searched across the flat plain and the wetlands in front of them, eagerly seeking this first indication that she was nearing her old home. They still had several hours of travel ahead, but the low chalk ridge which ran to the north-east of their farm was the only high ground for miles around and could be seen from a great distance. As a child she had often climbed to the top of that hill and gazed to the west, keen to see the smoke that indicated the growing settlement of Eboracum.

After an hour's travelling between small copses and square fields, they stopped by a stream and, while the mule drank and cropped the grass surviving on its banks, Senovara unwrapped the meat and bread and shared out the food. The air was drowsy with the sound of insects but this was a friendlier sound than the constant drone of the town flies and she felt herself relaxing. She and Matugenus used to pester their mother to be allowed to take some food down to the river at the farm when they were children and it seemed barely a year between those long-off days and now; but, as she looked at her son lying on his tummy, watching the small silvery fish flashing about in the shallow water, and her daughter contentedly picking a daisy to pieces, she realised how much time had passed since those days and sighed.

'Yes, we must be on our way,' said her brother, misinterpreting the sigh. 'Come on, children. We have a stream at home and you can watch the fish there.'

He picked them up, one under each arm, and set them in the cart before they could protest. Armea packed the basket and they all climbed back onto the cart.

'Now, Lucius,' said Matugenus, 'you can drive.' He put an arm round the boy and gave him the reins.

'Look. You hold the reins like this.' He folded a small hand round the leather. 'You don't need to pull hard, old Lampon knows the way.' He clicked his tongue and the mule obligingly started to move along the gravelled road.

As they neared the farm, Senovara was surprised to see that some of the harvest had been gathered in already and commented on this to Matugenus.

'Yes, we've already got the barley in and threshed it, too. It's been so hot and dry that the grasslands up on the ridge have burned, so we've had to thresh the barley earlier than usual to provide the sheep with some fodder. We couldn't bring them down because the lower clays have baked solid. I've never seen such deep, wide cracks – I could put my stick down them. The sheep would have broken their legs and I wasn't willing to risk the dogs on it, either, so I send a man up each day with barley straw for the flock. It wasn't a good crop this year – thin and patchy because of the weather – but I'm hoping for a good wheat yield. We'll probably start cutting the four-*iugerum* field soon.'

Matugenus took the reins from Lucius and guided the mule cart into the track that led to the farm. Up on the chalk ridge behind the farm compound Senovara could just make out the marooned sheep. Below the seared grasslands there were wheat fields on the clay lands to the north, while to the right of the track the shorn barley fields and a few small meadows ran off to the south-east. A herd of short-legged black cows sheltered from the heat in the shadow of a copse. Bees droned lazily among the plants that still flowered between the fields and along the edge of the track, accompanied by the chaffing of grasshoppers.

The track led up to an open gate in the stone wall that enclosed the farmhouse and its barns and outbuildings, as well as an orchard and vegetable garden. As Matugenus drove through the narrow opening with practised skill, Senovara felt a wave of affection for her old home. The farmhouse looked drowsy in the early afternoon haze; the sun reflecting off its whitewashed walls almost blinded her as she drank in the familiar scene. Several pigeons sat sleeping on the ridge of the red-tiled roof while, behind them, a wisp of smoke from the kitchen rose straight up from the decorative louvre over one gable-end. The wooden shutters were all closed on this side of the house to keep out the heat, and at first there appeared to be no one around. Then she noticed a figure by the beehives in the orchard and another working in the vegetable garden.

The mule cart drew to a halt in front of the verandah that ran along the front of the central range of the house, linking its two wings. Immediately, her grandmother came through the open door and hurried down the steps to welcome them, as energetic as ever despite the heat, followed more sedately by a tall, elegant girl of about Senovara's age. Senovara greeted her grandmother

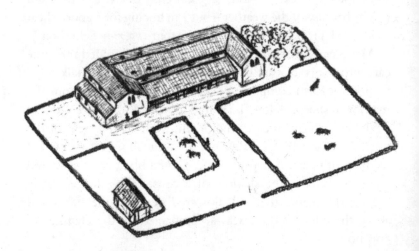

and sister-in-law cheerfully and handed down a sleepy Ertola. Lucius leaped down unaided. Armea's parents appeared from the back of the building, and welcomed Senovara courteously before hugging their daughter. All at once the peace of the summer's afternoon was shattered by the bustle of arrival as the other house servants and a couple of farmhands came out of one of the outbuildings and started to unpack the cart, with Matugenus supervising which packages needed to go into the house and which were destined for the barn.

All the servants, whether slaves or freedmen, hailed Senovara enthusiastically and she felt overwhelmed by their obvious delight at seeing her again. She had known most of them all her life, growing up with the younger ones, accepting the older ones as part of the scenery. There had been a close relationship between the children on the farm. She and Matugenus and their two cousins had played with the labourers' children, including them in their games, yet had not questioned why, as they got older, the other children gradually had more and more tasks to do and were not always able to play. Matugenus had always been the leader in their games, of course; even though some of the other children were older and bigger, there was an unspoken understanding that he was the young master and would eventually be their owner.

There had been a similar mixture of respect and familiarity with the farm workers and house slaves. If any of the children misbehaved, the servants reprimanded them – although they had, on occasion, conspired with the children to keep some of their misdeeds from her father's ears. If she fell down, one of the farm slaves always picked her up and comforted her, yet if she ordered one of them to fetch something they obeyed without argument. Senovara couldn't remember anyone explaining to her the relationship between those in the landowner's family and those who were owned by him; she had just grown up surrounded by a certainty and understanding of the way their small world worked. Now, as she noticed Lucius and Ertola eyeing two farm children peeping round the corner of the house, she knew they would also be absorbed in the same easy way into the complex community which made up the farm.

After they had eaten that evening, Matugenus rose from the table and looked at his sister with a smile.

'I need to look round the farm to see what has been happening while I've been in Eboracum. Would you three like to come with me?'

'I think I need to put Ertola to bed – she's already falling asleep – but take Lucius; it will give him a chance to get to know the farm.'

Her son jumped down from his stool, delighted at this unexpected treat. Senovara wiped his face with a cloth, then watched from the door with Ertola in her arms as the two headed off across the farm courtyard. Matugenus had strode off holding Lucius' hand firmly but forgetting that his nephew only had short legs. The child had to run as fast as he could to keep up.

Matugenus reported back on the success of this trip later that evening, after Lucius had at last been persuaded to go to bed.

'He wasn't too interested in the chickens but the ducks on the pond fascinated him.'

'I'm not surprised,' Senovara laughed. 'Some of our neighbours keep chickens but there are no ponds in Eboracum. Lucius has seen ducks hanging up on stalls in the market or when you've brought us one, but they've always been dead or in crates. He probably didn't realise that they can swim. What did he think of the other animals? He's seen cattle, sheep and pigs being driven through the streets to the market, but I usually keep the children in the house when the drovers bring the stock through; the animals are so frightened when they find themselves in the streets that you can't trust them.'

'He was a bit wary at first, but a few of the calves are still quite small so he soon got used to them. He said the old sow and her piglets were his favourites.'

Senovara smiled. 'He certainly couldn't stop talking about them when I put him to bed. He declared that meeting the old sow was the best bit of the most exciting day of his life.'

Ahteha laughed. 'I hope you'll be able to stay with us long enough for the children to get to know the animals. The last time you all visited was when Matugenus and I got betrothed. Ertola was just a baby then and Lucius was too young to remember much about it.'

'I'm only grateful that you and Matugenus were willing to let us escape the drought and disease in Eboracum, but you're right, it will also be a good opportunity for Lucius and Ertola to get to know what life is like on a farm. So many children who live around the fortress have never been outside the *vicus*, which is odd when you think how far some of their parents have travelled to get to Eboracum. Lucius' friend Castus has never been out of the town, yet his father comes from Mauretania and his mother from Gallia. No doubt when Castus gets older he'll join the army, too, and see more of the Empire, but that won't be for another twelve years.'

'Lucius told me he's decided that he doesn't want to be a soldier any more. His visit has already persuaded him to become a farmer instead,' chortled his uncle.

'We'll get him working in the fields and see if he's still of the same mind in a few days' time,' Enica said cynically.

Senovara soon settled into her old home, with Lucius and herself automatically talking in her old dialect to her family and the farmhands. She had been anxious about how Ertola would react to finding herself surrounded by people who didn't speak Latin in their everyday conversations but realised that her daughter had become used to listening to her talking to Armea and seemed to understand what was said to her, even if she didn't answer. Armea was obviously delighted to be home again, and whenever she had a spare moment took the children round the farm, showing them the animals, flowers and trees.

Ten days after their arrival, Matugenus decided it was time to harvest one of the wheat fields. When Senovara said she was looking forward to it, her brother teased her that she had forgotten what hard work it was; but she had been surprised by how easily she had adapted to the work of the farm after all the years she had been away and thought she would be able to play her part in the harvest like everyone else. It was decided that Ertola would stay with Enica in the house, because it was too hot in the fields, and Senovara and Ahteha would take Lucius with them to join the farm workers. Senovara covered her son's bare legs with mud mixed with animal fat to keep off the sun and warned him to keep his hat on all day, and they set off.

Although they arrived early, they found Matugenus and one of the farm men already working their way at a steady pace through the big four-*iugerum* field, the sharp iron blades of their sickles flashing in the sun at each stroke. They had started by cutting a strip round three edges of the field and one down the centre, dividing the field into two, and were now moving towards the centre of one half. Women and children were twisting bands out of the straw to bind the short stems of the cut wheat together into sheaves, two men following each team to stook the sheaves. Senovara showed Lucius how to twist the straw to make a stout binding, gradually drawing more straw in to form a rope. He couldn't get the hang of it straight away, but she was pleased to find that she hadn't lost the knack.

Throughout the day Senovara worked alongside her sister-in-law binding the sheaves. Everyone found it too hot to talk and the work was done in a silence broken only by the screaming of the many birds that circled around, landing every now and again to snatch some fallen grain, until driven away by the two gleaners, who were also salvaging what they could of the precious wheat that had been shaken out during the harvesting. Sweat trickled down the workers' faces and Senovara's eyes and nostrils smarted and tickled as the dust and chaff stuck to her skin. She took off her shady straw hat and wiped her forehead with her arm. It was a long time since she had done this sort of work, and she was ashamed that her hands were cut across the palms from the sharp edges of the straw. Her ankles itched with many small scratches from the stubble. She flexed her shoulders, reflecting ruefully on how stiff she would be the next day, before bending again to her task.

At the end of the day, when the cutters had got to the centre of the diminishing stand of wheat, the dogs were sent in to flush out the hares that had retreated before the advancing harvesters. The dogs yelped and snarled as they drove the hares into the nets of the waiting men, encouraged by the shouts and yells of the other harvesters and the whooping cries of Lucius and the farm children, who capered about excitedly, getting in everyone's way. When a hare was caught, the net was twisted quickly round to secure it before a skilful pull on its neck killed it. Only three hares were caught on the first day, and everyone hoped for a better bag when they cut the second half of the field the following day.

By the fourth evening they had finished the big field and a pair of smaller, two-*iugerum* fields. Senovara was tired, yet restless as well. After the evening meal she let herself out of the house and walked through the fields to the stream.

It was good to be back. Although she had got used to living in Eboracum with its noise and bustle, she was sometimes overwhelmed by homesickness for green fields and woods. Particularly on a summer evening like this, when she sometimes dreamed of doing just what she was doing now – sitting on the old fallen oak by the side of the stream, watching the kingfishers flashing in and out of the banks. It had been a hot day but here in the country it was different. In Eboracum the air would have been stifling, hardly moving between the close-packed houses, the natural heat of the day mingling with the heat of cooking fires and workshop hearths. Here in the fields, the air moved and stirred with the breeze from the stream. Even in the house it was cooler than her own home would have been. The kitchen was hot – all kitchens were hot – but in the rest of the house the shutters kept the heat out and the cool stone floors made walking comfortable. There was none of that sense of having to push through the air that she had felt in town over the past few weeks. She missed Quintus and was worried about how he was coping on his own. She hoped he would be coming to check on his family soon. She intended to try to persuade him to stay, rather than go back to disease-ridden Eboracum. Playing with Lucius and Ertola in the fields and woods and walking round the farm with his brother-in-law would be good for him, and much safer than working in Eboracum.

The children were having a wonderful time. They had already become familiar with the kitchen slaves, particularly Armea's mother, Alogiosa, whom they could rely on for titbits. Lucius spent every minute he could with his uncle and was turning brown from running about in the sun – Quintus would hardly recognise him. Senovara thought again how strange it was that so many of her neighbours never left the confines of the town or took their children out into the country. She had mentioned this to Broginara one day and the Pannonian woman had laughed and said, 'You're right. Until I started to travel the world with my brother I had never set foot outside Aquincum. Army families tend to stay put until they have to move, and then they often move to new provinces, not to the next town, crossing oceans rather than mere hills.' Senovara gazed at the stream in front of her. This was as much water as she wanted to cross. She had often looked at the ships in the quayside in Eboracum and wondered at the bravery of the sailors and merchants who sailed in them. She had heard tales of mighty tempests and dreadful sea monsters. No wonder the ships had good luck symbols painted on them.

A dark shape wheeled over her head. The bats were coming out from their roosting places in the roof of the barn. She must remember to show Lucius and Ertola how they hung there upside down, like bunches of black grapes. Her grandmother was putting the children to bed tonight. No doubt both of them would be badly spoiled if they stayed much longer, but Enica enjoyed pampering her great-grandchildren so much.

Ahteha and Matugenus had been married for over two years now, but there was no sign of a child. Enica was beginning to get worried and had confided in Senovara earlier that day.

'You couldn't send a charm or potion from Eboracum when you go back, could you?'

'I certainly couldn't,' Senovara had responded firmly. 'It's up to Ahteha and Matugenus to worry about that, if they are worrying. They might be waiting for a while.'

'Waiting! What do they need to wait for? This is a good farm and Matugenus needs a son to learn from him and take over in time, as Matugenus did from his own father.'

Senovara had made soothing noises; her grandmother had been just as impatient for her and Quintus to start a family but she had, to be fair, been quite satisfied when they had decided to stick to the usual custom and have only two. Enica had declared that she was not an advocate of large families: they led to the unnecessary division of land and wealth and the exhaustion of women. Senovara privately thought that Lucius' energy would eventually wear her grandmother out and she would become less keen to fill the house with small children, which would take the pressure off Ahteha. She grinned when she remembered their arrival. Enica had rushed out of the house and enveloped Lucius in a great bear hug and smothered him with kisses. Lucius was not always a demonstrative child and he had emerged from this great-grandmotherly enthusiasm as stiff as a spear. Senovara still didn't feel she knew her sister-in-law very well, even though she had been brought up only a few farms away to the west, and she had been impressed when Ahteha had noticed Lucius' discomfort and had simply laid a hand on his head when she greeted him. She would make a good mother if Enica would let her alone.

The breeze began to freshen and she shivered. It was time to get back to the house. Tomorrow they would start to cut another wheat field and they would have to make an early start to get as much done as possible before it got too hot.

As she walked back, Senovara searched the reddening sky for signs of a break in the weather, but there were no clouds and on the lower ground the breeze disappeared completely. The great expanse of sky was full of stars, their subtle colours beginning to deepen as the light faded. The night insects began to call and whisper; there was never total silence anywhere on the farm, and the sounds of the animals, the birds and the insects made a friendly background hum to the daily round.

When she reached the courtyard she was puzzled to see a cart being led into one of the barns. It seemed rather late for any of the farm hands to have been out – everyone had been too busy with the harvest for a man to be spared for errands. She shrugged. There was probably a perfectly good explanation; perhaps Matugenus had wanted something urgently.

The family had got into the habit of sitting out on the verandah after their evening meal, and in the light of a flickering candle she could see Ahteha bending down to pour a tankard of beer for someone. As her sister-in-law straightened up and moved away, Senovara recognised with joy the grizzled figure of Quintus.

She rushed up the steps onto the verandah and hugged her husband. 'I didn't expect you to come for a few more days yet. Are you all right? How is everyone? Where's Hylax?'

'I left him behind to guard the house,' said Quintus, answering the last question first. 'The army's patrolling the streets in case of looting – there are so many empty properties – and I didn't like to leave the house completely empty, particularly with Hairan and Aqmat being away. Ursa's boys have promised to look after him, so he'll be fine. I'm perfectly fit too, but there didn't seem much point in staying behind any longer; trade in Eboracum has ground to a halt. Everyone is just doing what they have to and the rest of the time they stay in their own homes, trying not to breathe tainted air. There's hardly any water – the army has been bringing it in in barrels and rationing it; what will happen if there's a fire, I dread to think. And people are still dying: the carter from the next street went the day before yesterday, and his widow said that if I'd drive her to her brother's farm near Derventio I could keep his cart and mule. She was pretty desperate to get away. It seemed a sign that I should leave as well, so here I am.'

Senovara listened to this with alarm and began to question him about the welfare of their friends.

'No one in our street has fallen ill yet, thank Salus. I don't know how our military friends fare, though. The fortress has closed its gates – no one is allowed in or out except those soldiers bringing water. If you want water, you have to go to the *porta praetoria* and it's doled out, but there are such queues that it's impossible to ask how anyone inside is or hand over messages. I presume Veturius' family is still well – I haven't heard to the contrary. Surilla is finding life a bit difficult at the moment, though. There is so little water that she can't take in any washing and her income has dried up as much as the Abus.'

'It's all this living in towns that brings the pestilence,' Enica announced. 'People were never meant to live so close together, relying on others to provide their food. Small farms were always good enough for us before the Romans came. I don't know how you can live in Eboracum, surrounded by strangers.'

'Have you always lived here, Enica?' Quintus asked in an attempt to distract her from her well-worn anti-Roman theme.

'No, I was born a few miles to the west in the territory of the Brigantes and came here when I married. Of course, it was very different then,' she reminisced. 'When I arrived my husband still lived in a roundhouse with his parents and his brother, Dignus. It was only when Dignus got married as well that they built the main part of this house – only three rooms to start with. My husband thought it would be better if we had separate accommodation and he preferred the new Roman house plans. I wasn't very impressed, myself; I much preferred the big old roundhouses.'

'What were they like to live in? In Germania we always had rectangular houses; it wasn't until I came to Britannia and served up on the frontier that I saw roundhouses. I never had the opportunity to see inside any, though.'

'Well, they were much bigger than most of the houses in Eboracum are today – I would reckon about as big as our paddock here. The walls were about Lucius' height and were made of split tree trunks. The roof was thatched, of course, so they were very cosy inside. No matter how much it rained or blew outside, inside we were always nice and snug. There was a hearth in the centre, where we did all our cooking, and that fire was never allowed to go out. It was a friendly sight when we trudged back from the fields on a cold night to see the smoke leaking out through the thatch and lying around the roof like a friendly fog.'

'Weren't they smoky inside as well?' asked Senovara.

'Not particularly. The roof was conical and the centre was very high, you see, so all the smoke gathered above our heads. The air did get thick sometimes if the door was open and the wind was in the wrong direction, but usually it was no problem.'

'But who kept the fire going?' Senovara was entranced; her grandmother had often told her stories when she was a child but they had mostly been about spirits or gods; she had rarely talked about her early life.

'Oh, because we all lived together there was always someone at home to keep the fire lit and attend to the cooking; that person was usually the oldest woman in the family. In our case it was my mother-in-law, your great-grandmother. My, she didn't like the new houses at all. Insisted on staying in the roundhouse, but of course she couldn't live in a big hut like that all by herself. First she lived with my brother-in-law in the house which is now the big barn, then with us, then back to Dignus' house, but she never really settled once they'd pulled the old place down. She was always complaining about the noise of the wind battering against the gable-ends of this house – in the old hut you never heard the wind, you see, with it being round. I notice the difference, myself, on a stormy night, but I've got used to it now.'

'Was it the same sort of farm in those days?' Quintus was fascinated by this tale of a life so different to any he had known.

'As far as the animals are concerned. We had more cattle and fewer sheep and also some goats, of course. You had to watch the goats, though. If they got near the roundhouse they'd pull the thatch away from the roof – sometimes jumping up onto the straw and eating great patches so that the rain came in.'

Quintus laughed.

'It was no laughing matter, I can tell you,' the old lady remonstrated. 'If they pulled too much straw away from the edge, the rain got into the walls and rotted them. One of the young slaves had a permanent job keeping the goats away.'

'Is it true that there were wolves around in those days?' Matugenus asked lazily, a wooden tankard of beer in his hand. He was sitting on a stool which he had tipped so that he was leaning against the house, his feet up on the low wall of the verandah. He sounded drowsy after his hard day's work in the wheat field and Senovara suspected he had asked the question in an attempt to stay awake.

'Wolves, bears and wild boars. We had them all in this area but we rarely saw them. They mostly lived up on the moors to the north or in the forests. It was only in the bad winters that they ventured down onto the farmlands to look for food. We sometimes heard the wolves howling on winter evenings, but the dogs kept them away from the buildings and we made sure all the stock was in the compound at night, just in case.'

Senovara shuddered. She remembered hearing the wolves a few times when she was a small child, and the unnerving sound of the farm dogs howling back at them. Decidedly, one of the benefits of the growth of Eboracum, with its roads and the increased prosperity of the surrounding countryside, was that there were more people about, so the wild animals had had to retreat further into the uplands.

'My brother, up on the frontier, says they often hear the wolves in the winter. He's seen bears there as well,' Quintus said.

'I'm amazed there are any bears left,' Matugenus snorted. 'Last time I was down at the quayside at Eboracum I got talking to a merchant who said he'd made most of his fortune shipping bears from the north across to Italia for the games. Apparently the Romans pay huge sums for a good Caledonian bear and then all they do with it is put it in the amphitheatre and cheer a gladiator on to kill it. Seems ridiculous to me – the real sport was catching it in the first place.'

Quintus roared with laughter. 'Come to think of it,' he said, 'it's amazing there are any wild boar left, either. Army officers will ride for miles for a good wild-boar hunt. They even put up altars thanking Silvanus if they catch a particularly big or ferocious one. I had a commanding officer once who wore a great boar's tusk round his neck and considered it a marvellous talisman.'

'Wild boar can do a lot of damage on farmland, particularly when they come in after the farm sows when they're in heat,' put in Enica. 'Mind you, deer do a fair bit, too, and they're still about. Even a small herd can destroy all your crops in a single night, particularly when the shoots are just coming up. That's why we have the big ditches round the farm that Senovara and Matugenus were so fond of rolling down when they were children. Even having venison to eat doesn't make up for the loss of a whole wheat crop at the beginning of the season. But at least you can just shoo them away – a wild boar is a bit difficult to shift if it doesn't want to go. I remember coming across one a few months after I was married. I'd gone into the woods over there to pick blackberries. I walked round the end of one big bush and there was this wild boar glaring at me, his little piggy eyes glittering and his tusks gleaming.'

'Weren't you frightened, Grandmother?' asked Ahteha.

'I'll say I was. I just froze – I couldn't move, I was so frightened. Luckily, my husband and his brother came along just then with some of the farm dogs and they chased the boar off before I'd even thought what I should do next.'

Senovara looked at her grandmother in awe. She had always been warned about the dangers of wild animals when she was a child but it had been a winter problem, brought on by bad weather. She couldn't imagine what it would be like to be surrounded by such dangers all the time, and she realised, with a shock, that her grandmother was talking not about a period lost in the mists of time and recalled only in fireside tales, but of a time only two generations ago. There had indeed been changes since the Romans arrived.

The next morning everyone set off for the fields as the sun rose. Quintus had offered to help, but pointed out that he had no skill in farming.

'Your new cart and mule will be useful, though,' his brother-in-law had declared as they had gone to their beds the night before. 'If you bring them to the fields we'll be able to get on really fast. We've only got two more fields to go.'

So Quintus and Lucius became waggoners for the day and spent a busy time fetching and carrying. When the sun was at its highest, Quintus drove out with Enica and Ertola to bring beer and bread for the workers and was welcomed with a cheer. Everyone headed for a small copse at the edge of the field and settled thankfully in its shade, mopping their brows.

'By the Gods, it's hot today,' complained Matugenus. 'Not a breath of wind.'

'It's going to rain,' announced Enica.

They all looked at her in surprise, then looked up at the sky. There was not a cloud to be seen.

'You mark my words, there will be a storm tonight,' the old lady said firmly. 'I can feel it in my bones.'

Matugenus looked alarmed. Enica's weather forecasts tended to be accurate and he had learned to take them seriously.

'We'd better get on, then,' he said, getting to his feet. 'We've nearly finished this field. If we work hard we might get the smaller field done before the rain starts. We can't afford to lose any of the crop. Briginus!' he shouted to one of the farm hands. 'You take Cenuacus and start on the small field – take a few of the women to help.'

'Ahteha and I will go with them,' his grandmother said, instructing one of the younger women to take Ertola back to the house. Matugenus didn't argue – he knew she'd work until she dropped, and her years of experience told on these occasions.

Halfway through the afternoon, Matugenus looked up at the sky with a frown on his face, aware of a change in the atmosphere. He snapped off an ear of wheat and tasted a grain thoughtfully between his teeth before coming to a decision.

'Quintus,' he called urgently to his brother-in-law. 'It looks as if your new cart is going to be our lifesaver. This corn is already pretty dry – I've never known it to be ready so early

– and I don't want it getting wet again if this turns into a big storm. Take some of the men and start taking the sheaves down to the barn. You might begin with the big field, as that's been stooked for a couple of days already.'

Quintus saluted and urged his mule into a trot across the stubble, calling to two of the men to jump on board.

There was no further rest for anyone that day and they all laboured long into the evening. The two carts had made many journeys between the fields and the barn and the bats were swooping about in the gathering gloom when Matugenus finally declared that they could stop. Joining the workers in the small field, Senovara was amused to see her grandmother and Lucius working as a small yet efficient team, her son determined not to be outdone by the elderly Enica.

Every now and again Senovara had also looked up to check on the weather and when the sun began to sink down towards the west she saw black clouds gathering on the southern horizon. Enica was going to be right again. The air had become heavier and heavier throughout the afternoon, and Senovara found gathering the stalks together into sheaves increasingly difficult as her limbs became weary and unwilling to move. She was relieved when Matugenus at last called for the dogs to be sent in after the hares, and the final stands of wheat could be cut.

Eventually everyone piled onto the two carts and headed slowly back to the compound. Lucius fell asleep as soon as he was lifted onto their new cart and many of the labourers followed his lead. When they reached the house, Senovara lifted her son down and put him to bed, still fast asleep and filthy dirty – he would no doubt wake up in the middle of the night and complain of hunger but she couldn't face him waking up now, querulous with tiredness, when she was worn out herself. Ertola trotted into the bedroom full of energy, having spent most of the day in the kitchen with the cook, and flung herself at her mother.

Senovara groaned. 'I'm sorry, my pretty pet, but I'm too tired to play now. Let's go and see what you and the cook have been doing in the kitchen – I'm hungry.'

Ertola looked disappointed but smiled and, putting a small, confiding hand in her mother's, led the way to supper.

That evening everyone was too tired to sit on the verandah and most of them were in bed almost as soon as they had had their meal. Senovara and Quintus were both asleep the minute they laid down their heads, too tired even for their usual discussion of the day's events.

It seemed to Senovara that she had been asleep for only a moment when she was woken by a great crash of thunder. She sat bolt upright in bed, confused as to where she was. She got out of bed and opened the shutters. Immediately, there was a bright flash as another of Jupiter's lightning bolts was flung down to earth. She flinched, then waited for the thunder to follow. There was a short gap between the two and she knew that the storm was not yet fully upon them. So far there was no rain and she hoped that this would not be one of those summer storms when there was thunder, lightning and wind but no rain – they needed rain badly and wind on its own could be very destructive.

Almost as though Jupiter had heard her, a few raindrops pattered down on the ground in front of her, raising small puffs of dust; then a few more, until there was a curtain of water pouring down from the sky. Behind her, Quintus stirred and woke.

'Is that rain I hear?' he asked, swinging his legs out and coming over to the window.

'Yes, thank Jupiter. But it's quite a downpour – if it stops soon it will just run off and not do any good at all.'

'At least the weather's broken. This will fill the ponds and rivers – it's water we need.'

Senovara shook her head. She was too much a farmer's daughter not to realise that in order to recover from such a severe drought the ground needed steady rain over several days, not a short, heavy cloudburst.

The next morning they woke to blue skies again, but there was a change in the air. No longer was it close and humid. Now there was a stiff breeze from the east and small fluffy clouds were heading purposefully towards them.

As Senovara stood on the verandah looking about her, Matugenus strode in through the gate of the compound.

'Hail, sister.'

'Hail, Matugenus. Has the storm done much damage?'

'No, thank the Mothers. It's lucky there was no wind, but it's a good thing we got the wheat cut yesterday. I've just been up to look at the clay. Some of the cracks are full of water and it's going to take a while for that to soak in – we're not over the hump yet but those clouds look good to me. A few days of steady rain is what we want to soften up the land. I want to marl the four-*iugerum* field this year, you know, and we haven't been able to get a spade into the ground for weeks now.'

'What do you mean by "marl"?' Senovara jumped as her husband spoke behind them.

'Oh, that's when we dig through the topsoil to get to the chalk underneath; we pile the chalk into heaps and let it rot down before spreading it over a field. It puts the strength back into the land.'

'I've never heard of it before. Is it just you Britons who do this?'

'So I've been told. Certainly, my father used to tell me that the soldiers from the old fort down the road – the one abandoned during Vespasian's reign, you know – used to ask why some of our fields were white; none of them had ever seen marling before and they thought he was mad. It's hard work but it does make a great deal of difference to our yields. Anyway, I can't stand round here all day talking to you lazy town dwellers. I've got a farm to run. You know what they say: "The fine profit of a farm is the work of the farmer."'

Quintus laughed. 'I must admit I ache all over today. Ahteha had to find me some garlic and honey ointment for my blisters last night. I can't remember when I last worked so hard. Is there anything we can do to help today?'

'Not really, although I was grateful for your help yesterday; without it I doubt if we'd have got all the wheat into the barn in time. Today,' he said with the air of one conferring a great favour, 'you may consider yourself on leave, soldier.'

He waved in salute and set off towards the barn, leaving his sister and brother-in-law standing on the verandah.

'Do we have to go back to Eboracum yet?' asked Senovara apprehensively.

'No. Your brother's right. There needs to be more rain before we can be sure the drought's over. It won't take long for Eboracum to get back to normal, but it would be foolish to go back too soon. I reckon we should see how it goes; if it rains today and again tomorrow, we might return the next day. In the meantime, I intend to enjoy myself. It's years since I had a "leave pass". What shall we do?'

'Well, I've got chores to do – you may be on leave but I don't think my grandmother would agree that I am. Why don't you take the children up onto the ridge? You can point out the great river mouth and the sea to the east and the smoke from the forges of the ironworks to the south. The climb will wear them out.'

As she said this, she realised that it didn't sound much of a treat but to the children, who had never seen the sea, it might seem like one. Quintus was of the opinion that it was a reasonable way of spending the morning, and he strode back into the house to find his offspring. She was delighted that he didn't want to return home immediately. Except for ceremonial occasions, the only times she could remember him taking a whole day away from his workshop were the day when he came to the farm to arrange their betrothal and the day they got married a year later. Since then, their only visits to the farm had been hurried affairs, leaving Eboracum early in the morning, when it was still dark, and arriving back late at night. She almost found herself wishing that it wouldn't rain so that they could stay longer. Then she heard her grandmother calling her from the house, and grinned to herself. A few more days of running round at Enica's bidding and she could see herself pleading with Quintus to take her back to Eboracum.

September

THE NOISE IN the marketplace was overwhelming and it was clear that trade had returned to Eboracum in force, despite the drought and disease of the past two months. On every side, merchants bawled the praises of their wares. Every chicken seller offered the plumpest fowl; each fish seller's perch and herring were the freshest and the cheapest. As she passed, Senovara glanced at the fish lying on the trestle tables and shuddered. The dull eyes and skin of most of the fish suggested that the traders had tarried too long on the road from the coast. Her nostrils also told her that few of the fish were at their best. She would wait until she got nearer home before deciding what to buy for supper.

She carried on along the rows of traders, marvelling at the increasing number who had set up their stalls or built shops over the past year. People of free, freed and slave status were all represented among the shopkeepers and there seemed to be traders from every province of the Empire, selling every type of commodity. There were vegetable sellers offering the newly introduced leeks and lettuces and the expensive, imported white carrots which, on the one occasion she had tried them, she had found tough and tasteless. There were also many more stalls selling the traditional cabbages, onions, chives and turnips brought in by the local farmers. The ripe smell of apples, pears and late cherries reached her as she passed the fruit sellers and there was even someone selling imported figs. She walked past quickly, not daring to look at the price. Senovara held her breath as she went past the liquamen sellers. Fish sauce might be a necessary ingredient in most Roman recipes but it still smelled revolting, particularly here in the marketplace where it was ladled into small bottles or the buyer's bowls from great amphorae set into the shop floors.

Senovara was in the market to purchase a mortarium. Although her grandmother always asserted that an old-fashioned stone mortar was good enough for her, a pottery mortarium with its gritted inner surface was, in Senovara's opinion, much more efficient. She could not manage nowadays without a mortarium. When hers had got broken the previous night, she couldn't help but fear that it was a bad omen.

Not that the accident had been her fault. She had been happily preparing the evening meal of chicken in green sauce, one of her family's favourite dishes. She was grinding up the mint, coriander, lovage and thyme with her stone pestle and had just stirred in the vinegar, wine, oil and liquamen. She'd picked up the mortarium and was pouring its aromatic contents over the chicken pieces in the pan when Hylax came hurtling in from the garden, snarling and snapping at the shrew he was chasing. She let out a yell as the shrew ran between her feet. Hylax dashed round her and, as the two animals ran back and forth, she swayed, still yelling, but holding on to her mortarium for dear life.

Quintus stuck his head round the door to see what all the noise was about and laughed at the scene.

He whistled, and shouted, 'Here, Hylax! Here, boy!'

The dog took no notice, far too excited by the thrill of the chase, and cornered the shrew in the fuel store under the stove.

All at once, the shrew had made a bid for freedom, again through Senovara's legs. This time Hylax followed, but got entangled in Senovara's long skirts and she lost her balance. Over she went, with her skirts flying up over her head. She could still feel the bruises where her buttocks had hit the cold stone floor. She had sat there winded, surrounded by broken fragments of pottery, dripping with the strong-smelling green sauce.

Quintus had roared with laughter, holding on to both doorposts. She gave him a piece of her mind, but he went on laughing until she pointed out in a chilly voice how much a new mortarium would cost. That sobered him up.

'Can't we put it back together again?' he asked. 'I've got some strips of lead in the workshop which could fix it.'

But the mortarium was in too many pieces. It would have to be a new one. It had nearly meant a new tunic as well, because the sauce had soaked into the wool, but luckily – or not, now she came to think of it – it was her old brown tunic. Armea had soaked it immediately in hot water and managed to get the worst of it out, so she had no excuse for buying a new tunic.

Senovara chuckled as she continued through the market. She must have looked a sight, sitting on the kitchen floor dripping with green sauce. But it was a shame about the mortarium. It had been a wedding present from one of her friends; already well used when given, but with fine, sharp, quartz grits. It would have been good for a few years yet, if it hadn't been for Hylax's hunting instincts.

Quintus had said she shouldn't complain too much – getting rid of vermin was one of their reasons for getting Hylax in the first place.

'It certainly wasn't for his looks,' she retorted.

As she walked along, recalling the events of the previous evening, she heard her name being called and, looking up, saw Pervica, Catia and Surilla talking to a couple of their friends.

'Hail!' boomed Pervica. 'When did you get back?'

'Just a few days ago. I've hardly stopped since then, trying to get the house cleaned and the garden back in order. Everything seems to have bolted now the rains have come. How are you all?'

'Fine, now things are getting back to normal. I never thought I'd be so pleased to see rain,' said Surilla.

'Has business improved? Quintus told me you didn't have much custom during the drought.'

'I couldn't get enough water to wash a handkerchief. Luckily, now everyone wants their clothes washed again and business has never been brisker. I've just popped out to do some shopping before I tackle another load. How was your trip to the country?'

'It was as if I'd never left,' sighed Senovara. 'The children loved it and it was wonderful having plenty of people around to help me with them. But it's good to be back in my own kitchen again, even if Lucius keeps complaining about leaving the pigs behind and Armea is wandering about looking miserable at having to leave her family again.'

'It was sensible of you to take them away,' declared Catia. 'Eboracum hasn't been a pleasant place recently. They say two hundred people died.'

'Have you heard how Adnamata is?' asked Senovara anxiously. 'I've been worried about her.'

'I saw Broginara the other day in the market and she said Adnamata was doing well. I thought I'd call this afternoon – she must be about due now. I'll tell her you were enquiring about her.'

'Where are you off to, Senovara?' asked Pervica. 'You were looking very purposeful as you strode along.'

'I'm going to buy a new mortarium. Mine got broken last night.' She told her friends the sorry tale of Hylax and the shrew, grinning sheepishly as they all roared with laughter.

'Do you know what sort of mortarium you're going to get?' asked Surilla.

Senovara shook her head. 'I've never bought one before. Have you any suggestions?'

'Well,' said Pervica, 'there's no point trying to get one of the local ones. I've heard that all Vitalis' and Mercator's wares are being bought by the army as fast as they can make them. What you need is one of Martinus' mortaria from Verulamium. They've got good grits and nice wide rims, so you can get a good grip or fix them into an iron stand, if you prefer.'

'Nonsense,' said Catia. 'Get yourself one from Camulodunum if you can. I've had one for years. They're a nice creamy colour, so you can see what you're grinding.'

'Yes,' Pervica snapped, 'and what you ground last. That nice creamy colour stains.'

All the other women had different mortaria to recommend, and the names of potters, preferred grit shapes and favoured colours began to fly through the air.

'All this is very well,' Surilla said eventually, 'but Senovara needs a mortarium today. It will depend on what is in the pottery market. She can't wait until the next shipment comes up from Verulamium or Camulodunum.' She turned to Senovara. 'I'd see what's on offer and choose the one you think will serve you best. I wish you luck. Now I must get back to my washing.'

'And I to my housework,' declared Pervica. 'Are you coming, Catia?'

Catia's homely face coloured slightly. 'I thought I'd just see if I can find some liver for my supper tonight. I'll come with you part of the way, Senovara.'

Pervica snorted derisively. 'I thought you got your meat delivered these days,' she said with an outrageous wink at Senovara. Catia glared at her but said nothing, and she and Senovara set off together.

They chatted amiably, catching up on the gossip as they carried on through the market until Catia turned down the alleyway which led to Bonosius' shop.

'Farewell, Senovara. I hope you get a good mortarium; it makes all the difference to one's cooking, in my opinion.'

Senovara watched her for a moment as she made her way down to the butcher's shop, pleased that Catia's romance seemed to be surviving Pervica's teasing. A horn blowing at the fortress reminded her that time was passing and she hurried on. At last she came to the section of the market where pottery was sold. The merchants in this part were more established and sold their wares from wooden counters built between the pillars at the front of their shops. The first trader offered grey cooking pots; the second the shiny red pottery imported from Gallia. Then she spied some mortarium sellers, each selling wares from different potteries. Which should she choose?

Ignoring the glowing descriptions of their vessels which issued from the pot sellers, she tried to remember her friends' advice. Looking at the bewildering choice now before her, Senovara wished she could wait for a few days. She would prefer to think carefully about her purchase, but a mortarium was a necessity and she would have to decide quickly. Perhaps the best thing to do was to decide on the trader first. She looked along the line of shops, considering their proprietors. Which one looked the most honest? She walked slowly down the row, looking at the pots on offer while surreptitiously assessing the merchants. One man she discounted on the grounds that he looked like a weasel, with a sharp, acquisitive nose and eyes set too close together for her liking. A plump, prosperous trader she gave up on because she couldn't understand his strong accent; she thought he must come from one of the south-western tribes of Britannia but he could equally have come from Gallia. She was finding the purchase of a mortarium too stressful to risk a misunderstanding because the buyer and the seller were both speaking in their second language.

Eventually she settled on a man and a wife who were working together. At least the woman would know how to use a mortarium and might have better advice to offer than the traders who simply wanted to make a sale.

She opened negotiations by asking if they had any of Martinus' wares.

'No, I'm sorry to say, we haven't,' the woman answered amicably. 'We've had some in the past, but his wares are now so popular that the traders in Londinium can offer him better prices – they don't have such high transport costs, so they can still sell the pots at a decent profit. I'm sure we can offer you a good alternative, though. What do you need it for?'

Senovara was puzzled. What could a mortarium be used for, other than to prepare food?

Seeing her confusion, the pot seller added, 'Some people use them for grinding up pigments or the ingredients for medicines and, of course, some cults require mortaria for their rituals.'

'Oh, no. I just want one for cooking,' Senovara explained.

'And do you do much entertaining? Will you want to be using the mortarium in front of guests, to add spices to their wine, for example?'

Senovara shook her head; this was clearly a more complex purchase than she had feared.

'So what you need is a basic bowl, not something to show off, and, presumably, not too expensive?'

'I want a good, solid mortarium which has nice sharp grits, a well-shaped lip so I don't spill anything when pouring, and a wide rim that I can grasp comfortably – I don't use a stand; I just put my mortarium down on a cloth to stop it sliding about,' declared Senovara firmly.

The mortarium seller smiled at her. 'We've just had a consignment in from Manduessedum, in the territory of the Coritani. Fine mortaria, they are, made from a good, hard fabric with sharp quartz grits. I'd recommend one of them – they're very popular round here. I've even heard a rumour that some of the potters are thinking of setting up kilns in this area. You can have a choice of the plain cream-coloured ones or the brown-slipped ones. All of them are stamped with named potters, so you know who to curse if your recipes go wrong,' she added cheerfully.

Senovara grinned at her. She'd heard several of her friends curse the mortarium maker when they couldn't get their sauces to blend properly and she had often thought that using name stamps on their wares was a risky advertising ploy for the potters.

The two merchants started to pull a selection of mortaria out from under their bench and Senovara concentrated on selecting one. She immediately rejected the brown-slipped versions; Pervica had warned her that the slip just rubbed off if one did a lot of cooking and the mortarium soon looked the worse for wear. She also rejected a couple which had painted decoration; they were too expensive and too fancy for kitchen work.

After much debate, she settled on a mortarium whose rim stamp declared it to be from the workshop of Bonoxus. Handing over the necessary *sestertii*, she turned away from the stall, thankful that she had completed her task successfully. A mortarium was a major purchase; buying the wrong one would be a costly mistake which she would have to work with for some years. Looking down in her basket at the vessel nestling there, however, she was confident that she had made the right choice and that Bonoxus would continue to live and produce pots free from her curses.

She set off for home, trying to think what to cook for dinner that night. It would be good to prepare something which needed a sauce or a mixture of herbs so that she could try out her new purchase.

As she neared the fortress she was overtaken by Grata, whose bulging leather bag indicated she was on her way to a woman in labour.

'Hail, Senovara,' puffed the stout midwife. 'I can't stop to chat. I'm on my way to the fortress. Your friend Adnamata has started. Her husband's just sent a messenger to fetch me.'

'Give her my best wishes.' Senovara responded. 'I hope she and the baby come through well.'

'Don't see why they shouldn't, if the gods wish it,' declared Grata, confident in her own skill and the general goodwill of the deities who concerned themselves with childbirth.

They reached the corner where Senovara turned off towards her home and she repeated her good wishes as she said farewell to the midwife. She stood for a moment, watching Grata moving purposefully through the stalls which lined the road to the fortress gate. Senovara did so hope that Adnamata and her child would be protected by the gods and that her labour would be short and without complications. She herself had been lucky in that both her children had been born with dispatch and without fuss, but not all women were so fortunate. Grata was a skilful midwife, though, and had a range of potions, like honeysuckle leaves boiled in wine, to ease delivery and bring away the afterbirth. Senovara remembered the egg-shaped amulet she had given Adnamata a few months ago, and hoped that the young woman would find it a comfort.

As she stood in the road, a cry of 'Marrows! Fresh marrows!' caught her attention. A farmer had manoeuvred his cart into a space between the stalls and was preparing to sell his produce.

Quintus was very fond of marrows and these were the first she had seen for sale this year. Stuffed marrow would be an ideal dish to cook tonight, she thought, and the recipe would be perfect for testing her new mortarium. She hurried over, selected a fine marrow and bore it home in triumph, thankful that she hadn't had to buy any of the stale fish or present her family with a patina again.

She sent Armea back into the market to buy some sheep's brains which she boiled up immediately on the slave's return. When the meat was cool, she chopped it up as finely as she could. While Armea hollowed out the marrow after cutting out oblong sections from its side, Senovara measured pepper, lovage and some origanum into the mortarium and pounded them together. So far, so good; the grits of the new mortarium seemed to catch at the herbs and spices in a very satisfactory manner and made short work of the task. Pleased with her purchase, she added a splash of liquamen and mixed everything together before pouring the sauce into the bowl of chopped brains. She beat in some raw eggs, stuffed the marrow with the mixture, then replaced the cut-out pieces and tied them tightly into position with string made from plaited straw. The bulging green marrow was then lowered into her biggest bronze cauldron, already full of boiling water. It wouldn't take too long to cook and the liquid left behind would make a good basis for tomorrow's soup. Some people liked to slice their boiled marrow and then fry it, but Senovara's family preferred it boiled and served with a little wine sauce.

There was still no news of Adnamata, and Senovara decided she needed to keep busy; worrying wouldn't make the baby come any faster. Armea could keep an eye on the boiling marrow, so Senovara went out into the garden to see if there was anything useful she could do there.

The apple tree's boughs were hanging heavy with fruit but they needed a few more days of rain before they were ready to be picked and stored in the roof space over the shop. The garlic bulbs had already been pulled up and were now hanging in pungent bunches from the rafters of her kitchen; the onions had had their tops bent over and were drying on the ground. The pea plants had been picked clean and the plants left drying in the sun; the haulms would be useful in the winter to protect other plants from the frost. The peas themselves had also been dried and were now stored in a small sack. There were still some beans hanging from the plants on the supports she had built out of sticks. She tried one between her thumb and forefinger and decided they needed to be picked before the pods burst.

Senovara fetched a basket from the kitchen and started to strip the plants of all their surviving beans. Some she would boil to serve with the marrow but most of them could be salted down for use later in the year.

She was pulling up the bean plants so that they could dry on the ground, when Armea called to her from the house.

'The marrow's nearly ready, Mistress.'

'I'll be right there. Take in this basket of beans, will you, while I finish doing this? Could you cut up some of the beans for tonight and put them on to boil?'

Armea came down the beaten gravel path and picked up the basket, its spiky green contents sticking out at all angles. 'This is a good amount, Mistress. I didn't think there'd be so many left.'

'Beans are very good at hiding behind leaves,' Senovara said, 'and the rain we've had since the end of Augustus has plumped up the stragglers nicely. It's just as well we watered them as much as we could in Iulius and Augustus, though, otherwise they'd never have recovered. These late beans are likely to be better than some of the earlier ones, for a change.'

She pulled up the last of the bean plants and gathered up the sticks for next year. They would need to be cleaned ready to be stored, so she left them propped by the back door.

As she entered the house, she heard a plaintive cry from the *latrina*. 'Mater! The last of the moss has just dropped to pieces.'

Senovara groaned; she had forgotten to buy some moss when she was out shopping. Some of her friends had adopted the Roman habit of using a sponge held on a stick to clean themselves after using the *latrina*, but sponges were expensive and the supply was erratic because it depended on ships coming in from the Mare Internum. There was always plenty of moss available, but it did tend to drop to pieces after it had been used and rinsed a few times.

'Hang on, Lucius. I'll pick you some dock leaves.'

Senovara headed back down the path to the bottom of the garden, where there was a patch of uncultivated ground which provided her with nettles for food and dock leaves for medicines. She grabbed a handful of dock leaves, enough to deal with Lucius' immediate needs, and returned to the house to rescue her son from his predicament. Armea could pick some more later, in case anyone else needed any before she could get back to the market.

By the time she had helped Lucius and washed the garden dirt off her hands, the marrow and beans were ready and she called Quintus and Ertola in from the shop.

The marrow looked splendid on one of her best plates, its dark green skin glistening against the shiny red surface. Senovara handed Quintus a knife and he started carving. He had just served Ertola with a small slice and Senovara was chopping it up into smaller pieces, when there was a rapping at the front door.

'Go and see who that is, Armea,' said Quintus.

'Are you expecting anybody, Quintus?' asked Senovara, wondering if this was a late customer or a message from the fortress, but before he could answer Armea ushered Grata into the kitchen.

'Hail, everyone. I've just come from the fortress and I thought you might like to hear the news.'

'Oh, yes!' cried Senovara. 'Do sit down and join us. Armea, bring another plate and spoon. Quintus, carve Grata a slice of marrow. How is Adnamata? Did everything go well? Is it a boy or a girl?'

'Thank you, that marrow looks just what I need. Yes, everything went very well, but it turned out to be *two* boys. One was born mid-afternoon, then his brother popped out about an hour later.'

'Twins!' Senovara was thrilled. She had never known anyone have twins before. 'And Adnamata is well?'

'She's fine. Very tired, of course, but she'll do. Her husband is beside himself with excitement. When I left he was handing out wine to all the men in his century, so I hope Adnamata will get some rest; having eighty drunken men in the same building doesn't make for a good night's sleep.'

'Did you have plenty of help?'

'Oh, yes. Broginara was there, of course, and she did very well, considering that she hadn't helped at a birth before – intelligent girl. One of the other centurions' wives offered to assist as well, so we had the three women necessary. Luckily, Marcus Anicius Ingenuus sent in a proper birthing stool; I don't think any of us would have been strong enough to support Adnamata on our knees throughout the birth as we used to have to do – even though it wasn't too long a labour. Do you know, I had to send Broginara back to my cottage for more swaddling when the babies arrived? It's the first time I haven't had enough with me, but then twins aren't that common.'

'I thought she was big when I visited her in Iulius but I just thought she'd miscalculated her dates.'

'Same here, but both boys are quite small, which is why I was fooled into thinking that she wasn't big enough for twins.

They both cried lustily when I laid them on the ground to introduce them to their household gods, though, so I reckon they'll do. I formally declared them worth rearing, anyway.'

'Did you plunge them into cold water before you made your declaration?' asked Quintus. 'That was the custom in my tribe. My mother always swore it toughened babies up, as well as being a good check on which were likely to survive.'

'I've heard of that practice, but I reckon I've been doing this long enough to tell if a child's going to be worth rearing without having to treat it like a freshly caught fish,' retorted Grata.

She finished her plateful of marrow and Senovara hastened to offer some more.

'Thank you, I will. It's been a long day and I've had little opportunity to eat or drink much.'

Quintus topped up the midwife's wine beaker. 'Veturius will be proud to have two boys.'

'I know he wanted a son,' agreed Senovara, 'though whether he has any idea what it will be like having two little boys around the house, I doubt,' she added, glaring at Lucius, who was trying to whirl a ring of marrow skin round on his spoon.

'Oh, I expect he'll treat them as though they are part of his century,' declared Quintus jovially.

Grata and Senovara exchanged the look of women who pity men who think that small children will do what they are told, despite all the evidence to the contrary. Secretly, Senovara thought that Veturius was likely to resent not being able to control his sons' inevitable tantrums and that Adnamata would have a hard time keeping the peace as they grew up.

Grata put down her spoon with a sigh. 'That was wonderful, Senovara. It would have taken ages to get my fire going again when I got home and I doubt if I'd have bothered to prepare a hot meal, I'm so tired. I'll be on my way now, with grateful thanks to you both. Drop in and see Adnamata tomorrow; she'll be ready to receive visitors by late morning.'

She rose to her feet looking searchingly at Ertola. 'Still not talking?'

Senovara shook her head. 'No. She's worn your amber amulet every day but nothing's happened yet. Have you any further suggestions?'

'I'll give the matter some thought,' said Grata. 'It could still just be a matter of time, though. I wouldn't worry.'

As she showed her guest out through the shop, Senovara had to admit that she and Quintus were very concerned about their daughter, and Grata repeated her promise to consider some further treatments. She patted Senovara on the arm in a comforting way and looked out into the night.

'The nights are really beginning to draw in now,' she declared. 'We'll be having frosts soon; there's definitely a nip in the air. I prophesy a fall of snow before the Saturnalia.' She pulled her cloak hood over her head and set off down the street with a cheerful wave.

The next day, Senovara rushed through her tasks in order to have time to visit Adnamata, but even so the fortress horn was blowing the sixth hour before she got to the centurion's house. She hoped she wasn't arriving just as the family were about to have their midday meal, but when Broginara opened the door the sound of crying babies and the sight of the normally neat Pannonian woman's hair escaping from its combs suggested that the household's usual routine was in tatters.

'Oh, Senovara. Hail. Do come in.'

'Hail, Broginara. I've come to congratulate Adnamata and Veturius and see how you all are, but if this isn't a good time, I can come back later.'

'No, I'm delighted to see you and I know Adnamata will be. Veturius is with the Legate.'

Broginara ushered Senovara through the living room and into the bedroom beyond. Adnamata was sitting up in the large wooden bed, with a crying baby held to her breast. In a cot by the side of the bed another small bundle wailed.

'Oh, Senovara, I thank the Matres you've come. Both of them are crying but they don't seem to want to feed. What am I doing wrong?'

'I doubt if they need milk this early.' Senovara hurried over and picked up the baby in the cot. Immediately he stopped crying, as did his brother in Adnamata's arms.

'Well, look at that,' exclaimed Broginara. 'What did you do, Senovara?'

'Nothing.' Senovara laughed. 'I think this little chap just wanted some attention; probably wondering where his brother is. I don't believe you need worry about feeding either of them yet, Adnamata. My grandmother always told me that babies should be put to the breast before the cord's cut, but Marcus Anicius Ingenuus says modern writers recommend not feeding babies for at least the first two days, and this little mite doesn't seem to be hungry.' She touched the nearest downy cheek of her sweet-smelling armful but he didn't turn towards her. 'No, he's not looking for food. Just making his presence felt. Tidy yourself up and give them a cuddle. Hold them both firmly; newborn babies like to be close to their mothers but they also like to feel that they're in experienced hands.'

'I've got a lot to learn,' admitted Adnamata, pinning the front of her tunic together while Broginara held the baby. 'I presumed they must be hungry when they both woke up and started to cry.'

'Grata will be along to see you later on today, to make sure you and the babies are doing well. She'll tell you when to start feeding them – she usually smears a little boiled honey on their lips after two days, in order to encourage them to suck, and after that lets the mother start breastfeeding, but if your babies look as if they're starving she might suggest starting earlier.'

'I was beginning to worry that I had no milk when neither of them would suckle. I don't have large breasts and I was thinking I'd need to employ a wet nurse.'

'It takes time for the milk to come, but it also takes a while for a baby to learn to suck, so don't give up too soon. As far as I know, the size of your breasts isn't important – as long as they're neither excessively big or very small – but I've never known anyone with twins before, so you may need a wet nurse. If you do, Grata will be able to find you one, no doubt. It's important to get the right one.'

Broginara handed one of the swaddled babies to Adnamata and when the new mother had him comfortably held in the crook of her left arm, Senovara tucked the other child into her right arm. Adnamata shifted her elbows cautiously, moving the twins into a more settled position.

She looked up at Senovara and smiled proudly. 'Aren't they lovely? Do you think they look like Veturius?'

Senovara agreed that they were wonderful babies but felt unable to confirm whether they bore a resemblance to their father; they had been so well swaddled by Grata's professional hands that all that was visible within the folds of linen bandage were their closed eyes, their noses and their tiny mouths, the last reminding Senovara more of the wild strawberries she had gathered in Iulius than of the authoritarian centurion.

'I'd better get on with preparing some soup,' said Broginara, 'now that peace is restored. Senovara, will you keep an eye on her while I get on with some work?'

'Of course I will,' declared Senovara, and she settled herself on the wooden birthing stool, which was still by the bed.

'That won't be very comfortable, Senovara. Bring in a stool from the other room,' said Adnamata.

'No, I'm fine. Birthing stools aren't too bad if you've got layers of woollen cloth between you and the gap,' Senovara assured her. 'How are you feeling?'

'Exhausted. I thought these two would never arrive. No one warns you about how bad childbirth really is and how long it takes. Please tell me I won't have to go through all that again.'

'Not if you don't want to,' Senovara reassured her, trying not to laugh. 'You've managed to have a whole family in one go. Veturius would be a very unreasonable man not to be satisfied with two sons, and I doubt if he'll be urging you to increase the size of your family. There are plenty of ways of avoiding having more children; Grata will be able to give you some ideas. Personally, I'm a great believer in inserting plugs of wool soaked in olive oil and wiping with vinegar after intercourse, but some women use alum.'

'I was told to drink honey water afterwards but it doesn't seem to have worked.' Adnamata looked fondly down at her sons, who were now sleeping peacefully.

'No,' laughed Senovara. 'Some people might say rather that you've been taking too much mistletoe syrup to help you to conceive.'

'I don't think I'd even consider using mistletoe ointment for scabrous nails now, just in case,' retorted Adnamata stoutly.

Both girls were giggling when Veturius strode into the room.

'Hail, Senovara. What do you think of my new family?'

'A fine pair of boys. You should be proud of them.'

'I am, I am. A splendid addition to the legion.' He turned to his wife. 'The Legate sends his felicitations, my love.'

Adnamata seemed overwhelmed by this attention from her husband's commanding officer and blushed.

'I will leave you now,' said Senovara. 'I'll call in again in the next few days, but if you need anything don't hesitate to send for me. Don't show me out, Veturius,' she added, as the centurion opened the door for her. 'I'll say farewell to Broginara before I go.'

She found Broginara in the kitchen, stirring a cauldron of vegetable soup.

'How do you think Adnamata's looking, Senovara?'

'Fine. She'll be tired for a few days but she'll soon be back to normal. It's important that you don't fuss her, though,' Senovara added warningly, aware that there was little experience of childbirth in this household and a general tendency to over-react.

'No, Grata told me that. I'm more concerned about the babies; they're so small and fragile. I'm terrified of them.'

Senovara roared with laughter. 'Babies are tougher than they look, don't you worry.'

Broginara grinned sheepishly. 'I know, I'm being ridiculous, but I've had no experience of babies.'

'You'll have to marry and have some of your own,' said Senovara.

'After what Adnamata went through yesterday I'm not sure I'm so keen on that idea. I suppose I do regret not marrying, but it hasn't been possible. You see, I was still under twenty when my father died and I came to live with Veturius. Because I was so young, Pater hadn't started any marriage negotiations for me and Veturius has been transferred too often since then for there to be time to get me betrothed. Of course, when Adnamata joined us she was just a child and I was needed to look after her.'

'Have you ever met anyone you might have wished to marry?' asked Senovara curiously.

'Many. I had a great friend and admirer when I was still living with my father but, sadly, he was killed when he fell from a barge he was helping to load on the Danuvius. There was also an *optio* in Veturius' century when we were stationed at Moguntiacum – he had the most astonishing black eyes.' Broginara's own eyes misted over momentarily. 'But,' she continued robustly, 'probably nothing would have come of it. As I recall, he wasn't a likely candidate to be promoted to centurion quickly, so we'd probably have had to wait for years before we could have married legally; Veturius wouldn't have let me marry except with the full protection of Roman law. Now it looks as if I have a new career as an aunt, which threatens to be a full-time job if those two nephews of mine go on being as demanding as they've been in the one day they've been here.'

Senovara smiled. 'I think you'll find they've only just started with their demands. Small children are selfish little brutes, if you allow them to be.'

As she left the fortress, Senovara reflected on the way the Fates arranged people's lives. Broginara was a handsome, intelligent woman; it seemed a waste that she should spend her life looking after her brother and his wife. She knew that, had she herself not married Quintus, Matugenus would have been willing to give her a home with him and Ahteha, and she had no doubt that they would both have tried to make her as happy as possible, but it would have been second best in her opinion. Having her own husband and children, her own house, even her own slave, made Senovara feel that the Fates had dealt kindly with her.

When she got home, she found that Quintus had already left to attend a meeting of the *cives Romani consistentes*, the town council that had recently been formed to look after the interests of the Roman citizens in Eboracum. Armea had fed the children and all three were in the shop.

'I hadn't realised it was so late, Armea. Did you give Quintus something to eat before he went?'

'Yes, Mistress, and there's some soup left for you. I'll stay minding the shop, in case any customers come in.'

Senovara bustled through into the kitchen, feeling guilty that she had spent so long at the Pannonians' house. She was now well behind with her household tasks, and this was one of the busiest times of year. Before the end of the month she would need to pick the apples in the garden and she must also find time over the next few days to go out of the town and search for blackberries and elderberries. The weather had been so wet recently, making up for the earlier drought, that it was likely there would be plenty of mushrooms if she could get to the meadows early enough in the morning, before other people had been out and picked the lot. If there was a good quantity of mushrooms, she would be able to dry some to see them through the winter. Matugenus usually brought her a supply at this time of year, but dried mushrooms were a useful standby and you couldn't have too many of them.

One of her fondest childhood memories was going out on misty September mornings with her father to hunt for mushrooms. The fields around the farm had seemed totally different in an autumn dawn, with the grass sparkling with dew and the mist lying in low streaks across the fields. When she was small, she had thought it magical that mushrooms the size of a plate could appear overnight in fields where the cows were grazing. Puffballs had seemed even more amazing; when he was ten Matugenus had found one bigger than a man's head and had struggled back to the kitchen with it clutched to his chest, barely able to see past it. Her mother had sliced it up and dried it on threads which she had hung about the kitchen; there was so much of it that the whole room had been festooned with mushroom garlands.

Senovara finished her soup and went back into the shop to relieve Armea. As she sat there waiting for customers, she planned her harvesting for the next few days. If the weather was right, first thing tomorrow morning she and Armea would take the children mushroom hunting. They would take several baskets so that if they came across any wayside fruit it could also be gathered. She would need to check that she had plenty of bottles to contain the fruit once she had preserved it – she always saved the square vinegar bottles for the purpose but never seemed to have enough. Both blackberries and elderberries could be kept for a long time if you stored them in a glass bottle in their own juice mixed with reduced wine. She'd already bottled some cherries in honey; she'd seen some being sold for a reasonable price in the market and hadn't been able to resist buying a quantity to store.

She was happily anticipating a storeroom full of pale green glass vessels, each containing preserved fruit, and grey pots full of salted vegetables, when Quintus returned.

As he stood in the doorway, shaking the raindrops from his bald head, she ran over to take his cloak from him.

'It's turned bad out there again. Having been too dry all summer, it now looks as if we're to be flooded all autumn,' he grumbled. 'How was Adnamata?'

'Stunned at finding herself the mother of two sons and not sure quite what to do with them, but she'll cope.'

'Did you see Veturius?' asked Quintus, leading the way into the kitchen to warm himself over the stove.

'Just for a few minutes. He's very pleased with himself.'

'I should think so. Twin sons would make any man proud. I must call in and congratulate him in the next few days.'

Senovara smiled to herself; Quintus, as always, saw the matter purely from the man's point of view.

'How was the meeting?' she asked.

'The usual – a great deal of debate and few decisions. We were supposed to be arranging the Ludi Romani in honour of Jupiter but the Legate had sent his tribune along – you remember, Marcus Pontius Sabinus? He came here when Minicius Natalis ordered his purple boots.'

Senovara nodded; she did remember the rather elegant young man.

'Well, apparently, the Legate wants the Ludi Romani to be limited to the sacrifice to Jupiter because he's decided to organise some chariot races for the Ides of October.'

'Chariot races? I remember you telling me he was a famous charioteer before he took command at Eboracum, but to have a race you need more than one entrant. Is there anyone else in the area who could compete?'

'That's why he wants to wait until the Ides of October. Apparently, the new Governor, Mummius Sisenna, has some young men in his entourage who are skilful charioteers so Minicius Natalis has invited them to Eboracum to give him a race. Pontius Sabinus said that ordinary horse races would be included in the programme, so it should be a lively event!'

'Can we go, Quintus?' Senovara's eyes were shining. When she was younger the local farmers had often organised horse races and she had been thrilled by the excitement of a good race; she'd never seen a chariot race, though.

'We'll certainly go. I'm not missing out on seeing a four-in-hand chariot race, particularly one in which an Olympic champion is driving.'

Quintus poured himself a tankard of beer and stood warming his bottom in front of the stove. Senovara sat down on the bench; she couldn't get on with her cooking if he was standing in the way, so she might as well wait in comfort.

'Was there any more talk about building a theatre in Eboracum?' she enquired.

'No. I reckon it will be a few years yet before we get a theatre. But there was plenty of talk about the new bath-houses and plenty of complaints about why they're taking so long to build. Felicius Simplex was particularly incensed about the delay. I suspect his wife has been giving him a hard time.'

'She was certainly very annoyed that time when she couldn't get in on women's day,' Senovara agreed. 'There are so many people in the town now that we women have to go earlier and earlier on our day in order to get in.'

Quintus chuckled. 'Poor old Felicius Simplex will be able to give her a progress report when he gets home, but I wager he won't tell her about the run-in he had with the military representatives. You know we have a rule that no one can attend the meeting carrying weapons?'

Senovara nodded.

'Well, Felicius Simplex is a great one for rules and he happened to be at the door of the chamber when the tribune arrived. He took it upon himself to tell Marcus Pontius Sabinus and his attendants that they had to hand over their swords and daggers, but one of the soldiers thought he'd said "sausages" not "daggers" and that he was making a rude personal remark. The soldier had to be held back from demanding an apology with his fists.'

Quintus saw that Senovara was looking puzzled and hastened to explain.

'The soldier thought he'd said *"isiciis"* – sausages – not *"iis sicis"* – those daggers. Well, we all roared with laughter, which upset pompous old Felicius Simplex; he's always prided himself on his Latin accent, you know.'

Quintus put down his tankard. 'I must go and check how many hobnails I've got left. Sacer was telling me that the price is likely to go up from two *asses* per hundred in the next few months, so I want to make sure I've got enough. I don't want to buy at the higher rate before I have to.'

Quintus left the kitchen, still chuckling over the misunderstanding at the council meeting, and Senovara started to prepare the evening meal. Personally, she was amazed that there were not more misunderstandings in a town full of soldiers and civilians from all over the world. She often found some people's Latin difficult to understand, although she had managed to avoid making such an embarrassing public mistake as Felicius Simplex so far. She always made sure she pronounced the old word '*bracis*' very carefully when ordering grain; it was too easy for it to be heard as the Latin '*bracae*', which meant trousers, and she could well imagine the hilarity that misunderstanding could cause. Life was full of pitfalls, she thought. She decided it would not be a good idea to cook sausages that night as she had planned; Quintus wouldn't be able to eat them for laughing. Armea would have to run out and buy some pigs' trotters instead. Hopefully, '*ungellas*' couldn't be confused with anything else.

October

SENOVARA PICKED HER way through the rubbish littering the quayside, holding her skirts up and stepping carefully past the mooring ropes of the vessels. She clutched her basket nervously to her side as she was jostled by the merchants, stevedores and sailors who thronged the busy wharf. She rarely visited the docks by herself, and today was distracted with the worry of having to carry out Quintus' commission on her own.

He had ordered some hides from a merchant of the Atrebates tribe and it had been arranged that the delivery would be made by sea. The ship that was supposed to have his cargo on board had entered the river a few days previously, but no consignment of hides had yet appeared at their shop. Quintus had become increasingly agitated that the leather had been sold to someone else by mistake. The previous evening, as they sat round the kitchen stove after their meal, he had declared his intention of going down to the quay the next day to find out what was going on. But the Fates had decreed otherwise; he had woken that morning with a bad toothache and in no condition to carry out the business himself. He'd felt better after Senovara had given him a draught of poppy tears, but she didn't want him to leave the house and venture into the cold north wind, which was loosening the last of the leaves on the trees.

Quintus was getting toothache more often as he got older and his teeth wore down. Senovara decided that she was going to have to start baking her own bread regularly again; it was the only way to ensure that there was no grit in the flour. Millers often put a handful of coarse sand into the hopper of their milling-stones when grinding corn, in order to make their flour finer, and there had been several times in recent weeks when Quintus had complained about jarring his teeth on grit when he ate his bread.

The quay at Eboracum had been just a jetty when she had first visited it with her father, but as she walked through the rain-filled wind, she saw all around her the signs of a busy and prosperous port. The whole of the waterfront had been revetted with great square-cut timbers a few years ago, before the surface of the wharf was levelled and covered with the packed gravel she was walking on. A row of great warehouses ran along the landward side of the wharf, their ground floors made of roughly adzed timbers, their upper storeys of wooden planks or whitewashed clay. On the red-tiled roof of one of the buildings, a couple of seagulls squawked and fought over a titbit, while several sparrows darted around, hoping to catch some crumbs. The small rectangular spaces under the eaves of the warehouses, which let air and light into the gloomy interiors, were all fitted with iron grilles to stop the birds flying in. Big wooden doors filled the front of each building; the planks of these doors could be removed to allow the stevedores to run cargoes straight into the open storage areas from the ships' gangplanks. Some were bursting at the seams with crates, bundles and bales; others were almost empty.

From each warehouse there drifted strange smells, some revolting, others pleasantly exotic. From one warehouse, the pungent whiff of Baetican fish sauce surged out to catch at the throats of passers-by. From another emerged the distinctive smell of damp fleeces; Senovara wondered where they had come from and how long they had been travelling – it was too late in the year for the local sheep to have been recently sheared. Many of the warehouses presented the subtle scent of the straw and hay used to pack the crates of imported pottery or to protect the square glass bottles containing preserved fruit, medicines, or reduced wine products, such as *sapo* or *defrutum*. Occasionally, Senovara caught the heady aroma of spices. The rich smell of olive oil rose from a broken amphora, whose contents oozed across the landing stage and dripped sluggishly into the black water. A young boy was spreading straw over the spillage to stop anyone else slipping and having another expensive accident. All the smells mingled against a background tang of sewage, river water and fish.

On both sides of the Abus, and in the lower reaches of its tributary river, flat-bottomed river lighters lay, rocking lazily in the sluggish water that lapped the waterfront timbers, their high prows and sternposts decorated with the heads of birds and animals. As she watched, a barge laden with barrels was rowed past, its crew working to the rhythm of their chanted song. Next to the lighters were the small sailing ships that plied their trade up and down the estuary, their hulls protected from rubbing against the quay by strakes of timber. In midstream sat the larger seagoing merchantmen, their great mainsails furled and their steering oars at rest. Each ship, whether large or small, had eyes painted on her prow so that she could see where she was going and to ensure the protection of the gods. Sculling in and out between the larger vessels were several hide-covered curraghs and small skiffs with blunt prows. There was constant movement between the ships and the shore as men loaded and unloaded cargoes – rolling barrels, lifting crates – cursing and complaining as they did so.

Despite the activity, Senovara knew that this was nearly the end of the shipping season and that soon the only trade on the quay would be from the fishermen who worked the river and the estuary throughout the winter. Many of the ships moored to the huge iron rings set into the edge of the quay were from Germania and Gallia; they would want to make a run for their home ports before the weather worsened and their crews found themselves stranded abroad. Within the next few days most of the cargoes would be distributed around the country, either by waggon or by the smaller boats and barges, and the big merchant vessels would be gone.

The merchants themselves, only too aware of the limited time available to them, were determined to finish their trading season in profit. Wherever Senovara looked there were men in stout woollen tunics, leather leggings and waterproof capes haggling over prices, counting bales and crates, or making lists on large wax tablets. One merchant was making notes with a stylus in a tiny book made from small bone tablets hinged together with gut. Senovara wondered where she could buy such a notebook; it would be an ideal present to give Quintus at the Saturnalia.

The noise and bustle bewildered her and she wondered how she was to find the ship holding Quintus' missing hides. She stood in the middle of the landing stage trying to make out the name symbols painted on the bows of the ships. Suddenly, she was startled by a dull rumble and a loud warning cry. Before she could look round to see what was the matter she found herself being lifted bodily to one side as a large barrel, which had escaped during its journey down a gangplank, careered past the spot where she had been standing.

'That was close, Senovara,' grunted her rescuer.

'Oh, thank you, Bruccius.' Senovara was relieved to recognise Pervica's husband, the river pilot. 'This seems to be a dangerous place for those who aren't used to it,' she said as she dusted herself down.

'Aye, you need the eyes of Janus round here. But what are you doing down on the quayside? Isn't Quintus with you?'

'No, he's got toothache this morning so he sent me down to see if I can find a ship called the *Margarita*. She's a coastal vessel which is supposed to have arrived from Noviomagus Reginorum with a consignment of leather for Quintus. We'd heard she'd arrived in the river but we've not had any delivery yet. Quintus is getting worried that his order has been resold or even that it's been forgotten.'

'I can see why he'd be worried. It's late in the year; anything forgotten this trip isn't likely to be sent until the spring now.

But I can give you news of the *Margarita*. I piloted her in myself a few days ago, but there wasn't room for her to dock at the quayside until this morning. There are so many vessels in at the moment that she's had to lie off in midstream. She's just starting to unload now. That's her down there, fourth vessel beyond that big lighter. I'll take you along and we'll make enquiries about Quintus' leather.'

Bruccius set off down the quay with his hand under Senovara's elbow to guide her round the gangplanks and crates. Senovara was thankful that she had met him; her nerve had been starting to fail her and she wondered if she would have been brave enough to approach the *Margarita* and ask about the missing goods on her own.

'Hold back there! Make way!' The hairiest man Senovara had ever seen barred their progress. The black hair on his head mingled with a huge bushy beard; more hair sprouted along his arms and down his bare legs. He looked like a bear in a dirty green tunic, and as he smiled ingratiatingly at Senovara and Bruccius his huge yellow teeth added to this impression.

'Just shifting these slaves, Madam. We'll be out of your way in a moment.'

He shouted at a line of slaves who were trooping down the gangplank of a small seagoing vessel. From the look of them, the vessel had been all round the Mare Internum gathering up men and women of all the provinces before fetching up in Eboracum. As they passed her on their way to the slave market, which had been set up temporarily in one of the warehouses, Senovara thought the slaves looked tired and defeated but clearly glad to be on dry land at last. She was pleased to see that they were neither bound nor shackled, but then there was probably little need; where could they go if they escaped? They were in a foreign country with no money, no possessions except the clothes they stood up in, and no friends or relations to help them.

'You lot might as well sit down. The sale isn't due to start for another hour,' directed the slave trader. The slaves all slumped down onto the wooden floor of the warehouse, silent and apparently uninterested in their fate. Senovara hoped they would all be bought by decent people and not end up being worked to an early death in mines or brothels.

'Do you need a good slave, lady?' asked the slaver as she and Bruccius tried to get past. 'I might be able to offer you a discount if you buy now, before the auction starts.'

'No, thank you. I have a house slave already,' Senovara responded politely.

She thought with affection of Armea, who'd been left at the shop that morning with instructions to keep the children from pestering their father and to make sure Quintus had enough warm beer to ease his toothache. She was a good, steady worker, who had fitted into the family so well that she seemed more like a younger relative than a slave. Senovara had encouraged her to join in with Lucius' lessons at the kitchen table and she had proved a more willing pupil than the lively six-year-old. Armea could now write a reasonable hand on a wax tablet, although she was not yet proficient with pen and ink, and she could read shopping lists without difficulty. Her counting still needed practice, but when she was more confident she would be useful in the shop, which would mean that Quintus could concentrate on making his shoes and leave Armea to deal with the customers.

It seemed extraordinary that Armea had arrived only in Februarius. Senovara could hardly remember how she had managed without her. She hoped Armea was happy; the girl certainly seemed content and was often heard humming as she went about her household tasks or laughing as she played with Lucius and Ertola in the garden. Looking at the bearded slave trader roughly pushing some of his merchandise out of the way as he entered the warehouse, Senovara knew he would be astonished that anyone should worry about whether a slave was happy or not, and she shuddered to think what Armea's fate might have been had Matugenus not considered it his duty to ensure that she had a good home with considerate owners.

But surely her family were not alone in their attitude? thought Senovara. Some army officers travelled with entourages which included freedmen and freedwomen who had decided to continue to work for their previous owners after manumission; they would hardly have done so if they had been badly treated as slaves. Even in Eboracum market there were now freedmen and women trading who had set themselves up in business, either using their own savings or money supplied by their manumitters. Indeed, Senovara knew of several free families who used their freed slaves to trade on their behalf – a system which seemed to benefit both parties but relied a great deal on mutual trust. Senovara supposed that, on the whole, domestic slaves had a better life than those who were bought by tavern-keepers, mine owners, tanners, or even the big landowners, but she understood that the gods decreed who suffered and who didn't and she hoped the deities would oversee today's slave auction in a benign mood.

A trumpet call broke into her musings, making her jump.

'What was that, Bruccius?'

'There's a ship coming in; they always blow a horn to announce their arrival. I recognise that one, though – she belongs to Glaucus, a local trader who's been over to Gallia with a load of cloaks and rugs. He told me he wanted to do one last trip this year, to collect a consignment of pottery figurines to sell as Saturnalia presents. I thought he was leaving it a bit late in the year, so I'm glad to see he's got back safely.'

Bruccius stopped to watch the small sailing ship tacking towards the far shore.

'It's a good thing the wind's dropped; trying to get berthed along here when the wind's blowing from the north can be tricky. See how he's using just the mainsail and the *artemo* – that's the little square sail projecting beyond the bow. He's got the *siparum* furled – that's the triangular topsail. Can you see that fellow in the stern holding the brails? Those are the ropes which furl the sail; by pulling on different ones he can alter the shape of the sail, while the helmsman angles it by pulling on the lee sheet.'

'Do they steer the ship just with the sails, then?' asked Senovara.

'No. Those two big steering oars at the back do most of the work, particularly in these confined waters. You can see the oars hitched up at the sterns of those vessels over there.'

Senovara looked where he was pointing and saw that each of the sailing vessels moored alongside the quay had two great wooden oars jutting out horizontally from their sterns, the blades held well above the waterline. She had noticed these oars before but had presumed that they were used to propel the ships; she hadn't realised that they were for steering.

'There. He's got her in very neatly,' said Bruccius approvingly, as a sailor jumped down onto the quay to moor the incoming ship and an enormous iron anchor was lowered down into the water at the end of its line.

He strode on until they got to the gangplank of a small coaster with the image of an open oyster, complete with pearl, painted on its bow. This must be the *Margarita*. An elderly man was leaning over the railing that ran along the ship's side, having a spirited argument with a trader who stomped off crossly as Senovara and Bruccius drew near. Bruccius hailed the sailor as the captain of the *Margarita*.

'Don't say you're another one who thinks I can make the *Margarita* leap across other vessels to get a berth, just because you've got a consignment on board,' said the captain irascibly, peering down at them. 'Oh, it's you Bruccius; I didn't recognise you for a moment. Come aboard.'

Bruccius shook his head and indicated Senovara. 'This lady is enquiring about a shipment of hides for Quintus Flavius Candidus. Have you got it aboard?'

The captain looked down at a wax writing tablet in his hand. 'Yes, I have but I doubt if it will get unloaded until tomorrow; as you know, we only got berthed this morning and I've got to wait my turn to be unloaded. It was one of the first cargoes aboard so it's right down in the hold and will be one of the last bales out. Can you come back tomorrow with your own transport, lady, or do you want a carter to deliver it?'

That was a poser. Tomorrow was the Ides of October and she and Quintus were planning to attend the races organised by the Legate. Armea would be staying behind to look after the shop and the children, but she wouldn't be able to manage a big bale of hides on her own. They had rented out to a local potter the cart and mule that Quintus had been given by the old carter's widow in Augustus, not having any daily need for the transport themselves nor anywhere to keep them. Because he knew the equipage was worth quite a lot, Quintus had felt worried about keeping it, but had eventually decided that he could salve his conscience by offering the widow a share of the rent. Luckily, the potter was always willing to let them borrow the cart back if he wasn't too busy. If she called in on the way home, she could check that the cart was available and then Quintus could come down first thing in the morning before they went to the races, assuming his toothache was better. In fact, she suddenly thought, the cart would be useful for carrying them to the flat area north of the fortress which had been laid out temporarily as a racing circuit; they could offer some of their neighbours a lift and the cart would be a handy viewing platform from which to see the races if there was a big crowd.

Senovara made a decision. 'We'll come back tomorrow but it will have to be early – before the fourth hour.'

'That will be fine, lady. I'll make sure that your husband's bale is placed at the front of the warehouse so you'll be able to find it easily.'

Senovara thanked him and turned to go. Bruccius went with her, clearly feeling that his escort duty would not be over until she had left the wharf.

'Are you and Quintus going to the races tomorrow?' he asked.

'If Quintus is feeling better, and I hope he is – we've both been looking forward to the event since we first heard of the Legate's plans. I was just thinking, though, if I can get the cart to pick up the hides, we might be able to keep it for the rest of the day and use it to go to the races. Perhaps you and Pervica might like a lift?'

'That's a kindly thought and I'm sure my wife would be happy to accept. Unfortunately, I'm due to take an outgoing vessel down to the estuary later today but I'm hoping to get back in time to see at least one race. Here we are at the street. You should be safe from being knocked into the river now. I'll say farewell until tomorrow – I must go and find those lazy sons of mine, otherwise we'll never get away before the tide turns.'

Senovara said goodbye and repeated her thanks for his rescue and his help with the ship's captain. She then hurried to the potter's workshop, where she was relieved to be told he wouldn't be needing the cart the next day. She arranged with him that the mule would be in the shafts ready for Quintus to collect around the third hour, and then headed home to see if Quintus was feeling better and if he approved of her arrangements.

The wind dropped, and the rain started in earnest. Senovara wrapped her cloak tightly round her, pulling the hood up over her head. She shivered; this was the sort of autumn weather which made it clear that winter was closing in. As she walked home she was thankful that she had worked so hard in September to fill her store cupboards with food that would keep; unless it was a very long, hard winter, she should be able to provide the family with an adequate and varied diet until the spring. Some housewives never seemed to think ahead and often had to put an unending procession of porridge or gruel on the table around Februarius. Senovara had made a pledge with herself when she first got married that she would carry on the country tradition of bottling, salting and drying food in preparation for winter and that she would never rely on being able to find provisions in the market.

Thinking of her store cupboard reminded her that she needed to turn her thoughts to that evening's meal. She had bought some mutton the previous day and had asked Armea to heat the oven while she was at the quayside so that it could be roasted during the afternoon. It had to be cooked or it would go off, and they couldn't afford to waste meat, but Senovara wondered if Quintus would feel like chewing roast mutton. She decided to put the meat in as soon as she got home, then if Quintus' teeth were still giving him trouble she would have time to chop some of it up for rissoles.

When she arrived home, Quintus was firmly of the opinion that they should have rissoles, even though he declared himself to be feeling much better. He was very relieved to hear that his bale of hides was safe. Senovara was worried that he wasn't as well as he pretended but, since she was told to stop fussing in the same breath as she was praised for having carried out his business at the quayside efficiently, she decided not to say anything. Quintus was determined he would be fit enough to go to the races the next day and, while she mixed the finely chopped mutton with egg and lovage, they discussed her idea of taking their neighbours on the cart with them.

'It would be a good idea to set off early,' he warned. 'Everyone seems determined to go, so there'll be a tremendous crush. If we take some food with us we can set off before the seventh hour – the races are due to start at the eighth hour, you know. I just hope this rain stops; if the track gets waterlogged the races will have to be cancelled. I'll wager the Legate is pouring a libation to Jupiter in the hope of a drying wind tonight.'

After she had put the children to bed, Senovara ran next door to talk over her plan with Ursa and Lurio before going along the street to include Pervica and Surilla. Everyone was enthusiastic about a lift to the races, despite the rain, and promised to be outside the shop in plenty of time.

To everyone's relief the next day broke dry and clear. Quintus seemed to have got over his toothache and was in a jocular mood. As soon as it was light enough he set off for the potter's to collect the mule cart while Senovara prepared some food to take with them.

The fort horn was just signalling the fifth hour when Armea stuck her head round the kitchen door.

'Master's back. He wants help lifting down the bale.'

Senovara wiped her hands on her skirts and ran out to the front of the shop, where the mule stood waiting patiently. Quintus was standing on the cart looking down at a large bale of leather tied firmly with plaited ox-hide.

'This is heavy,' he commented. 'I think the best way to move it is if Armea gets up here and pushes it to the edge of the cart and you and I take it from there. I don't want it to land on the road – this leather is too expensive to risk getting any of it dirty. Armea, you can help at Senovara's end when the bale is off the cart.'

He jumped down and Armea scrambled up to take his place. Senovara and Quintus positioned themselves at the back of the cart, while Armea struggled to move the bale towards them, bracing her feet against the front board. The bale tipped suddenly over the edge and Senovara felt her knees buckling as she grasped the ox-hide straps and took the weight. She managed to keep her balance and, puffing and struggling, the three of them staggered into the shop to drop the bale thankfully just inside the door.

Quintus wiped his brow with the sleeve of his tunic. 'I'll unpack them when we get back. They look like good-quality hides,' he said with satisfaction.

Senovara hoped they were; they had come a great distance and had caused a great deal of trouble, but these days the army used so many hides that civilian leatherworkers had to go further and further afield to get their raw material.

It was getting close to the seventh hour when Pervica and Surilla appeared at the door and were courteously helped onto the back of the cart by Quintus. He winked at Senovara as the cart creaked ominously under Pervica's weight and the mule shifted his feet restlessly as the shafts moved.

'I'm really looking forward to this,' declared Pervica as she made herself comfortable. 'I've been to horse races before but I've never seen chariots being raced.'

'I doubt if the horses will be pushed to their limit,' warned Quintus. 'I've heard the Legate has organised the layout of the track as close as he can to a real circus but it won't have been worth stripping off the turf and laying a proper surface. You can't race chariots at full speed on grass, you know.'

'I'm sure it will still be exciting,' said Surilla, her eyes gleaming in anticipation of the treat in store.

'Aren't you bringing Lucius and Ertola, Senovara?' asked Pervica.

'No. We decided that they're too young. I'd spend the whole day worrying that they were going to dart under the horses' hoofs. Lucius is having a good sulk at the moment, I can tell you. Ursa's sons are coming, though; Lurio reckoned they were old enough to behave themselves.'

'Where are Ursa and Lurio?' fretted Quintus. 'If they don't hurry up we won't get a good vantage point. Go and knock on their door, Senovara.'

At that moment, however, the door of their neighbours' house opened and Ursa's two sons came rushing out. They tumbled onto the cart, followed at a more stately pace by their mother. Lurio locked the door of his workshop behind him and, putting the key into the leather pouch at his belt, hurried over to join them.

'I'm sorry if we've kept you, Quintus,' he said, 'but we've just had a letter delivered – the final confirmation that our two boys are now registered as legitimate. We had to read it several times over before we could believe it; it's taken so long to resolve.'

'That's tremendous news, Lurio,' said Quintus, clapping his neighbour on the back enthusiastically.

'You must be relieved,' said Senovara to Ursa as she joined her on the cart.

'We are, and very grateful to Quintus for all his help. If he hadn't been willing to act as witness I don't know what we'd have done. With my brother still up at Vindolanda, there was no one else who knew us before the children were born and who could attest that Lurio was their father.'

'Delighted to be able to assist, Ursa,' declared Quintus jovially. 'Now sit tight, everyone, and we'll be off.'

He clicked his tongue at the mule and the cart moved off down the street to the accompaniment of excited chatter as everyone discussed Ursa and Lurio's news and the day's outing.

Progress to the temporary circus was slow. The streets were thronged with people, all heading the same way on waggons, carts, mules, horses or on foot. When they got to the *porta principalis dextra* of the fortress the crowd was swelled by those soldiers lucky enough to be off duty. Everyone seemed to be in a good mood and there was much laughter as people hailed old friends and exchanged pleasantries.

At last, Quintus turned his mule onto the grassland where the races were to be held and Senovara saw that they were not the only ones to think it might be a good idea to arrive early. The field was already thronged with people. A number of soldiers were acting as stewards, trying vainly to instil some order; as Senovara gazed around her in astonishment, one approached their cart.

'There's still some room on the far side if you want to park your cart by the ropes,' he informed Quintus. 'Could you leave some space right by the ropes so that bystanders can see? Also, when you've got your cart into position, I recommend that you unhitch your mule from the shafts and take him to the compound over there; even mules can get excited when the races start and we don't want any accidents with unofficial runners joining in, complete with carts.'

Quintus laughed. 'I've seen that happen before; the chaos was indescribable,' he told Senovara, as he moved the cart off. 'Now, where shall we settle ourselves?'

Lurio stood up and scanned over the heads of the crowd. 'There's some space left on the far side, over to your right, Quintus. Head down towards the turning post.'

Quintus followed Lurio's directions and they soon found themselves in a good place near the midpoint of the track, almost opposite the finishing line, with the cart alongside the ropes separating the track from the racegoers. Quintus unhitched the mule and Lurio led it off to the compound, accompanied by his two sons, who were hopping from foot to foot with excitement.

'We've got some time before the first race,' said Quintus. 'Let's all have a look round. We can have something to eat between races.'

'You all go off,' declared Pervica. 'I'm quite happy sitting up here and watching the crowd. I'll wait here and mind the cart and our belongings.'

Senovara, Surilla, and Ursa scrambled down to join Quintus, and the four of them set off to explore.

The track itself had been set out as a long rectangle with one rounded end. Down the centre there was a double line of widely spaced fence posts with two horizontal bars, the first of which was set almost as high as Senovara's shoulder. This fence was the *spina* and it ended in a great wooden obelisk at the rounded end of the track. This, Quintus explained, was the turning post. He'd once seen chariot racing in the Circus Maximus in Roma, and told them that the turning post there was gilded with a great ball on the top. At the open end of the track, twelve white lines were painted on the grass to the right of the central fence, making lanes, so that none of the competitors had an unfair advantage at the start. Quintus explained to his female entourage that at a proper circus there would be wooden starting gates, but it was likely that today's races would be started by a man blowing a trumpet. At the moment, the course itself was quiet and clear of all activity; outside the ropes there was noise and bustle and Senovara wondered if the trumpet would be heard above the din. Many of the Eboracum traders had grasped the opportunity to make money, and wooden stalls had sprung up selling a wide variety of food and drink. Street traders mingled with the crowd, carrying baskets of fruit, toys and trinkets. There were a lot of ribbon sellers but their wares were confined to red, green, white and blue. Senovara commented on this to her friends, and Quintus explained that at the Circus Maximus there were four teams and that they were distinguished by these colours, which were also worn by their supporters. He seemed amused that the idea was being copied at Eboracum.

Senovara began to feel dizzy from all the noise. Not only were the racegoers being assailed from all sides by traders' cries, but there were also a number of men offering to take wagers on the result of the races. These men had attracted the interest of a few civilians but were mostly surrounded by soldiers, many of whom were clearly convinced they would make a fortune during the course of the afternoon. Quintus said it was more likely that they would lose the whole of their last quarter's salary like several of his friends in the past.

'Look, Quintus, isn't that Veturius over there?' Senovara pointed to where the Pannonian centurion was watching some soldiers from his century trying to negotiate better odds.

'It is. Hail, Veturius. Are you here on your own?'

'Hail, Quintus. Hail, ladies.' Veturius acknowledged Senovara and her friends punctiliously. 'Broginara and Adnamata aren't here, of course, but there's quite a contingent from the fortress as you can see.'

'How are Broginara and Adnamata? Are the twins thriving?' enquired Senovara.

'They're all doing well, thank you. Adnamata found that she couldn't feed both boys – they both seem to have the appetites of true legionaries – but Grata has found us a good wet nurse from among the soldiers' women on the other side of the Abus. A sensible woman; sadly not a Greek, as the medical writers advocate, but that wasn't to be expected. She's had two children of her own so she's a great help in advising Adnamata and she seems to be of a steady temperament, which is important. Gaius and Aulus are doing really well now they're getting properly fed. Grata has even recommended removing their swaddling bands already and they are only thirty days old.'

'That is early. They must be doing well.'

Veturius continued to extol the virtues of his sons until he spotted the young tribune who had accompanied the Legate to Quintus' workshop.

'Excuse me. I must just have a word with Pontius Sabinus,' he muttered, and he hurried away.

'He seems to be in a rush,' commented Senovara, feeling that his departure had been somewhat peremptory. 'But I suppose military business has to take precedence over manners.'

'Not in this case,' snorted Basilia, who had just arrived behind them with her husband, Anicius Ingenuus. 'Haven't you heard? Marcus Pontius Sabinus has been showing interest in Broginara. Everyone up at the fortress is expecting him to make an offer for her soon. Veturius won't want to miss any opportunity of making himself pleasant to the young man.'

Senovara was amazed. 'Really? I had no idea. When did all this start?'

'After Adnamata had the twins. Pontius Sabinus is an only son and his parents have been stressing the need for him to marry again – his first wife died in childbirth, you know? Although at nearly thirty Broginara is older than most Roman brides, the fact that she comes from a family which produces male twins makes her an attractive proposition.'

'I'd have expected him to wait until he got back to Roma and could choose a girl from another equestrian family,' commented Quintus, who was as intrigued by this turn of events as his wife and her friends.

'I get the impression that the tribune isn't interested in marrying a child but rather likes the idea of a sensible wife who's well educated and can make intelligent conversation, play musical instruments and is skilful at board games,' said Anicius Ingenuus. 'He's a bit quiet and reserved, you know, but he seems to know his own mind.'

'There's no reason why he shouldn't marry her,' Basilia added. 'She may not have a huge dowry but neither is she a pauper. She's a free woman and is in all respects perfectly eligible.'

'Do either of you know what Broginara thinks of the idea?' asked Senovara.

'Haven't seen her to ask,' admitted Basilia. 'Those babies are keeping the whole household occupied at the moment. She's not been visiting anyone and I didn't come across her at the bathhouse the other day. Haven't you seen her, Senovara?'

'Not for a while. I went to visit Adnamata when the babies were first born and I attended their naming ceremony on the ninth day, but I've been too busy preparing my stores for winter these last few days to pay social calls.'

Senovara was thrilled by this latest piece of gossip. It was only last month that she had thought it would be a good thing if Broginara could have her own household and now, all of a sudden, it seemed possible. It would be an excellent marriage for her and she would make a good wife for the young tribune.

'Are you here in your professional capacity, Marcus?' asked Quintus.

'I'm afraid so. If any of the riders falls off I'm expected to stick them back together again and mend their sore heads. Titus Flavius Virilis, the *veterinarius*, is here, too, but I don't think he'll have much to do; most of the officers up from Londinium have brought their own horse doctors with them. But it does mean that Basilia and I get an official seat and a good view. How are the children?'

'Both well, thank Jupiter,' answered Quintus, 'but Ertola still isn't speaking.'

'Why don't you bring her along to see me? Sometimes the gods help us doctors when they won't respond to the patients' own pleas.'

Quintus and Senovara looked at each other. They had tried most things; this might just work. They thanked the *medicus ordinarius* but before they could settle on a date for the appointment he was called away to deal with a soldier who had been kicked by a horse.

Senovara and Quintus, accompanied still by Surilla and Ursa, completed the circuit of the track. Back at the cart, they found Pervica holding court with several acquaintances, including Aqmat and Hairan, who had returned to Eboracum a few days earlier.

'Hail, Aqmat. I wasn't sure if you would be well enough to attend today,' said Senovara.

Aqmat had found her journey back from the frontier at the end of September, in the pouring rain, a great trial and had succumbed to a feverish cold as soon as she crossed her own threshold. Senovara noticed that she had her blue cloak tightly wrapped round her body, although she had left her head uncovered and was not peeping out with one eye as she normally did, in the Palmyrene way. Her hairpins and earrings glittered in the fitful sunshine, drawing the attention of passers-by.

'I'm feeling much better now, thank you, Senovara, and I didn't want to miss an event like this. Our cart is over there – we arrived too late to get close to the ropes.'

'Join us,' invited Quintus hospitably. 'We've managed to get an excellent spot and there's plenty of room on our cart. Just let me get to our baskets and I will pour some wine for everyone – have you got beakers with you?'

'I think we could all do with something to eat as well,' suggested Senovara. At these words, Ursa's sons appeared by her side as suddenly as if they were messengers of the gods. Quintus laughed and ruffled the hair of the taller boy when Ursa slapped her son's questing hand out of a basket.

'I've brought plenty of bread and meat,' said Senovara. 'Why don't you all help yourselves? It looks as if racing is going to be a hungry business; we can share the contents of the rest of the baskets later.'

Soon everyone was either perched on the edge of the cart or standing around it, munching contentedly and catching up with gossip – the news of Broginara's romance being of particular interest.

'How's our other local romance going, Pervica?' asked Senovara of her old friend, who was always the first to hear the gossip.

'You mean Catia and Bonosius? Well, it's difficult to tell. They attended the Ludi Romani celebrations together, but Catia didn't seem very relaxed about it.'

'Is she coming today?' asked Ursa.

'I believe Bonosius is bringing her in his cart but I haven't spotted them yet.'

Suddenly there was a great fanfare from the four trumpeters standing in front of the platform that had been set up by the edge of the track, next to the finishing line. The Legate and the other senior officers from the fortress took their places on the dais. When the crowd was quiet, one of the tribunes stood up and announced the first race, which was to be for twelve horses. The crowd looked towards the end of the track, where grooms were leading the runners into their positions. The race was for soldiers in the Sixth Legion Victrix, and the riders, dressed only in their red tunics, sat on their saddles looking tense. The horses' harness was made from narrow leather straps without the usual metal decoration. At first Senovara presumed that the harness mounts had been left off in case their jangling distracted the horses, but then she remembered Matugenus once telling her that a racing harness needed to be very light so that the horse carried the least possible weight. She was sorry that he and Ahteha had not been able to come – they would have enjoyed the outing – but Ahteha had been ill with stomach cramps for several days and Matugenus didn't want to leave her.

An *optio* ran back and forth in front of the line of horses, making sure that none was over the starting line. When he was satisfied, he ran to the edge of the track and a soldier standing on a small plinth blew a sharp blast on a trumpet. They were off.

The twelve horses thundered down the far side of the fence, came sharply round the turning post and galloped up towards Senovara's party. The ground shook as they passed and clods of earth, gouged up by their hooves, flew in every direction. The crowd erupted, everyone yelling encouragement to their favoured mount. Even those racegoers sitting on carts or who had provided themselves with seats were on their feet, carried away with excitement.

The field finished the first lap neck and neck, turned smartly at the open end and headed round again. The races were all to be of seven laps. As the horses approached the turning post for the third time, a bay horse stumbled and his rider fell heavily. Immediately, some soldiers ran on with a wooden stretcher and carried him to one side, while the loose horse carried on with the race. At the end of the sixth lap, the bay suddenly realised that the open end of the track offered him an escape route and he veered off to his right, nearly bringing down two other horses. The whole crowd held its breath as the two soldiers struggled to keep their seats and cheered unanimously when they held on.

'Those two won't be pleased,' commented Quintus. 'They'll never catch up with the rest now.'

A great cheer went up as the leaders crossed the finishing line in front of the Legate's platform. It had been a close-run race and everyone applauded when the winner trotted up to be presented with his palm branch. As the Legate came to the front of the platform to present the prizes, Senovara suddenly clutched Quintus' hand. Lucius Minicius Quadronius Verus Natalis, Legate of the Sixth Legion Victrix, was wearing his new purple and gold boots. Quintus' chest swelled with pride and he squeezed her hand tightly, but he said nothing.

The next race was for civilians. The riders wore trousers with their torsos naked to the freshening breeze, and, unlike the soldiers, they rode bareback. Mostly they were farmers from the surrounding district who could afford to carry on the old tradition of keeping horses for racing. As children, Senovara and Matugenus had often been taken to races organised by the local landowners, many of whom were descended from the great warrior families who had ridden into battle generations ago. Although her family had never taken part in the races, Senovara couldn't remember missing a single meeting. Not only did her family enjoy the races themselves but her father always said it was the best way he knew of keeping in touch with what was going on in the district. It was at the races and at religious festivals that business was done, daughters looked over as prospective brides, and old feuds fought out.

Quintus and Lurio knew several of the riders in this race and a spirited argument broke out between them as to who was likely to win. In the end they each put an *as* down on the seat of the cart and declared that whoever chose the winner would have both coins; if neither of their chosen jockeys won, they would each have their coin back. As it was, both their choices fell before the field had gone round twice and they picked up their coins to derisive comments from their friends.

The trumpeters blew their *cornua* again and the tribune stood up to announce the first chariot race. It was for *bigae*, chariots drawn by two horses, and there were four contestants. Senovara craned her neck to see the chariots being led to the starting line by grooms. The charioteers, each dressed in a leather cuirass and leather trousers with a wide belt in his team's colours, strolled out, nonchalantly acknowledging the cheers of the crowd. Before mounting onto the platforms of their vehicles, they saluted the Legate and then put on their bronze helmets with wide brow-bands and grilled visors. Senovara thought they looked quite sinister as their expressions disappeared behind these defences. Once again, the worried *optio* ran around arranging the contestants to his satisfaction before the trumpeter started the race.

Senovara had never seen anything like this before. She had seen farmers race each other in their mule carts if they happened to meet along the road on the way back from market, but those races had been run at a lumbering trot, not at the gallop. The charioteers stood on a tiny wooden platform balanced over the axle between the two wheels. They were protected from the rear hoofs of their horses by a curved basketwork barrier, but the back of each chariot was open. As they shot round the turning post they leaned into the curve, their off-side wheels off the ground, and Senovara wondered how they kept upright. They galloped past her and she could hear them cursing their horses and exhorting them to go faster, the thunder of the horses' hoofs and the rumble of the wheels increasing as they got nearer and then subsiding just as quickly when they had passed, leaving a shower of dirt and grass behind them.

Even though the chariots did the full seven laps, the race seemed to be over in an instant, such was the tension. The winner wheeled over to the Legate's platform to be presented with a garland and then trotted round on a lap of honour before leaving the track.

'Well, that was something!' declared Pervica. 'How do they keep those tiny chariots from falling over, that's what I want to know? You'd think they'd blow away in a stiff breeze, the way they lift off the ground.'

All around them the crowd was eagerly discussing the race, and the trumpeters had to blow the signal for the next event twice before the tribune could make himself heard. The afternoon progressed with more horse races and another two *biga* races before the event they had all been waiting for was announced: the *quadriga* race. The Legate had disappeared from his platform during the last event and now emerged from a small tent behind the platform, dressed in his leather racing garments. A great cheer went up as he made his way to the starting line, where his chariot and three others were being lined up. Each assemblage had two grooms to hold the heads of its four horses as they danced about nervously. The Legate acknowledged his rivals courteously before donning his helmet and climbing into position. He gathered the reins in his hands, and flexed his shoulders, settled his feet slightly apart and crouched forward. He looked at the starter and nodded. The crowd fell silent and then, as the chariots sprang forward, everyone started to shout, mostly for the Legate, who was known to them all, but the other competitors had brought with them their own supporters who tried their best to out-shout the rest.

Round and round the chariots raced, swaying as they cornered. At one point one of the Legate's horses slipped and there was a gasp from the crowd, but he retrieved the situation with a practised hand and no one was surprised when he crossed the finishing line first. The tribune who had been announcing the races came down from the platform to hand the Legate a gilded palm leaf. Minicius Natalis then drove his chariot round the track slowly, waving the palm branch at the cheering crowd.

As he left the track, the sounds subsided. The afternoon was over.

'I'll go over to the compound and get the mule,' said Quintus, 'but it may take me a while; everyone will be wanting to leave at the same time.' He strode off.

Senovara and her friends started to pack up the remains of their picnic, and Aqmat and Hairan said their farewells and went off to collect their own cart.

Bruccius and his two sons appeared.

'You didn't miss it all, did you?' asked Pervica.

'No. We arrived just in time to see the last race. I can see there'll be plenty of young men round here wanting to take up *quadriga* racing, though. That was wonderfully exciting.' His two sons looked sheepish at their father's teasing.

'No one in our family is taking up *quadriga* racing!' said Pervica firmly. 'You three eat enough as it is without us having to feed four great horses as well.'

Quintus returned with the mule. 'Hail, Bruccius,' he exclaimed. 'I must thank you for helping Senovara down at the quayside yesterday. She told me how kind you were.'

'Only too happy to assist, Quintus. You got your hides, did you?'

'I picked them up this morning. Can we give you and your boys a lift back? I think the old mule can manage three more.'

'No, we must get down to the quay, but if you'd take Pervica back I'd be grateful. I'll help you harness the mule,' said Bruccius.

As they made their way home, Senovara felt her eyelids getting heavy and it wasn't long before she fell fast asleep, her head resting on Quintus' shoulder. It had been a very tiring few days, what with her visit to the quayside and all the excitement of the races. She was so tired that she didn't even wake properly when they arrived home and their neighbours said goodbye.

She stirred when Quintus lifted her down from the cart and carried her into the shop. 'He was wearing your boots, Quintus,' she said sleepily. 'That was the best part of the day.'

November

THE MONTH STARTED mild, for which Senovara was grateful, since it meant it was possible to dig the vegetable beds over in preparation for winter without the usual discomfort. She set Armea to work on the last area one fine morning, as soon as it was light enough to see, while she herself started to earth up the leeks to blanch them and protect them from the frost so that they could be dug out as needed over the next few months. Traditionalists like her grandmother might scorn leeks as foreign imports, but Senovara considered them a fine introduction; so few vegetables could be left in the ground to see a family over the lean winter months and these could be used in so many recipes and medicines.

The garden was looking gaunt. The leaves had already fallen from most of the surrounding trees, weakened by the summer's drought, but the apple tree was still green and a robin, hidden among the leaves, was noisily commenting on their work. Senovara was pleased with her first real harvest from the young tree and had stored the apples in the roof space above the shop where there was room to spread them out. Hopefully, they would keep well and there would still be some left for the hungry days of early spring.

Senovara was so absorbed in her thoughts and her work that she started when she heard her name spoken just behind her.

'Basilia! This is a rare visit – there's nothing wrong, I hope?'

'No, nothing wrong. I simply bring a message from my husband. He hasn't forgotten the promise he made to Quintus at the races last month and says that, if you'd like to bring Ertola to see him tomorrow, he'll see if there is anything he can do for her.'

'Oh, that is kind of him. We've tried everything we can think of and his opinion would be most welcome. Did he say any particular time?'

'No, any hour will do. As you know, he usually spends the day before the Ides of each month at home so that civilians can consult him without having to go to the *valetudinarium*. If he has another patient you may have to wait, but the usual round of winter coughs and chills hasn't started yet, so I doubt if you'll have to wait long.'

Senovara wiped her hands on the piece of sacking she had tied round her waist to protect her skirts from the mud.

'Have you got time to have a beaker of wine?'

'That would be very welcome, Senovara, but I can't stay long. I've got to get my shopping done.'

In the kitchen, Senovara offered her guest a seat and turned to encourage the embers on top of the stove to give a cheerier flame. After adding a little more fuel, she took a couple of beakers down from the shelf and poured some red wine into each. Her guest added a generous quantity of water to her wine and settled down to catch up on the gossip. Senovara took a small box of honey cakes down from the high shelf where she had put them out of the children's reach, and put it open on the table.

'Have you recovered from the races yet?' Basilia asked as she selected a small oval cake from the box and peeled the bay leaf from its base.

Senovara laughed, recalling how she had fallen asleep on the way home. 'No one round here has talked about anything else since. Lucius is still cross because we wouldn't let him go; Ursa's boys have been playing charioteers almost every day and he feels left out because they were there and he wasn't. Quintus has had to promise to make him a model of a chariot for his Kalends present. It was certainly exciting, though. Did your husband have much work to do that day?'

'There were a few accidents,' said Basilia. 'One cracked skull and a couple of broken legs, but Marcus was liberal in his application of boiled lard and they all seem to have survived to boast about their exploits. There were plenty of bruises and sprains as well – the *seplasarius* told me he had quite a run on dried boars' manure in water for a few days.'

'I hadn't realised what a dangerous sport chariot racing was,' said Senovara. 'I kept expecting someone to be killed at any moment. Did you see how that chariot was smashed to pieces when it turned over?'

'I did. I thought they'd be more solidly built than that, but Marcus says a well-built chariot would be very heavy and would hold the horses back. The lighter the chariot, the faster it will go, but the easier it is to smash into kindling too.'

For a few moments the two women relived the thrills of the circus before moving on to other matters.

'Is there any further news about Broginara and the tribune?' asked Senovara. She had been bursting with curiosity about this exciting development in her friend's life, but had felt uncomfortable about calling on her, in case it was thought she was being nosy.

'The betrothal looks likely to be held in Ianuarius. I think Marcus Pontius Sabinus is waiting to hear what his parents think of the idea before making a formal announcement, and it could take a while for their letter to arrive at this time of year. I haven't had a chance to talk to Broginara about it alone; she's always in the house with Adnamata and the twins these days. How about Catia and Bonosius? You see more of them than I do. Any developments there?'

'I think she's going to accept him.'

'Really? The last I heard she was trying to put him off again.'

Senovara grinned at her friend. 'I met her the other day at the water trough. She declared that he'd worn her down.'

'Well, she could do worse. But where would they live? Did she say?'

'I suspect it's that sort of detail which is stopping her making a final decision.'

'It would probably be better if they lived in Catia's house,' mused Basilia. 'It's a good size and it would mean Bonosius could improve the storage space behind his shop and expand his business.'

'I shouldn't start planning a betrothal gift for them yet,' warned Senovara. 'The way the two of them have been behaving, the whole thing might still be called off. When I saw her at the trough she said that, if he was anything like her first husband, she'd probably see less of him after they were wed than before, and that this was an argument in favour of the marriage. Those didn't strike me as the words of a woman deeply in the thrall of Eros.'

Basilia laughed. 'And if they marry, we'll all have to find something else to gossip about.'

'Oh, there'll always be plenty for us to talk about,' said Senovara. 'The way the town's growing there'll be lots of new people to keep us interested. Have you been over the bridge recently? The army families who arrived in Iulius have been putting up houses at a great rate. I was worried that many of them would have to spend the winter in their carts but they all seem to have got proper roofs over their heads now.'

Basilia shook her head. 'I have few reasons to go over there at this time of year but, as everyone keeps telling me it has changed so much, I might just take a walk over there out of sheer curiosity.'

'Have you heard from either of your daughters recently?' asked Senovara.

'Not since I had a letter from Calpurnia in Augustus. It takes such a long time for letters to arrive these days. She and her husband are with the Thirtieth Ulpia Victrix in Germania, you know, and they seem to have settled in well. Marcia's husband has a position in the *operum publicorum* in Roma; whenever she writes, she always says there's nothing to say, but it would be nice to know how my grandchildren are getting on.'

She finished her wine and stood up. 'Well, I must be getting on myself, or the day will be over before I have finished anything. Thank you for the wine. I'll see you tomorrow, no doubt, when you bring Ertola to see Marcus.'

Senovara ushered her friend out through the shop, then turned to Quintus. 'Did Basilia tell you that her husband is willing to see Ertola tomorrow?'

'Yes, and I call it kind of him to remember, though I have my doubts as to whether he will be able to do anything for her,' Quintus responded gloomily.

The subject of their concern was sitting in a corner of the shop, playing with her doll. Senovara had at last finished the set of doll's clothes for Venus, and Ertola enjoyed nothing better than to sit for hours taking them off and putting them back on again. For her third birthday, at the beginning of the month, Quintus had made a tiny pair of boots for the doll, which had been a great success. Now, hearing her parents mention her name, she looked up, gave them a sunny smile, then lurched to her feet and came over to show her mother what she had been doing.

'Oh, you've plaited her hair, just as Ursa taught you. What a clever girl,' exclaimed Senovara, looking at the strips of wool which covered the doll's head and which were now pulled back into a single, rather untidy plait.

She beamed down at her daughter. Even though she didn't speak, Ertola was more advanced in other ways than her brother had been at a similar age, and, as she gazed down at her daughter, Senovara felt the frustration of not hearing the childish prattling which would normally be expected from a three-year-old.

'We're going to see Marcus Anicius Ingenuus and Basilia tomorrow morning, Ertola. You'll like that, won't you?' Senovara asked anxiously.

Ertola, having no reason to expect that she wouldn't enjoy the outing, nodded amiably before trotting off down the kitchen passage, followed by her mother.

The next morning, Senovara woke to find that the bowl of water she had left on the bedroom cupboard after the family's evening wash had frozen solid. There had been a hard frost in the night, the first of the winter. As she looked out of the back door at the cold, grey light of morning, Senovara silently thanked the Mother Goddesses that she and Armea had finished digging over the garden and had protected the remaining vegetables. Everything in the garden was rimmed with silver, from the dark clay ridges of the vegetable beds to the edges of the leaves on the apple trees. The pea haulms heaped over the last of the cabbages looked like loose tangles of silver rope. Senovara stood for a moment, entranced by the sight. If the frozen wastes of the Underworld were like this – as some people claimed – eternity would certainly be uncomfortable, but not without its compensations.

Quintus came into the kitchen, wearing trousers for the first time that winter. He rubbed his hands together vigorously. 'It looks as if winter has arrived,' he said. 'I thought all that mild weather was too good to be true.'

'I'm just thankful we got most of the gardening done yesterday,' said Senovara. 'If it's going to be as cold as this, we might not get another chance. When shall we go to see Anicius Ingenuus?'

'I thought we might leave here about the ninth hour. I know he tends to see most of his patients in the morning, so if we wait until after he has had his midday meal we shouldn't have to wait long to see him. I've got too much work to finish to hang about while someone gives him a long account of all their aches and pains.'

Senovara agreed that this seemed sensible. Since word had got round that Quintus had made the elegant boots worn by the Legate at the races, many people from both the fortress and the settlement had asked him to make them boots or sandals, and he now had a respectable order list. Unfortunately, everyone seemed to want their footwear produced by the end of the year, which meant that Quintus was working long hours to fill the orders. That he was willing to spend valuable daylight taking Ertola to see the *medicus ordinarius* was a sign of how concerned he was about his daughter's health. Senovara felt tears welling behind her eyes and blinked them away quickly, grateful that she would not have to take Ertola to visit the *medicus* on her own.

The frost soon lifted and the sun shone with the sparkling clear light of a fine winter's day. Despite her worries, Senovara found herself humming as she went about her household tasks. Bright days at this time of year were to be welcomed for the chance they gave for drying laundry, and she and Armea were kept fully occupied washing clothes and draping them over the boughs of the apple tree until the time came for Senovara to make some soup from her store of dried mushrooms.

She called down the passage to Quintus that the soup was ready. When he entered the kitchen he looked a little preoccupied.

'What's the matter? You look as if your teeth are hurting again. Do you want some mustard seed to chew?' asked Senovara anxiously. With such a long list of customers waiting for boots, Quintus would not be pleased if he was hampered by toothache again.

'No, my teeth are fine. I've just had a letter delivered from Gaius. He says that young Lucia isn't well.'

'Does he say what's wrong with her?'

'Not really. Here, have a look for yourself,' said Quintus, handing her the familiar wooden strips. Senovara sat down on the bench and read the inked words quietly to herself.

> *From Gaius Flavius Naso, Centurion of the VIth Legion Victrix at Vercovicium, to Quintus Flavius Candidus, his brother at Eboracum, many greetings. I pray that you are enjoying the best of fortune and are in good health. My daughter, Lucia, is not as well as I might wish, having spots and a fever. It would be a kindness if you could send a fever cure by return, for the medicines here are not helping her. Flavia and Alana are well and send their wishes for your own health and prosperity.*

Senovara looked up at her husband, who was morosely dunking lumps of bread into his soup.

'It's just as well that we're seeing Anicius Ingenuus in a few hours,' she said. 'We can ask him to recommend a good fever cure. Then we can call in at the fortress on the way home and see if Veturius knows of a messenger going up to the frontier tomorrow who could act as carrier.'

'Aye, Anicius Ingenuus is a clever man and well versed in the latest ideas from Graecia. Hopefully, he'll have some idea what's causing Lucia's spots, as well as what ails young Ertola,' he added, ruffling his daughter's shiny curls. 'When I've finished my soup, I'll bank up the brazier in the shop and check that everything is left tidy so that Armea can find the boots which are due for collection, and then we'll be off.'

Within a short time, they had got themselves organised and Ertola was wrapped snugly in her cloak, with a stout pair of boots on her feet, and a bright yellow scarf round her neck.

'Can I come too?' enquired Lucius, as he observed these preparations.

'Not this time, son,' said his father. 'The *medicus ordinarius* is just going to have a quick look at Ertola's throat to see if he can help her speak.'

Lucius scowled, annoyed at being excluded from an outing. 'Being a *medicus* he'll probably want to do something really nasty to her, like cut off one of her ears,' he announced, rolling his eyes horribly at his sister. Ertola's own eyes widened in terror and she ran whimpering to her mother's skirts.

'No, he won't,' said Senovara in exasperation, and she picked her daughter up. 'He's just trying to help, unlike you. Don't listen to him, Ertola; he's just being unkind. Pater wouldn't let anyone hurt you, would you, Quintus?'

She hoped she was right about Anicius Ingenuus. In her experience, doctors attached to the Roman army were capable of almost anything. Quintus, of course, was confident that anyone trained in Greek medicine knew what they were doing; even if they wanted to operate on their patients with knives and probes; she preferred treating ailments with potions, in the northern way.

'No, I wouldn't,' her husband responded firmly, 'although I might be tempted to do something unpleasant to you, Lucius, if you behave like that again.'

Lucius glared at his parents.

'If you want something to do while we're out, you can practise your writing,' said Senovara. 'That should keep you out of mischief. The wax tablet and the stylus are on the table.'

Lucius didn't look very pleased at this suggestion, she thought, as she wrapped her own cloak round her shoulders, but it would keep him from plaguing Armea while she looked after the shop. He would be going to school next year and the schoolmaster, who taught a small group of children in his house in the next street, would expect him to be able to read and write. Lucius was going to have to work hard over the next few months whether he liked it or not.

As Senovara, Quintus and Ertola turned into the road to the fortress, they had to stop for a moment to give way to a herd of small black cattle being driven in the same direction. There must have been at least thirty of the beasts, destined for the military abattoir where, at this time of year, their meat would probably be smoked in case supplies of fresh meat couldn't get through when the snows came. The animals' breath steamed in the cold afternoon air, forming a cloud around their heads, and they seemed more nervous than usual; the two herdsmen and their dogs had their work cut out to keep them on course. Quintus snatched Ertola up hurriedly as one of the bullocks kicked its heels and tried to escape down an alleyway between two houses.

One of the herdsmen ran round with a loud cry, bringing his stick down on the beast's rump to encourage it back onto the road.

'I don't know what's got into them today, really I don't,' panted the man as he passed Quintus and Senovara. 'They've been like this since we crossed the river. I've been bringing cattle in for the military for years now and I've never had such problems.' Despite the chill in the air, the man looked hot and bothered, his face the same bright red as the kerchief tucked into the neck of his hooded *byrrus*.

'You haven't got far to go now,' said Quintus, sympathetically.

'I know and I thank the Gods for that,' replied the herdsman. 'Nor – and I'm particularly grateful to Bacchus for this benefit – do I have far to go to get a good, hot flagon of beer down me after I've been paid. I reckon me and Quartio have earned our time in the tavern today.'

He waved his stick cheerily and set off again, exhorting his stock with loud cries and curses.

'That was curious,' said Quintus. 'I wonder what's wrong with those beasts? Something has obviously upset them, yet there are no insects about in this weather to bite them.'

The cattle's peculiar behaviour was quickly forgotten, however, when they reached the door of the house where the *medicus ordinarius* lived and had his civilian practice. It was opened by Basilia herself.

'Hail to you all. Come on through to the consulting room. Marcus is waiting for you; there's no one with him at the moment.'

She showed them into a room which opened off the entrance chamber. Senovara looked around with interest. Although she had known the Greek couple for many years, she had never been in the consulting room. In some ways it reminded her of Grata's cottage, with its couch against one wall and its rows of shelves laden with boxes and pots for pills, medicines and amulets; but it was neater and more businesslike, and lacked the cheerful, domestic touch provided by Grata's stove and battered furniture. Instead of a large, central table, there was a small wooden desk under the glazed window, with a bronze box and writing equipment on it. In front of the desk, there were four small stools with padded leather seats for the comfort of the patients and physician during the consultations. Basilia had told Senovara that the *medicus ordinarius* had another room where his freedman made up pills and potions and stored all the medical ingredients; Senovara presumed that was why there were few of the herbal aromas so much in evidence in Grata's cottage.

Marcus Anicius Ingenuus was reading a papyrus scroll when they were shown in, but he jumped up to welcome them, rolling the scroll up and handing it to his servant to put away in its cylindrical box.

'Hail. Come on in and sit down. Can we offer you any wine?'

Quintus shook his head. 'Thank you, but no. I must get back to my workshop as soon as possible.'

'Then I'll leave you all to it,' Basilia said and she left the room, closing the door softly behind her.

Her grey-haired husband smiled at them. 'You're here about your daughter, aren't you? Come here and let me have a look at you, young lady.'

Senovara undid the little brooch at her daughter's neck, took off the child's cloak and scarf, and gave her a gentle, encouraging push forward.

Ertola stood sturdily between her parents and the doctor, looking slightly unsure what was expected of her. The physician winked broadly at her and she smiled back, reassured by his avuncular manner. To Senovara's relief she submitted patiently as he examined her. First, he ran his hands behind her ears, over her head and around her neck, occasionally asking her if any part hurt, to which she shook her head solemnly. Then he turned to his desk and slid back the lid of the bronze box. Senovara and Ertola both looked at the box with curiosity. Inside there were a number of small compartments, some square with knobbed lids, some oblong and holding a selection of neatly arranged bronze and iron instruments. Most of the instruments looked benign, but a row of iron scalpel blades made Senovara nervous about what the next stage in the examination might entail. Marcus Anicius Ingenuus selected a bronze probe and, opening Ertola's mouth, inserted one bulbous end. He peered down her throat, moving her head this way and that so that he could see better in the light of an oil lamp which hung from an iron bracket on the wall.

After a while he put the probe back in the box and slid the lid into place. He picked Ertola up and sat her on his knee.

'Does she come when you call her?' he asked Senovara.

'Yes. She's very obedient.'

'So she doesn't have tantrums or get frustrated when she can't do a task she has set herself?'

'Not as often as her elder brother,' remarked Quintus.

'Do you speak many different languages at home, or just Latin?'

'Usually Latin,' said Quintus. 'Senovara speaks her tribal dialect sometimes with our slave and I speak my old tongue if any other Germans are present – or if I lose my temper,' he added with a grin.

'What about Ertola's brother? Did he learn to speak easily?' the physician continued.

'Noisy from the start. Nowadays he can switch from local speech to Latin without thinking – and swear in my language and several others, I regret to say.'

Marcus smiled, then bounced Ertola on his knee absent-mindedly, clearly deep in thought.

Eventually he looked at Quintus and Senovara, who had followed his every move with anxious eyes. 'I can't see anything or think of anything which might be stopping her talking. The uvula and tonsils seem perfectly healthy, so removing them would probably do no good,' he said encouragingly. 'What remedies have you tried so far?'

Quintus mentioned the amber amulet provided by Grata and the decoction of wine and blackberry shoots, the gargle of mustard and goose grease, and the tincture of sage that had been recommended by various friends. He then listed the gods they had made offerings to in the hope that some divine good will could be directed to his daughter: the Matres, Fortuna, the healing god Salus, Jupiter, and of course their own household deities.

'And we've been very careful to use her proper name whenever we made the sacrifices, so that the holy gods know who she is,' Senovara broke in eagerly.

Marcus Anicius Ingenuus looked surprised. 'Is Ertola not her real name, then?'

'No. She was named Flavia, as is right and proper for our family,' explained Quintus, 'but my sister-in-law is also called Flavia, as is her own elder daughter, of course. It got very confusing, so we slipped into the habit of calling our daughter Ertola and my brother calls his child Alana – both are old names in our family; names we used for girls before we became Roman citizens. Senovara has been worried that in saving ourselves confusion we may have muddled the gods.'

'I doubt if it has confused the Holy Ones,' laughed Marcus, 'and I'm sure they'll allow Ertola to speak in their own good time.'

'That's what Grata said,' commented Senovara with relief.

'Grata is a wise woman,' responded the Greek physician, gravely acknowledging the skills of a fellow professional. 'We don't always agree about treatments but she understands women and children.'

Quintus rose to his feet and thanked Marcus for seeing them. A short, polite skirmish then ensued over payment for the consultation.

'There's no charge, old friend,' declared Marcus. 'I've only looked at the child and offered reassurance. It will be the gods who will require payment when she eventually speaks.'

Quintus looked concerned at this generosity; he was a proud man and preferred to pay his way. 'In which case, there will be no charge the next time you have any boots to mend,' he asserted.

Senovara tugged at the sleeve of his tunic. 'Don't forget about Lucia,' she whispered.

'Of course!' Quintus turned back to the *medicus ordinarius*. 'My brother's younger daughter, up on the frontier, has a fever and spots. He has written to ask us to send up a cure. Can you recommend one?'

Marcus frowned. 'Did he say where the spots are, or what they look like or how long she has had the fever?'

'No, but she must have been ill for a few days; the letter implied that they had tried several treatments already, and it will have taken some time for the message to get down to us.'

'My colleague at Vercovicium is a sound man and I'm sure he'll have offered the best advice, but I can let you have a medicine based on vervain and coriander which is very good for all fevers. It's only two *asses.*'

He called to his young servant and instructed him to fetch a flask of the medicine from the store.

'Here you are,' he said, as the freedman came back into the room holding a glass flask with its wooden stopper firmly held in place with wax. 'That should work. How are you going to get it up to Vercovicium?'

'We thought we'd call in at the fortress on our way home and ask Veturius if he knows of anyone going north tomorrow,' replied Quintus, giving the freedman two coins.

'No need to do that. I've just arranged for a consignment of medical supplies to go to Vindolanda. The rider's due to start at first light tomorrow and he won't dawdle. They've had an outbreak of inflammation of the eye there and they need more eye salve urgently. The satchels will be well packed with straw so the bottle won't get broken. I'll make sure it's clearly labelled as an urgent delivery for Vercovicium.'

Quintus and Senovara were expressing their gratitude to Marcus for this offer when Basilia stuck her head round the door to announce the arrival of another patient.

'We must go, Marcus,' declared Quintus. 'We've already taken up too much of your time. Farewell to you both.'

Senovara stepped from the building feeling much happier than when she'd gone in. If both Marcus Anicius Ingenuus and Grata thought there was nothing seriously wrong with Ertola, she was confident they were right. She was particularly relieved that Ertola would not have to undergo the horrors of an operation, and resolved to offer special veneration to their household gods tomorrow in thanks.

She was also glad that a fever cure would reach her niece within a few days. It was always worrying when a child was ill and, while the military doctors were well versed in dealing with broken limbs, eye problems and wounds, she often wondered how good they were with the ailments that beset children. Most women married to military men tended, she knew, to deal with illness in the home themselves or relied on a local woman with experience in sickness.

She and Quintus walked home at a brisk pace, Ertola skipping along between them holding their hands. Several garden owners were out with shovels claiming the cow pats that marked the earlier route of the cattle. Where the road was still littered, Senovara and Quintus lifted Ertola up by her hands over each steaming pile, their hearts gladdened by the gleeful chortling that came from the child as she swung through the air.

'Could we go by the marketplace, Quintus? I need a bottle of vinegar.'

'Just as long as it doesn't take all day,' he grumbled, keen to get back to his bench.

They turned off into the large open space of the market. There were few stalls laid out today; the farmers had less produce to sell at this time of year, and the travelling merchants usually gave up their wanderings as winter approached, preferring to stay safely at home. Even some of the permanent shops that sold imported goods were closed.

As Senovara and Quintus crossed towards the vinegar seller's shop, they saw that the few people in the market were all standing around in a group looking towards the west. Even the shopkeepers, who would normally be behind their counters, were out in the street.

'What's going on?' asked Quintus when they reached the small crowd.

'It's the sun. Look. A great piece has gone black.'

The setting sun could be seen in the gap between the buildings, hanging huge and red like a big Gallic plate just above the western horizon. Sure enough, there was a great crescent of shadow covering it.

'It's an eclipse,' declared Quintus with excitement. 'I saw one once when I was stationed in Germania.'

'Eclipse it may be,' said one of the traders. 'A portent it certainly is: no good ever came of such a thing.'

'True,' said someone else. 'The astrologers told us there was an eclipse of the moon in Maius – not that any of us saw it, it being at night – but look what happened afterwards: drought, pestilence, hunger. That's what happened.'

'Some of those same astrologers said there was a new star on the Nones of Februarius. Personally, I think that was more likely to be the cause of our problems this summer,' argued the vinegar seller, who had emerged from his booth and was standing with his arms folded, squinting up at the sky.

'Eclipse. New star. Who cares which it was? Anything like that causes trouble. It's a clear sign that the gods are displeased. We can expect trouble in the next few months, you mark my words.'

Senovara felt a shiver down her spine as she looked at the sun with its shadowy crescent. There had been so much trouble this year; surely the gods didn't still want the people of Eboracum to suffer?

'Well that explains the behaviour of those cattle we saw earlier,' said Quintus with satisfaction at a mystery solved. 'It's well known that animals behave oddly when there's an eclipse.'

Senovara was impressed by her husband's knowledge but could not stop watching the progress of the shadow across the sun. She shivered again. It seemed to be getting colder, even though the stiff breeze that had been playing with the edges of their cloaks when they set off had dropped and the air was completely still.

'Will the whole sun be covered?' she asked Quintus nervously.

'I don't know,' he said. 'Sometimes it is and sometimes it isn't.'

They stood with the crowd, unable to pull themselves away from this strange evidence of the power of the gods. Ertola fidgeted around their legs, not understanding what was happening and getting increasingly bored by their lack of progress. After she had tugged at his cloak for a second time, Quintus picked her up and held her closely, but he still didn't move off.

As the sun sank slowly down towards the horizon, the shadow edged further and further over its face and the light started to fade. The people in the market stopped talking and all the animals fell silent: it became eerily quiet. When they had entered the marketplace, there had been the usual late afternoon sounds of dogs barking, starlings twittering as they gathered at their evening roosts, cockerels crowing in their back-garden coops, and ducks and hens complaining as they waited in their boxes to be sold. One by one these, too, fell silent until there was not a sound.

Senovara clutched Quintus' arm. She really did not like this at all.

The fortress horn blowing the first hour of night shattered the silence, startling the watching crowd. As if it had also been shocked by the sudden noise, the half-covered sun slid out of sight and the shadows of the surrounding buildings deepened.

'Come on, you two, we'd better get home,' urged Quintus. 'It'll get dark very quickly now. Let's buy the vinegar and go.'

The crowd started to break up as the shopkeepers ran back to their premises to put up the shutters before thieves took advantage of the increasing darkness.

'Will the sun rise again tomorrow?' asked Senovara, trying to keep a note of fear out of her voice.

'I should think so,' replied Quintus reassuringly. 'It always has done before.'

Senovara wasn't too sure. There was a first time for everything, and the sight of the sun being engulfed in shadow as it disappeared over the edge of the world had been awe-inspiring and unnerving.

When she got home she couldn't settle and found it difficult to concentrate on making the sauce for the pieces of crows' meat she had had soaking in milk since morning. Her relief at learning there was nothing wrong with her daughter had evaporated in the short time they had watched the eclipse. Now she felt nothing but foreboding. Several times during the evening she slipped out into the garden and gazed up at the sky, anxiously searching for further portents.

Everything was normal, as far as she could tell. There was another sharp frost and each star was plainly visible, twinkling in its correct place in the heavens. The second time she ventured out, she was comforted to see the moon rising in its usual way. Animal noises came to her through the clear air: foxes barking out beyond the settlement, owls hooting in the trees, and the occasional small bird muttering to itself as it settled into its nightly sleep. From the surrounding houses she could hear her neighbours talking and laughing, kitchen pots rattling as evening meals were prepared. Everything was just as it was every evening, but she couldn't rid herself of a feeling of dread.

As they got ready for bed, Quintus scoffed at her fears, telling her that eclipses were regular occurrences and that it was only because the sun was low in the sky that the event had been noticed. He tried to explain the astrologers' theories about the phenomenon, but his own understanding was hazy and after a while he gave up.

'All I know,' he said, as he settled down under the blankets, 'is that there will be a dawn tomorrow and that's the main thing.'

The next day, Senovara rose at her usual hour, well before the sun was likely to rise on a November morning. Normally her first task would have been to light the kitchen candle and stoke the fire. Today, however, she ran past the stove and opened the back door to look out at the sky.

'Close the door – you're letting the cold air in,' complained Quintus as he came into the kitchen to collect the bowl they had left by the side of the stove overnight to stop their washing water freezing. 'It's too early for the sun to be up yet.'

'I won't feel happy until I see its light,' admitted Senovara as she wiped Ertola's face with a damp cloth. 'The way it was consumed as it disappeared last night was awful. I'm sure something dreadful's going to happen.'

'Nonsense, woman,' said her husband brusquely, but Senovara noticed that he kept looking towards the shuttered window while he ate his morning bread.

'I'll go and get the brazier from the shop,' he said when he had finished. 'It's cold enough for a fire, I reckon.'

He headed down the passage. Senovara could hear him moving about in the shop, then she heard the sound of the door bolts being pulled back, followed by Quintus' voice calling her. She ran through to see what he wanted.

'Come here, my love,' he said, smiling. 'Look down the alleyway between Surilla's house and the basket shop. There's the dawn, just as I promised you.'

Senovara went out of the door and looked towards the east. Sure enough, there was a definite light towards the horizon. As she stood gazing, the sky turned from the darkest blue of night to the colour of speedwells and slowly to the colour of a wheatear's egg. The sun had risen again!

She watched the dawn, with Quintus' arm round her waist, oblivious to the cold. Armea, Lucius and Ertola had followed them out of the house to see what was going on. Armea and Lucius had stayed in the kitchen the previous afternoon, so had not noticed anything odd about the sunset and they were now curious as to what was so fascinating about the sight of the sun rising. As Quintus tried to explain, other people came out of their own houses and stood watching.

'That is a good sight,' declared Aqmat as she emerged from her front door, pulling a shawl tightly round her shoulders. 'I wondered last night if we would see the dawn again.'

'I was worried as well,' admitted Senovara. 'I'd never seen an eclipse of the sun before.'

'Neither had I, but at home in Syria I have known the sun disappear for several days when we have had a big sandstorm. That is frightening enough, even though you know where the sun is and that it will eventually reappear. Last night it seemed to leave the earth behind as if for ever, didn't it, Hairan?' she added as her husband came out to join them. He nodded in agreement and hailed his neighbours.

'The people in the market yesterday were foretelling disasters. They reckoned that an eclipse is always a portent of ill luck,' said Senovara.

'I've heard that too,' said Hairan. 'Several catastrophes in the past have been preceded by an eclipse – or so I was always taught. Isn't there supposed to have been an eclipse before Lucius Sergius Catilina led his conspiracy against Gaius Julius Caesar?'

Quintus nodded. 'So I've heard, but there wasn't an eclipse as far as I know before Caesar was murdered, although there was one afterwards. And the eclipse when the army rebelled in Pannonia after the death of Augustus turned out to be propitious.'

'How was that?' asked Senovara.

'The soldiers serving in Pannonia were roused to mutiny by a man called Percennius – he'd been a professional applause leader in the theatre before becoming a soldier, so he knew how to excite a crowd. Soldiers always feel hard done by, of course, but they may have had good reasons for complaint in this case. Anyway, many officers were killed and Drusus, the son of the Emperor Tiberius, was sent to sort out the mutiny. By the time he got there the soldiers were out for blood and it is likely that they would have killed him if the light of the moon hadn't started to decline because of an eclipse. The soldiers took it as a sign that the heavens were sickened by their crimes and the rebellion was abandoned. All soldiers know this story.'

'But that eclipse was seen as a bad omen too?' asked Senovara, somewhat confused by this tale.

'Yes, but only for the mutineers. Because it led to the putting down of the rebellion, it was a good portent for the Empire.'

'Well, I think the priests should be encouraged to make a special offering to Jupiter on behalf of the town today,' said Aqmat firmly. 'After all, no one can tell a good portent from a bad one until it is too late. Precautions need to be taken if we are to avoid a catastrophe.'

'There certainly will be a catastrophe round here if I don't get some work done,' said Quintus amiably. 'Sadly, I haven't got time to stand around watching the sun all day. I'm just grateful I've got some good light to work by. Do you want to collect those boots you ordered, Hairan? They're ready.'

'Well, that's good news for a start,' said the Palmyrene trader, following Quintus into his workshop.

Senovara would have liked to have stayed talking to Aqmat, but it was too cold to stand around outside. She arranged to call in to see her neighbour later in the day to continue their discussion, and turned back into the house to get on with her own work.

Later that morning, while she swept the passage between the shop and the kitchen, she heard Quintus whistling cheerfully as he hammered hobnails into boot-soles. She smiled to herself.

She suspected that he had been as worried about the eclipse as she had, despite the air of detachment he had displayed in front of Hairan; but old soldiers hate to show fear. She thought of the story he had told of the Pannonian revolt, which seemed to prove that Aqmat was right: there wasn't any way of telling a good portent from a bad one. She put her broom back in its place in the corner of the kitchen hoping fervently that the eclipse would prove to be propitious; but she still couldn't rid herself of that feeling of dread.

December

THE COLD WEATHER that had started on the day of the
eclipse gripped Eboracum throughout November,
leading the marketplace gossips to assert smugly that they
had been right to warn that the event would be a portent of
troubles to come. Going out of doors entailed wearing as many
layers as possible, and shawls, gloves and socks became essential
accessories. Senovara and Armea started to wear two woollen
tunics over their winter-weight shifts as they went about their
household tasks. Quintus and Lucius also took to wearing two
tunics as well as trousers. Senovara even looked out an old pair
of Lucius' trousers and dressed Ertola in them after she found
the child almost blue with cold one morning. The whole family
wore socks inside stout boots, but they still had swollen, itchy
toes and fingers, despite Senovara preparing a hot decoction of
turnips which they all applied each evening.

A short thaw at the beginning of December was welcomed
by everybody, but within two days a heavy fall of snow cut
Eboracum off from the surrounding countryside. The town

was strangely quiet without the sounds of carts and animals being driven through the streets. Even the footsteps of the passers-by were muffled as they trudged along in their daily quest for water. The nearest trough froze solid, so Armea had to go to the well by the marketplace, where the queues grew longer each day when other water supplies also froze. Quintus made some sheepskin leggings for her, in an attempt to keep her legs warm while she waited her turn in the icy air, but the little slave's teeth were always chattering and her nose purple when she returned. Everyone shovelled snow into buckets, which were placed by their kitchen stoves to melt into an additional water supply. Even the long icicles that hung down from the roofs were broken off and added to the buckets so that trips to the well could be limited.

Inside Senovara's house, small pockets of warmth were produced by lighting braziers in the kitchen and the shop, but when she moved from room to room she was met by icy draughts. The passage between the shop and the kitchen seemed particularly cold, and anyone walking down it was preceded by clouds of their own breath. At night, Senovara warmed tiles on the stove during the evening to wrap in pieces of cloth and slip between the blankets for a few hours before any of them went to bed. This took the initial chill and damp off the bedclothes but the coverlets were still stiff when they woke in the morning and there was frost on the rough linen pillows. Getting out of bed each day required an effort of will – cold though their beds were, the air in the bedrooms was even colder. Armea was banished from the kitchen for a few minutes each morning, because Quintus demanded to be allowed to get dressed in the only room in the house which was reasonably warm at that time of day. Senovara began to think longingly of her next visit to the bathhouse; at least it would be warm in there.

Her promise to herself in October that she would bake her own bread was abandoned when the outside oven disappeared under a drift of snow. Even if she dug it out, she reasoned, it would take too much fuel to get it hot for long enough to bake bread or roast meat, and she was becoming increasingly worried about husbanding their supply of fuel. Aqmat showed her how to make thin unleavened bread discs in the Syrian manner, using a frying pan. It was a slow business and the family was not keen on the alien taste and texture, but it saved Senovara or Armea from having to trudge to the baker's each day.

The daily meals started to make inroads into Senovara's supply of salted and bottled vegetables and fruit. She was lucky in having plenty of bacon and smoked mutton, which Matugenus had brought her from the farm in October, and she had salted some fish in pots, sealing their stone lids with pitch to be sure the contents would not go off, but she began to long for a fresh piece of liver or a fragrant pig's trotter. She was thankful that she had been sensible about preparing her stores for winter, but was alarmed at the speed with which her shelves were emptying. She had not expected to use so much before the turn of the year – in previous years she had judged it so well. Perhaps she had become complacent about her housekeeping or possibly she hadn't made enough allowance for having Armea and two growing children to feed as well? If the weather didn't break soon, Februarius and Martius would be the lean and hungry months she had worked so hard to avoid.

She wondered how the settlers on the other side of the river were getting on. They had not had much time to plan for winter; indeed, most of them had been lucky to have got their houses reasonably weatherproof before the weather closed in. Senovara feared that many cupboards would be bare and several families would be going hungry.

As December drew on with no improvement in the weather, Senovara found herself getting increasingly irritable. She saw few people outside her own family and felt confined; even her nearest neighbours, Ursa and Aqmat, kept indoors and no one made purely social calls. Some days the sun shone and the light reflecting off the snow sparkled and made the few surviving colours seem brighter. On these days the children could go outside, and the laughter and cries as they played with their friends in the snow made a cheerful sound. But most days were dark, with barely a change when it became night. Even in the middle of the day, the world was a gloomy grey place with lowering clouds, flurries of snow and an oppressive silence. Everyone kept to their own firesides with the doors shut against the cold. Expeditions out of the house were limited to urgent trips to the market for essentials, though these were often doomed to disappointment as the traders' own supplies began to run low.

At least she got to see other people on these outings, thought Senovara, as she returned from a shopping trip which had yielded only some eggs and hard cheese. She joined the queue at the shop of Albanus, the *seplasarius*, thankful that he had proper premises and didn't sell his wares from a counter which opened onto the street. Her hot turnip decoction was not working well enough, and she was looking for a better salve to take the itching away from her family's swollen toes and fingers.

There were more people gathered in the snug little room from which the *seplasarius* plied his trade than Senovara had seen for days. The cold weather had exacerbated people's aches and pains and brought on coughs and colds, while the limited winter diet had led to an increasing demand for laxatives. The *seplasarius* looked harassed as he dispensed phials of wild chicory in wine for aching limbs, syrup of figs or hellebore for constipation, the expensive balm of Gilead for neuralgia, and horehound and Aminean wine for coughs and colds. Senovara always felt that the wizened little man, who had an unhealthy yellowish tinge to his skin and stained fingers, was not a good advertisement for his own wares, but she had to admit that his medicines often brought relief.

Senovara was the last in the queue and the drug seller relaxed when he realised that she was his only customer for the time being.

'What can I do for you, Senovara?' he asked.

'Ursa tells me that an ointment made from the lees of the dark olive is very good for the winter itch. Have you got any?'

'You mean for *ulcera hiberna*? Ursa's right, it does bring relief, but bears' grease and alum is better. I've got a few pots of that left.' He bent down and rummaged under his counter, then placed a small red vessel with a wooden bung in front of Senovara.

'That will be two *asses*,' he told her.

She handed over the money. Albanus leaned on the countertop, prepared for a gossip now that his first rush of customers was over.

'How's Quintus? I bet he's feeling the cold on that bald head of his. I've offered him some Greek thistle juice to rub in but he won't listen.'

Senovara laughed. Every time Albanus saw Quintus he offered him a new cure for baldness, despite the fact that Quintus always declared that at his age he didn't hold it a crime to be losing his hair. His own healthy riot of grey curls, Albanus asserted, was the result of trying these cures out on himself. He had never managed to persuade Quintus to believe these claims, but that didn't stop him trying.

'How long do you think this cold weather's going to last?' asked Senovara.

'Hard to tell. It can't go on much longer, I wouldn't have thought. Let's hope it starts to thaw before the Saturnalia, otherwise the feasting is going to be on the sparse side.'

Senovara agreed, but before she could continue the conversation the door opened and a customer came into the shop demanding a cabbage liniment to ease the pain in his arthritic hands. Senovara said goodbye and, drawing her shawl tightly round her head, set off for home.

Albanus' reference to the Saturnalia brought a frown to her face as she slithered cautiously along the snowy road. She had planned to cook a special meal on the first night of the Saturnalia but without any fresh meat that was going to be difficult. Unless there was a thaw in the next day or two, there was no likelihood of the drovers being able to get any animals in to be slaughtered in time for the five-day festival.

Having been brought up on a farm, she also knew that the farmers would be having difficulty in feeding the animals when the ground was covered in snow, especially as the drought in the summer had led to a poor hay and straw crop. She wondered how Matugenus was managing; he hadn't been able to get in to Eboracum since the beginning of October, and Senovara wanted to know if Ahteha had got over her stomach cramps. She wasn't worried about whether they had enough food; her grandmother would have been preparing for winter all through the autumn, and if they couldn't feed the animals they could at least eat the meat. It was the people in the towns who found it difficult to cope if there was any disruption in the usual supply system, not the country folk, but she still wished she could find out how they all were.

That evening, as she put Lucius and Ertola to bed, however, she felt that it was not as bitterly cold as it had been, and when she looked out of the kitchen door the next morning she was delighted to see evidence of a thaw. The sudden change had resulted in a thick frost forming on the walls of the buildings as the warmer air touched the cold plaster and stone: a sign, she knew, of a rapid thaw. That would bring its own problems, of course, but it was still welcome.

All through the day the snow and ice began to relinquish their grip. The road outside the shop became a quagmire of slush, which Senovara found even more difficult to walk on than the snow had been. Her long skirts seemed to soak up moisture whenever she ventured out, and flapped damply around her ankles for hours afterwards. The previous silence was broken by loud cracks as icicles snapped and there were sudden roars as avalanches of melting snow surged down from the roofs in an explosion of white, hitting the road and any unwary passers-by.

By the Ides of December, the snow had gone as quickly as it had arrived, leaving behind a sea of mud and flooded roads. Just as quickly, the market became crowded with farmers and their carts when they hurried in to sell their surplus beasts while there was still some meat on them and before the weather cut their farms off again.

Senovara and Armea were sitting in the kitchen, trying to decide what they needed to buy to last through the festival when most of the shops would be shut. Without knowing what was available it was difficult to plan recipes, and neither of them wanted to have to go to the market twice. Senovara probably had all she needed by way of herbs and spices to cook most meals, but it was worth running through the possibilities before setting out, just in case something obvious got forgotten.

She was interrupted by a great shout from Quintus in the shop, followed by the welcome, familiar tones of her brother's voice. Before she could get to her feet, the door burst open and Lucius rushed in, followed by Ertola.

'Mater, Uncle Matugenus is here and you'll never guess what he's brought.'

Senovara looked towards the door in bewilderment. Her brother strode into the room, clutching a struggling, squealing piglet under his arm.

'Hail, sister. We thought you might like one of these for your Saturnalia feast.'

'Matugenus, what a wonderful surprise! You've no idea how much we've missed fresh meat over the last month.'

'Aye, we reckoned it would be like that, so when the old sow produced a late litter Grandmother said we should let you have one as soon as the roads were clear enough for the cart to get through. She and Ahteha send their love, by the way.'

'Have you time to stay for a meal yourself, Matugenus?'

'Not really. I've just delivered the rest of the piglets to Bonosius and I've done everything else I needed to do. It won't be light long and I don't want to be out on the road after dark. Where do you want this little fellow? Do you want to slit its throat now or do it later?'

'We might as well do it straight away if we're going to have it for our feast tomorrow,' decided Quintus. 'Take it into the garden.'

Senovara collected a big pottery bowl, Quintus selected a large knife from the hooks on the wall, and everyone trooped out of doors, Lucius still capering about in excitement. Matugenus set the piglet down on the ground and held its squirming body between his legs. He forced its head up by both ears and Quintus quickly slit its throat. Senovara darted forward with the bowl to catch the blood. Matugenus held the body up by its back legs to allow the blood to drain out, then handed it to Armea, who had emerged from the back door with a sack to wrap round the piglet.

'Hang it from the shelf in the store, Armea,' said Senovara, preparing to carry the bowl of blood indoors. 'It'll keep nicely there until tomorrow. Put another bowl underneath to catch any more drips; there's no point in wasting anything – the blood makes good sausages. Would you care for something to drink, Matugenus?'

'I would that.'

'How about some warmed wine on this cold day?' suggested Quintus, wiping the blade of the knife on the sack before Armea bore the piglet away.

'That's an excellent suggestion.'

In the kitchen Quintus poured some red wine into a bronze pan, while Senovara selected some solid pieces of charcoal from the fire with the iron pincers. She knocked them against the iron griddle to remove any loose flakes before placing them in a bronze colander. She held the pan over the fire for a second, shaking it briskly to clear off any ash, then brought it over to the table and plunged the colander, complete with contents, into the waiting wine. The hot charcoal hit the cold wine and steam rose with a bubbling, hissing sound.

'That sounds and smells good,' declared Matugenus, as a rich, warm wine smell filled the kitchen. 'Just what's needed on a winter's day.'

Quintus poured the warm wine into three beakers and handed one to his brother-in-law, before raising another with the words: 'Good health to you and yours, Matugenus. And many thanks for our Saturnalia piglet.'

'Good health in our family indeed.' Matugenus beamed around at them. 'I must tell you, it looks as though Ahteha may be expecting a baby in late spring.'

Senovara leaped to her feet and hugged her brother gleefully. Quintus thumped him on the back with enthusiasm.

'That's wonderful news!' she said. 'I was so worried in October when you said that she was ill.'

'So was I,' Matugenus admitted. 'Grandmother thought she might have been having an early miscarriage, but it now looks as if she'd just eaten something which didn't agree with her. We reckon the baby will be born around Maius or Iunius.'

'That's a good time of year to have a baby,' said Senovara approvingly.

Matugenus drained his beaker and stood up. 'I'm sorry this is such a short visit but I must get back, as I'm sure you will understand.'

'Of course,' said Quintus. 'And thank you again for the piglet.'

Senovara called out of the kitchen door: 'Children, your uncle's leaving. Come and be polite.'

Lucius ran in from the storeroom, where he had been getting in Armea's way while she hung up the piglet, followed by the silent but smiling Ertola. They were both swept up under their uncle's arms and carried off at a gallop down the passage to the shop with loud cries from him and squeals from them. Quintus and Senovara looked at each other and smiled. Matugenus was clearly thrilled by the news he had brought them.

Now that her dilemma as to what to cook for the Saturnalia had been solved, Senovara felt she could relax a bit and look forward to the festivities. She had decided to prepare *melcae* to serve with bottled cherries for the second course, and she could now prepare it without any rush, because it would take Armea only a few moments to run down to the market to collect some fresh milk. She would have plenty of time after warming some leek soup at midday both to start the *melcae* and to prepare the cheese and salt-fish *patella* for that evening's supper.

The afternoon passed quickly as she prepared the meals for both days. After making the soup, she cooked the fish in oil, boned it and warmed it through with some hard-boiled eggs and cheese. She then pounded pepper, lovage and rue berries together and heated the resulting paste in a pan with wine and oil before stirring it into the fish mixture. This was then set aside to wait until it needed to be cooked with raw eggs and sprinkled with cumin that evening.

The next task was to start the *melcae*. Senovara selected her newest earthenware pot and poured in some vinegar. Using the iron poker, she pushed the gridiron to one side so that she could set the pot directly on the hot embers. While she waited for the vinegar to start to bubble, her mind drifted and she thought happily about her brother's news: a first baby on the way for Ahteha at last. Her grandmother would be thrilled, and was no doubt already planning the child's life in every detail. Senovara was pleased that Ahteha's illness in October had not been serious and that everything seemed to be going well for the family after the difficulties of the year.

The sound of the vinegar beginning to bubble startled her and she emerged suddenly from her daydreaming. It was dangerous to tempt the gods like that! Nervously, she put the thumb of her right hand between her first two fingers in the old sign to ward off the Evil Eye.

Turning back to her cooking, she carefully poured the milk into the warm pot and, wrapping a cloth round it to protect her fingers, lifted it up onto a shelf, where it would be undisturbed until wanted.

It was now time to gut the suckling pig while the offal was fresh. It took a while to clean out the entrails, largely because she didn't want to waste anything, but eventually the carcass was cleaned and scalded inside. She poked the fire on the stove to encourage it to burn fiercely and called to Armea to help her singe the hair from the pig's skin. It took the two of them to hold the piglet over the flame, turning it slowly until all the bristles had been burned off. The kitchen filled with the acrid aroma of singeing hair – a smell which took Senovara back to the midwinter festivals of her childhood. She opened the back door and flapped it back and forth to clear the kitchen of the fumes and lit a candle to help dispel the odours.

The next morning, Lucius and Ertola ran into their parents' bedroom and jumped on to the bed.

'Io Saturnalia, Mater! Io Saturnalia, Pater!' shouted Lucius while Ertola wormed her way under the warm covers.

'Io Saturnalia,' responded Quintus sleepily.

Senovara hugged Ertola, then hugged Lucius. 'Io Saturnalia, children. Let's get up and see what the day's going to bring.'

Quintus groaned and turned over. 'I'm staying here for a while. It's one of the few days in the year when I don't have to open the shop, so I'm going to have a little more sleep.'

Senovara picked up her clothes and took them into the kitchen so that she could get dressed in the warm without disturbing Quintus. She had a lot to do today if the suckling pig was to be properly cooked by the evening.

Armea was already in the kitchen and she greeted her mistress with a shy 'Io Saturnalia'.

'Io Saturnalia, Armea. And an excellent day it looks like being as well,' added Senovara when she peeked out of the back door. 'I was worried it would rain or snow again and we wouldn't be able to roast the piglet. Get the oven lit as soon as you can after we've had our bread, then I'll get on and make the pastry and honey stuffing and prepare the piglet while the oven's heating. We can then go out and watch the ceremony while the meat's cooking.'

It was some time since Senovara had cooked a sucking pig, and she set to with enthusiasm as soon as she had given Quintus and the children their bread. She crumbled some pastry made the day before into a pan and boiled it with pepper, honey and wine, adding some bay leaves and stirring it until it thickened. She tasted a small spoonful, added a pinch of salt, and stuffed the piglet with the mixture, securing the stuffing with some wooden skewers. Lastly, she rubbed salt over its skin before going out into the garden to check on the heat of the oven. It was still a little cool she judged but there was still some time before they needed to leave the house. It would probably be better to get herself and the children ready now, and put the piglet in just before they went out.

The streets were thronged with people making their way to the parade ground for the sacrifices and there were many loud cries of 'Io Saturnalia' as they greeted their friends. Quintus and Senovara led Armea and the children through the crowd until they could see the altar standing ready. There was a loud blast from a trumpet and the soldiers marched in to take up their positions. Everyone fell silent as the ceremony began.

'Mater.' Lucius tugged anxiously at his mother's sleeve.

Senovara looked down. 'What's the matter?' she whispered.

'Why hasn't the priest got his head covered? I thought if someone was sacrificing he had to have his head covered.'

'Normally that's true, but on the Saturnalia it is permissible to sacrifice with a bare head. It's such a happy day that the priest can take the risk of seeing an ill-omened portent without worrying.'

Senovara was glad to see that Lucius seemed comforted by this explanation. It reminded her that she had asked exactly the same question of Quintus the first time she witnessed the Saturnalia ritual after her marriage. While she watched the ceremony coming to a close she thought how familiar the ritual now was to her. Was this a sign that she was now more of a Roman woman than a woman of the Parisi? she wondered, a little frightened by the thought.

The crowd stirred at the end of the rites and the sudden burst of conversation broke into her thoughts.

'Time to go home, children,' said Quintus. 'I'm ready for our feast now, aren't you?'

It took a while to get home, however, as they were hailed by friends and neighbours, all keen to gossip and exchange news. This was one of the few days in the year when everyone was at leisure, though few went so far as to give their slaves the day off. Several times they were invited in to have some wine at friends' houses, and Senovara began to worry about the fate of their roasting piglet.

On their return Senovara rushed through the house and out into the garden to see how the meat was doing. When she lifted the iron cover from the front of the oven, delicious smells of hot pork fat met her nostrils. It would be ready soon; there was just enough time to give the children their Saturnalia *sigillaria* and prepare some vegetables.

Taking off her cloak she went back into the kitchen, where she found Quintus had poured them some wine and was settling the children on the bench.

'Shall we give the children their presents now?' he asked, grinning.

Lucius and Ertola bounced up and down in excitement as Quintus reached up to the highest shelf and pulled down the small white clay figurines, one of a horse and one of a pig, which he handed to them solemnly. The children's eyes lit up with delight and before long both were on the floor playing with their new toys.

Quintus left the room for a moment and then returned with a small wooden box. 'A present for you, my love,' he said, handing the box to Senovara. She opened it carefully and gasped when she saw the pair of small gold earrings sitting inside.

'Oh, Quintus, they're lovely. I've never had anything gold before. Are you sure we can afford them?'

'I kept some money back from my fee for the Legate's boots. Anyway, with all the extra work I've had since making those boots, I think it's about time my wife had some gold earrings. Unless, that is, you'd prefer a more traditional candle or figurine?' he teased. 'Here, let me put them in for you,' he continued, when Senovara shook her head wordlessly.

Senovara took out the plain bronze hoops she had put in that morning and he gently slotted the earrings into position. She ran into the bedroom and came back with her mirror. She stood looking at her reflection, turning her head this way and that to see the effect of the light catching the small gold bosses nestling against her earlobes.

'They are truly lovely,' she said breathlessly. 'But I have a gift for you as well.'

She turned to the cupboard and rummaged behind the pots to find the small linen-covered package she had hidden there last month. 'It's not a candle or a figurine, either. I hope you like it.' She placed the tiny bone notebook in his hand.

He opened it wonderingly, to see the smooth surface of four miniature wax tablets held together with gut. 'Wherever did you find this?' he asked. 'It'll be perfect for keeping a record of orders.'

'I saw one of the merchants on the quayside had one when I went to see about that consignment of hides for you in October and I asked Bruccius to find out where he got it. It turned out that the merchant had bought several when he was in Germania and he was willing to sell me one. I've been expecting you to find its hiding place ever since.'

Quintus hugged his wife and kissed her on the cheek. 'It's the best present I've ever had.'

Senovara smiled happily at him, then turned to Armea, who was sitting on a stool watching the children playing with their new toys. 'And this is for you, Armea,' she said, handing the slave girl a small bundle. Armea looked astonished at being included in this present-giving and her eyes were round with amazement as she unfolded a dark blue shawl. Senovara smiled at her when she tried to stammer her thanks.

'You're part of the family now,' said Quintus, 'so of course you should have a Saturnalia present. Anyway, this is the day when slaves are equal with their masters and mistresses, you know.'

Seeing tears come into Armea's eyes, Senovara said briskly, 'It's time we got the vegetables prepared or the pig will be burned. You chop the cabbage, Armea, and I'll prepare the leeks.'

Within a very short time the vegetables were ready and lying in their dishes on the table. Senovara handed Quintus the big iron carving knife and the whetstone, and he briskly sharpened the blade. Senovara put the roast piglet down in front of him. She had been worried about how to serve the dinner because she had no pottery plate large enough to take a suckling pig, but Armea had suggested putting it on the wooden tray she used for carrying beakers and wine into the best room when they had guests. It looked a little odd but Quintus didn't seem to mind as he started to carve slices of meat.

'This meat is done to perfection, Senovara,' he commented, placing the slices on the family's plates.

'I'm thankful for that. I was beginning to get worried it was going to be burned or dried out when it took us so long to get home from the ceremony. It looks as if there is plenty of it as well – it'll do us for several meals. Lucius, if you hand your plate over I'll give you some cabbage. Armea, would you pour out some wine for us all?'

Quintus scooped some of the stuffing onto everyone's plate and Senovara moved the tray onto the side table. Her husband sat down with a satisfied look on his face, lifted his beaker of wine and declared, 'Long life to us all!'

'Well, that was an excellent meal, Senovara,' Quintus said later as he undid his belt a notch and belched politely behind his hand. 'I'm sure I won't get anything half as good when I go to the Birth of Mithras celebrations.'

Senovara acknowledged the compliment, but made a mental note to ensure that she had a box of pine nut kernels handy for the seventh day before the Kalends of Ianuarius; Quintus always returned from the ritual meal that accompanied the celebration of the Birth of Mithras with terrible heartburn. Though he had never told her exactly what transpired during the rituals, she gathered that they ate the meal lying on benches in the Roman manner, which did Quintus' digestion no good.

The five days of the Saturnalia passed happily and the townspeople gradually all went back to their shops and workbenches. Another cold snap led to Quintus catching a slight chill on his way back from the Birth of Mithras celebrations; he recovered quite quickly but Senovara made sure that there was always a good fire going in his shop brazier every day, just in case.

By the time it came to the day before the Kalends of Ianuarius she realised that her store of fuel was getting dangerously low and needed replenishing so, after the family had had its midday meal, she wrapped her cloak round her and set off across the Abus to seek out Viducus the charcoal burner and arrange a delivery.

The newest part of the settlement looked totally different today. Gone were the waggons and tents of the summer, and in their place were timber and half-timbered houses and shops, all arranged with their narrow fronts to the street. The air was full of smoke and the smells of cooking. Even on this cold day there were children running around and the sounds of people gossiping and arguing in many languages, but Senovara did not dawdle – she needed to get her business over quickly and return home before it got dark.

She carried on through the roughly laid out streets until eventually she got to the hut at the edge of the woods where Viducus lived. She hoped he would be there and not tending a charcoal pile deep within the stand of trees. As she drew nearer, a small woman came out of the hut and threw some rubbish onto a heap by the door.

Senovara's footsteps on the twig-strewn ground broke the silence and the woman looked round to see who was there.

'Oh, it's you, Senovara. How are you?'

'Well, thank you, Ivixa. I've come to arrange for some charcoal to be delivered. Is your husband around?'

'No, he's got a burning about a mile away which is nearly ready, so he's gone down to check it. I can let him know you need some fuel when he comes back or you can wait if you like. He shouldn't be long; he has a couple of workmen tending the burning so if it's not ready he probably won't stay.'

'I must get back before dark,' said Senovara. 'Could you ask him to drop round with a couple of sackfuls in the next few days? With all the cold weather we had at the beginning of the month, I'm very low on fuel.'

'You and everyone else. But I know he still has a few sacks left, even if this new lot isn't ready. I'll let him know.'

Senovara thanked her and set off for home, worried that the light was going quickly and a faint mist was beginning to gather under the trees. She stepped out briskly, her cheeks starting to sting as the air grew colder.

Her way through the streets on the south side of the Abus was hampered by shopkeepers moving their goods indoors and putting up their shutters, and there were a few stars already shining high in the sky by the time she reached the river. As she neared the south end of the bridge, small flocks of starlings started to circle around her head. While she crossed, more and more birds appeared and soon there were thousands of black specks wheeling through the air, banking over the water then swooping up and away before returning once again. She stopped to watch, noticing a sense of order amid the apparent chaos. The flock appeared to be divided into smaller cohorts, each of which wheeled and soared in close formation, always separate from the other cohorts yet still part of the mass. Suddenly one group banked away and swooped down towards the bridge, perching for a second on one of the outer supporting timbers before moving further under the shelter of the bridge to make room for the next group, which was already circling ready to take its place. The number of roosting birds increased and the noise of their twittering got louder. Eventually, all the starlings were neatly stowed away for the night. By this time the din was tremendous and Senovara imagined them exchanging gossip with their neighbours about what they had been doing during the day, squabbling over their favourite roosts, and chastising the younger birds for their presumption in taking up more room than they were entitled to. She laughed at her fantasy, yet she wondered if her ideas were any more fantastic than those of people who believed that the flocking birds were an ill omen? This miracle of the roosting starlings happened most evenings, yet Eboracum continued to thrive.

She shook herself. She didn't have time to watch while the gods arranged the lives of birds. Quintus would be wondering where she was and when he was likely to get his evening meal. She hurried on.

When she got home she found the door of the shop closed but not locked, so she just shut it behind her, not knowing if Quintus had left it like that for her or because he was expecting a late customer. In the kitchen Quintus was sitting at the table helping Lucius with his writing practice by holding the child's chubby little hand as it grasped the stylus tightly. Senovara smiled, noticing the tip of Lucius' tongue sticking out between his teeth as he concentrated on forming the letters in the wax of the tablet. It annoyed him that Armea had learned to write much more quickly than he had, and he was determined to catch up. Senovara was glad that he had started to show an interest in his lessons, even if his concentration was still limited.

Lucius shook his head with irritation and started to upbraid his father. 'Don't hold on to my hand so tightly,' he said crossly. 'I can do it without your help and you're hurting me.'

His father laughed. 'Go on then, show me.'

Armea was sitting on the floor with a boot, showing Ertola how to tie the laces in a neat bow. Despite her young age, the child was nimble-fingered and it seemed to Senovara that her daughter was having no difficulty in picking up the tricky skill.

Quintus looked up when she entered the room, but before he had a chance to hail her the sound of hobnail boots was heard in the passage from the shop.

'We appear to have a visitor.'

The door opened and a soldier stood there, removing his helmet.

'Why, it's Aulus Postumus. Come on in and make yourself at home,' invited Quintus hospitably. 'We haven't seen you for some time. How are you and how are my brother and his family?'

'I'm well, thank you, and I bring a letter from your brother.' The soldier reached into his leather document case and brought out a writing tablet. He placed it on the kitchen table, its wax seal uppermost. 'I won't stay, though. I have to be getting to the fortress.'

He backed out of the kitchen and made his way back to the shop, pursued by Quintus, who wished to show the *optio* out courteously.

The writing tablet sat on the table and Senovara eyed it nervously. The *optio* had seemed in a hurry to leave and she had a feeling that the letter contained bad news and the soldier knew it.

Quintus came back into the kitchen, rubbing his hands. 'It's getting cold out there; we're in for a hard frost tonight,' he said, settling himself on a stool. 'Let's see what Gaius has to say for himself. I hope young Lucia is better.'

He slit the string holding the writing tablets together and scanned the contents quickly, paling as he did so. He looked up at Senovara, suddenly looking old and gaunt. He handed the letter over soundlessly.

Senovara read the inked words.

From Gaius Flavius Naso, Centurion of the VIth Legion Victrix at Vercovicium, to Quintus Flavius Candidus at Eboracum. Brother, I send bad tidings. Our most sweet daughter Lucia died on the last day of the Saturnalia. I, a pitiable victim of unfair hope, bewail her final end. Flavia and Alana are beyond grief. I will write again when my tears allow me to see.

As Senovara read the dreadful words, tears sprang to her own eyes and she could hardly see her husband. She groped for his hand and they sat silently. Ertola got to her feet and came over to her mother, setting the boot she had been playing with on Senovara's knee, as though consoling her. Senovara looked down at the child; although she had never seen her niece she knew that Lucia had been about the same age, and she was overwhelmed by the thought of her sister-in-law's feelings at losing something so precious. She swept Ertola towards her and hugged her fiercely, rocking from side to side.

'You're hurting me.'

The gruff little voice seemed to come from nowhere. Senovara looked down in astonishment then held her daughter away from her.

'What did you say?'

'You're hurting me, Mater,' Ertola announced in firm tones.

Lucius raised a great cheer and started to dance excitedly round the kitchen. Senovara and Quintus looked at each other, then jumped up from their seats and into each other's arms, laughing and crying all at once. The gods who could give as well as take away had answered their pleas for their daughter to find a voice.

That night, as she lay in bed, listening to Quintus snoring next to her, she felt the day had brought too many emotions for her ever to get to sleep. Tomorrow would bring a new day and also a new year. Lying in the dark she thought back through the past twelve months which had brought her so many experiences.

Her heart was full at the thought of Ertola suddenly finding her voice. The child had not said much more that evening, but at least they now knew that she could. Lucius had been so excited at hearing his sister speak that he had taken a long time to settle. Indeed, he had hardly stopped talking himself all evening as he had prattled to his parents about how he was going to teach Ertola to say rhymes and sing songs. He had learned so much himself during the year, particularly when he'd visited her family's farm in the summer. Senovara was glad her children had had the opportunity to spend time in the country, discovering how she had lived when she was their age. They had Roman citizenship through their father, and she and Quintus were trying to bring them up according to Roman ways, but she still felt pleased that they had had a chance to discover the Parisian traditions of her side of the family.

Many of her friends, too, had had a year full of interest and opportunity. She thought of Broginara, who was soon to be betrothed to Marcus Pontius Sabinus, and would eventually be travelling to Roma with him, and she thought of Catia who had finally agreed to marry the butcher, Bonosius. Senovara hoped that both women, so very different from each other, would find the happiness she had found with Quintus. She thought of Adnamata, now the proud mother of twins, and hoped with all her heart that the Pannonians would not be visited with the depth of sadness that had descended on her brother-in-law's house. She thought of Ahteha and Matugenus, soon to become parents themselves to a child who would be brought up in Senovara's old home; times were so very different now and she hoped that when their baby grew up it would be taught the best of the old traditions as well as learning the best of the new Roman ways. She thought of Armea, who had come to them in Februarius, a frightened little slave, away from home for the first time, and how she was now part of their family.

Quintus turned over in bed, throwing an arm over his wife's shoulder. Senovara thought of his year and how he had made the purple boots for the Legate and how proud they had both been when they were worn for everyone to see at the chariot races. The death of his niece had been a bitter blow for him. Tomorrow he would have to write a reply to his brother, offering what comfort he could. It would not be an easy task, particularly with their own news being so joyful.

All in all, it had been a good year, she decided, despite this latest grief. But what would next year bring for them all? she wondered, adjusting herself to fit more comfortably against Quintus' rough tunic. Only the gods knew, and they rarely let mortals know in advance. The future was always a voyage in the dark; no wonder people gave each other oil lamps as presents on the Kalends, she thought as she finally drifted off to sleep.

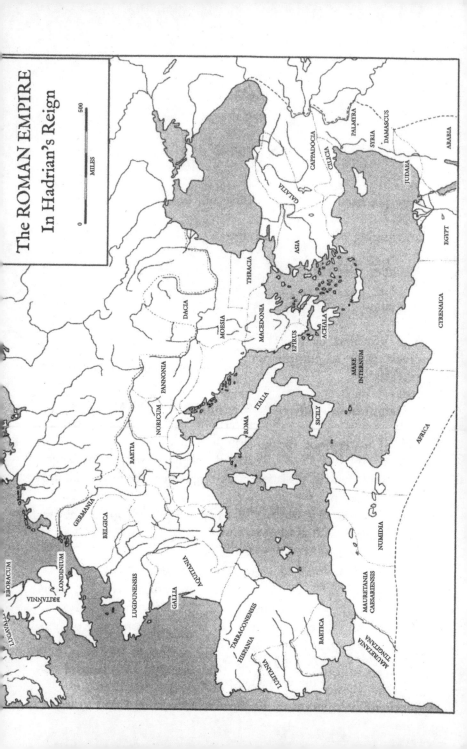

Glossary

AMPHORA: A large jar, used to transport olive oil, liquamen, wine, etc.

APODYTERIUM: The changing room in a bathhouse.

AQUILIFER: The soldier who carried a legion's eagle standard.

AS: The smallest denomination of bronze coin.

AUXILIARY: Troops provided by the allies and subjects of Rome, often with specialist skills to complement the heavy infantry of the Roman legionaries.

BENEFICIARIUS: Non-commissioned officer with administrative duties.

BYRRUS: A type of waterproof cloak.

CALDARIUM: The hottest room in a bathhouse.

CENTURION: Officer in charge of a century of eighty men. There were sixty centurions in a legion with graded seniority. Centurions could be transferred from legion to legion and were regarded as professional soldiers, in service until death.

CIVES ROMANI CONSISTENTES: A council formed to protect the interests of the Roman citizens in a town or city.

COHORT: Each legion was divided into ten cohorts, each with 480 men; the first cohort of a legion, however, had 800 men in five double-strength centuries. The number of men in an auxiliary unit varied depending on whether it was an infantry or cavalry unit or had a mixture of both.

COLLEGIA: Any private association of fixed membership and constitution, often a guild of workers in the same industry.

CONTUBERNIA: A room in a military barrack block, housing eight men.

CUIRASS: Body armour covering the torso.

DEA NUTRIX: A mother goddess, usually depicted suckling a child.

DENARIUS: Silver coin equal to 16 *asses* or 4 *sestertii*. In Hadrian's time, an auxiliary soldier was paid 100 *denarii* per year, a legionary 300.

DUODECIM SCRIPTA: A board game played with three dice.

FRIGIDARIUM: The cold room of a bathhouse.

EXPLORATORES: Native troops used as scouts.

GENIUS: Spirit, as in *genius loci* or 'spirit or guardian of this place'.

HOURS: Roman days and nights were each divided into twelve hours but the length of the hours varied depending on what time of year it was, the longer daylight hours being in the summer.

IDES: The fifteenth day of March, May, July and October; the thirteenth day of the other months.

IUGERUM: A land measure equal to 0.25 hectares.

KALENDS: The first day of a month. When used on its own, Kalends (or Diem Kalendarum) refers to 1 January.

LARARIUM: A domestic shrine in which the household gods were honoured.

LARES: The spiritual guardians of a home.

LATRINA: A lavatory.

LEGATE: A senatorial member of a provincial governor's staff used to command a legion or a detachment.

LEGION: Heavy infantry made up of Roman citizens. The Second Legion Augusta, the Sixth Legion Victrix and the Twentieth Legion Valeria Victrix built Hadrian's Wall. A legion consisted of 5,000 foot soldiers and 120 mounted men.

LIBRARIUS: A military record keeper.

LIQUAMEN: A sauce, made by rotting down fish entrails, which was used as a seasoning in most Roman recipes.

MANSIO: A building, usually just outside the main gate of a fort or fortress, which provided accommodation for official travellers.

MEDICUS ORDINARIES: A military medical doctor, probably with the status of a centurion.

MELCAE: A pudding, resembling junket, made from milk and vinegar.

MODIUS: A measure, usually used for corn.

MORTARIUM: A bowl with grits set into the clay of the inner surface, used for grinding food.

NONES: The fifth day of the month, except for March, May, July and October when it was the seventh day. So called because it was the ninth day before the Ides.

ONAGER: A term for both a donkey and a military catapult.

OPTIO: Second-in-command to a centurion.

OPERUM PUBLICORUM: Office of Public Works.

OPUS SIGNINUM: A waterproof surface made from lime mortar mixed with pieces of broken tile, giving it a blotchy pink appearance.

PATELLA: A recipe using eggs.

PATER FAMILIAS: The male head of a family. Under Roman law, every woman had to be under the guardianship of a *pater familias*.

PATINA: An egg custard.

PHALERA: A metal mount which hung from a harness or from armour, usually given to soldiers as a reward for valour.

PILUM: A legionary's throwing spear.

POPPY TEARS: A painkiller made from opium.

PORTA: Gate; Eboracum fortress had four: *porta decumana* (at Eboracum it was the north-east gate), *porta principalis sinistra* (at Eboracum the south-east gate), *porta praetoria* (at Eboracum the south-west gate), and the *principalis dextra* (at Eboracum the north-west gate).

PRAETENTURA: The front section of a fort or fortress.

PRAETORIUM: The house of the commanding officer of a fort or fortress.

PROCURATOR: A man employed by the Emperor in civil administration, often governing minor provinces, collecting revenues and paying the troops.

QUAESTOR: A magistrate.

ROSALIA: A festival on 5 May, when families gathered at cemeteries to honour their dead.

SATURNALIA: A festival held in mid-December. In Hadrian's time it lasted for five days and involved feasting and the exchange of presents.

SEPLASARIUS: A seller of medicines.

SESTERTIUS: A bronze coin equal to 4 *asses.*

SPINA: The fence or rail which ran down the centre of a race track.

TEPIDARIUM: The warm room of a bathhouse.

TERRITORIUM: The area around a settlement that was farmed or owned by people who lived within the settlement.

THREE-AS LOAF: A loaf big enough for one man for one to two days at the time of Hadrian cost 2 asses.

TORC: A thick metal necklet worn by Britons to ward off the Evil Eye and as a symbol of a warrior. Roman soldiers were awarded torcs to fasten to the front of their armour as a reward for valour.

TRIB. POT.: Short for *tribunicia potestas*: used as a dating aid, it referred to the number of times an emperor had had his power as a Tribune of the People renewed.

TRIBUNE: There were six tribunes in a legion, one of whom was expected to follow a military career and was second-in-command. The other five were from equestrian families doing military service to qualify for a senatorial career.

ULCERA HIBERNA: Chilblains.

VALETUDINARIUM: A fort or fortress hospital.

VETERINARIUS: Military veterinary surgeon, mostly working with horses.

VICUS: The civil settlement that grew up around the roads leading to a fort.